The Mystery of the Serpent Mound

In Search of the Alphabet of the Gods

The Mystery of the Serpent Mound

In Search of the Alphabet of the Gods

Ross Hamilton

Illustrated by
Patricia Mason

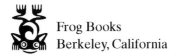
Frog Books
Berkeley, California

Published by Frog Books

Frog Books' publications are distributed by
North Atlantic Books
P.O. Box 12327
Berkeley, California 94712

Cover art by Andrew Bomkamp
Cover and book design by Paula Morrison

Printed in the United States of America

For more information about the Serpent Mound, visit www.greatserpentmound.org.

The Mystery of the Serpent Mound is sponsored by the Society for the Study of Native Arts and Sciences, a nonprofit educational corporation whose goals are to develop an educational and cross-cultural perspective linking various scientific, social, and artistic fields; to nurture a holistic view of arts, sciences, humanities, and healing; and to publish and distribute literature on the relationship of mind, body, and nature.

North Atlantic Books' publications are available through most bookstores. For further information, visit our Web site at www.northatlanticbooks.com or call 800-733-3000.

ISBN-13: 978-1-58394-003-7

Library of Congress Cataloging-in-Publication Data
Ross Hamilton
    The mystery of the serpent mound / Ross Hamilton.
        p. cm.
    Includes bibliographical references and index.
    ISBN 1-58394-003-0 (alk. paper)
    1 Serpent Mound State Memorial (Ohio)
2. Adena culture.   3. Sacred space.
4. Archaeoastronomy. I. Title.
E99.A18H35 1999
977. 1'86—dc21   99-29926
                                                    CIP

3 4 5 6 7 UNITED 13 12 11 10

There seemed to come to me a picture as of a distant time, and with it came a demand for an interpretation of this mystery: The unknown must become known.

Frederick Ward Putnam,
"Father of American Archaeology,"
Boston, 1888

This book is dedicated to Patricia Mason, without whose selfless help this manuscript would never have been brought up to a level of presentation worthy of the many years of effort put into it.

In Indian symbolism the serpent—especially the Great Serpent—corroborates other evidence pointing to the presence of the Mysteries on the North American continent ... Moreover, who can doubt the presence of the secret doctrine in the Americas when he gazes upon the great serpent mound [sic] in Adams County, Ohio...?

Manly Hall
Founder, Philosophical Research Society
Los Angeles, 1928

Were the various symbols from the ancient alphabet of the Greeks properly modified and placed together in a certain deliberate fashion, the image of what we are familiar with as the Great Serpent Mound presents itself. The design of the Serpent Mound, which goes back to the earliest period of North American earthworks, was somehow either brought to or taken from Ohio approximately five thousand years ago. Herein is the true mystery.

Ross Hamilton
Cincinnati, 2000

Table of Contents

List of Illustrations.........................ix

Preface....................................xiii

Author's Cut to the Chase xvii

The Great Light Bearer....................xix

A Unique Discovery.......................xix

Sacred Geometry...........................xx

How Old Is Serpent Mound?..............xxi

   A Forgotten Clue xxii

   Standing on Putnam's Shoulders xxiii

   A Tip of the Hat to Dr. C xxv

   From the Earth to the Stars xxv

The Draconian Serpent and Stonehenge..xxvi

The Egyptian Connection xxvii

The Lost Oracle of Delphi?..............xxvii

The Mystery of the Serpent Mound

**A Vision Beyond Politics:
Frederick Ward Putnam** 3

Putnam's Story...............................4

Science and the Horse of Reason 4

The Work of the Worm 6

The Fire and Stone Mystery 8

Archaeoastronomy.........................11

The Sun and the Moon 11

The North Star..............................15

The Draconis Mystery......................16

The Grand Dragon 17

The Serpent and Stonehenge...............19

**The Great Serpent and the Mysteries
of Geometry** 23

The Philosophy of Geometry...............25

The Spirit of Geometry.....................26

The Serpent as Universal Template 29

The Hexagon 29

   The Design of the Hexagon..............31

   *The Seven Spirits and the
      Twenty-four Elders* 32

   The Elders as the Human Form 33

   The Four Beasts as the Four Ideas 34

   The Vibratory Principle..................37

   The Timeless Wisdom....................37

   *Building the Hexagon:
      The Redoubtable Foot* 39

The Vesica Piscis............................40

   Construction of the Vesica Piscis.........42

The Pythagorean Theorem Connection.....43

The Serpent and the Golden Ratio..........44

   The Philosophy of Phi...................53

   Some Names for Phi.....................53

The Great Serpent and the Great Pyramid .53

**The Traditional Tree
and the Great Serpent**.......................61

Introduction 61

The Ank as Tree 62

Numbers and the Divine 64

Spirit and Matter 67

The Sacred Seven and the Sacred Ten.......69

The Serpent and the Ark...................71

Electricity: History and Mystery 72

Dharma: The Mystery
of the Electric Couple 73

The Current of the Land 75

    The Science of Natural Magic 76

The Great Anomaly 81

Soul and Spirit: A Connection to the Ark...84

Biblical Electrical Knowledge..............86

The Number of the Beast 89

The Great Serpent Mound
and the Number of the Beast..............92

The Hexagon Proper 92

The Measure of the Stars...................93

Over the Ocean and Back 94

Searching for a Piece of π 95

Putting the Foot to the Megalithic Yard—
In America................................95

Divination by Means of Light 98

Ohio Valley Metrology
and the Serpent Mound 98

Marshall's Rule...........................101

A Perspective on Miscellaneous Measure .102

The Mystery of Measure 104

The Serpent and the Mysteries............107

Apollo and the Python 108

The Python of Pythagoras.................111

Serpent Mound as Python.................112

The Revelation 113

The Woman in Revelation 116

The Name of Jesus 119

    The Term Christos 121

    The Resplendent Sun or Son:

    The Spirit of 1776....................122

    The Cardinal Number 1776 122

    The Measure of 1776 124

The Phoenix Mystery 125

Spiritual Chemistry.........................125

    The Alchemy of the Vesica..............127

    The Great Alchemical Furnace 128

    The Serpent and the Cross:
        The Mystery of Distillation 128

    The Worm and the Dragon 130

The Great Magnetic Line 135

    Phoenix Resting 136

In Search of the Alphabet of the Gods

The Power of the Word 141

**The Symbolism of the Serpent:
Alpha through Omega** 153

The Alpha Symbol 153

The Beta Symbol 154

The Gamma Symbol 156

The Delta Symbol 157

The Epsilon Symbol.......................159

The Zeta Symbol 161

The Eta Symbol 162

The Theta Symbol 163

The Iota Symbol..........................164

The Kappa Symbol........................165

The Lambda Symbol 166

The Mu Symbol 168

The Nu Symbol...........................169

The Xi Symbol 171

The Omicron Symbol 173

The Pi Symbol............................175

The Rho Symbol 177

The Sigma Symbol 179

   Sigma: The Final Doubling
      and Separation......................180

   Pythagoras and the Sigma 180

The Tau Symbol 181

The Upsilon Symbol 183

The Phi Symbol 184

The Chi Symbol 186

The Psi Symbol...........................188

The Omega Symbol 190

Epilogue...................................193

The Rosetta Stone Metaphor 194

The Vision 196

Notes 199

Bibliography 210

Index 213

List of Illustrations

Figure 1. Putnam's Diagram Showing a
   Cross-section of the Serpent Mound 7

Figure 2. Heartland of the Prehistoric
   Adena-Hopewell People 8

Figure 3. Solar Alignments at the
   Serpent Mound..........................10

Figure 4. Romain's Map Showing Lunar
   Alignments at Serpent Mound 13

Figure 5. The Hardman Summer
   Solstice Setting Sun Alignment
   Crossing Romain's Polaris Alignment....15

Figure 6. Romain's Serpent Mound Map
   Superimposed Over Draconis...........16

Figure 7. The Thuban Circle 17

Figure 8. Comparison of the Two
   Depictions of Draconis..................18

Figure 9. Polaris and Thuban Alignments ...19

Figure 10. Serpent Mound with Big and
   Little Dippers...........................19

Figure 11. The Arrows of Artemis 20

Figure 12. Stonehenge and Serpent
   Mound—A Sky Map....................21

Figure 13. Serpent Mound Relative to a
   Golden Mean Spiral.....................23

Figure 14. Serpent in Association with
   an Egg 24

Figure 15. Seven Circles—
   The Foundation of the Hexagon 26

Figure 16. The Hexagon of the Wise........26

Figure 17. Great Solar Hexagon:
   Throne of the One......................30

Figure 18. The Numbering of the Sacred
   Hexagon 32

Figure 19. Αμεν: 96. 37

Figure 20. Pi and the Geometry of the
   Hexagon 39

Figure 21. Vesica with Double Serpents
   from the Middle Ages 40

Figure 22. Womb of the Creative Forces 42

Figure 23. Construction of the Vesica
   Piscis Using Equilateral Triangles 42

Figure 24. Link Between Serpent Mound
   and the Vesica Piscis 43

Figure 25. The Great Serpent as the Word
   or Logos 43

Figure 26. The Pythagorean Theorem 45

Figure 27. The Python of Pythagoras 46

Figure 28. Astrological Symbols Associated
   with the Pythagorean Theorem. 46

Figure 29. Magic Square of Four 47

Figure 30. 816 47

Figure 31. The Enigma of the Cube 47

Figure 32. The Twenty-four Sides
   of the Cube 47

Figure 33. The Cube and the Magic Square
   of Four 48

Figure 34. The Figures 34 by 24
   Discovered in the Parthenon 48

Figure 35. Ophi—the Ancient Greek
   Name for Draconis and Serpent. 49

Figure 36. The Golden Spiral 50

Figure 37. The Arbelos 51

Figure 38. The Sacred Cut 51

Figure 39. Serpent in the Sacred Cut 51

Figure 40. Use of Sacred Number
   at the Serpent's Head. 52

Figure 41. Phi Ratio at the Tip
   of the Serpent. 52

Figure 42. A Further Example of the
   Phi Ratio at the Serpent's Head. 52

Figure 43. Tet and Tuat 54

Figure 44. Rediscovering the Base
   of the Great Pyramid. 54

Figure 45. Using Circle, Square and
   Triangle to Divine the Golden Mean. 57

Figure 46. Geometry of the Great Pyramid
   United with the Solar Hexagon 58

Figure 47. Serpent as Center of the Great
   Pyramid's Geometry 58

Figure 48. The Great Pyramid and the
   Measure of 777 59

Figure 49. Geometrical Reasoning behind
   the Architecture of the Great Pyramid. . . 59

Figure 50. Kircher's Sephirothic Tree. 63

Figure 51. Strange Orb 64

Figure 52. Magic Squares Sacred to
   Mercury. 65

Figure 53. Magic Square of Eight as
   Building Block for the Tree of Life. 66

Figure 54. Solar Hexagon and the Tree
   of Life. 66

Figure 55. The Mercurial Ank 68

Figure 56. The Tree of Life as the Ten
   Doors 70

Figure 57. The Ark of Moses 71

Figure 58. The Wheel of the Ages 74

Figure 59. Cryptoexplosion Anomalies
   in the Midwest. 82

Figure 60. Serpent Mound
   Cryptoexplosion. 83

Figure 61. The Box, the Tree, and the
   Sacred Serpent 85

Figure 62. The Great Solar Hexagon
   Showing True North Alignment 86

Figure 63. The Furnace of the Wise. 86

Figure 64. Square of the Sun................90

Figure 65. Number of the Beast 92

Figure 66. The Serpent Mound Unit
and 666 93

Figure 67. Starry Dragon 93

Figure 68. The Primary Hexagon 96

Figure 69. An Alternate Version of the
Hexagon 97

Figure 70. The Circle of Thuban 99

Figure 71. Romain's Serpent Mound
Units..................................100

Figure 72. Romain's Units in the Star
Pattern of Serpent Mound 101

Figure 73. Marshall's Units in the Star
Pattern of the Serpent Mound 102

Figure 74. How the Foot Relates to the
Megalithic Yard 103

Figure 75. Man in his Embryonic Stage
Awaits Maturation within the Great Egg...
107

Figure 76. The Delphi Circle 109

Figure 77. The Circle of Thuban and the
Delphi Circle 110

Figure 78. The Celestial Woman............116

Figure 79. Mysteries of the
Womb-Delphos........................117

Figure 80. The Seven Heads of the Beast ..117

Figure 81. The Tail of the Dragon 118

Figure 82. The Dragon Waiting before
the Womb 119

Figure 83. Numbering the Hexagon........120

Figure 84. Dawning of the Great Serpent..121

Figure 85. 888 and the Spiritual Son.......123

Figure 86. 1776 124

Figure 87. The Devouring of the Sun.......125

Figure 88. The Serpent and the Egg........127

Figure 89. The Mystical Number
of Jesus Christ 127

Figure 90. 777............................129

Figure 91. Symbol of the Fish 131

Figure 92. A Prehistoric Native American
Flying Dragon 132

Figure 93. The Great Seal 133

Figure 94. A Heraldry Phoenix............134

Figure 95. The Great Magnetic Line
and the Great Western Meridian........135

Figure 96. The Greek Alphabet 152

Figure 97. Alpha and Omega..............153

Figure 98. Alpha.........................154

Figure 99. Constructing the Miniscule
Alpha..................................154

Figure 100. Beta's Twin Serpents..........154

Figure 101. Majuscule Beta 155

Figure 102. Majuscule Beta Shown in
Transparency 155

Figure 103. Minuscule Beta 155

Figure 104. The Forerunner of the
Minuscule English *B* 156

Figure 105. Majuscule Gamma is Defined
by the Sacred Cut 156

Figure 106. The Comma and the Sacred
Cut....................................157

Figure 107. Majuscule and Miniscule
Gamma................................157

Figure 108. Daleth and Delta..............157

Figure 109. Majuscule Delta...............158

Figure 110. Minuscule Delta 158

Figure 111. Epsilon.......................159

Figure 112. Epsilon's Divining Bar.........160

Figure 113. The Thunderbolt of Creation
and Destruction 160

Figure 114. Majuscule Zeta 161

Figure 115. Minuscule Zeta 161

Figure 116. Theraen Double Square 162

Figure 117. Majuscule Eta.................162

Figure 118. Minuscule Eta.................163

Figure 119. Comparison Between the Eye of Horus and the Serpent's Head 164

Figure 120. Iota..........................164

Figure 121. Majuscule Kappa and the Golden Mean...........................165

Figure 122. Majuscule Kappa 165

Figure 123. Minuscule Kappa Within the Two Serpents 166

Figure 124. The Golden Vesica Details the Geometry of Kappa................166

Figure 125. Lambda 167

Figure 126. Mu 168

Figure 127. Nu............................170

Figure 128. Gamma and Nu 170

Figure 129. The Holy Spirit filling Adam with the Breath of Life making Man....170

Figure 130. Digamma.......................171

Figure 131. *Hexagrammon* 171

Figure 132. The Hexagon Within 171

Figure 133. The Cube in the Hexagon......171

Figure 134. Tetractys 171

Figure 135. Fifth and Seventh Coils 172

Figure 136. Majuscule Xi Upon the Coils ..172

Figure 137. Apollonian Severance 172

Figure 138. The Grafting of Minuscule Xi..172

Figure 139. How Xi Represents Sight......173

Figure 140. The Delphi Circle, the Arbelos and the Phi Ratio 174

Figure 141. The Serpent Revealing the Phi Ratio 174

Figure 142. Construction of the Two Omicrons...............................175

Figure 143. Plotting the Arbelos 176

Figure 144. Interesting Features of the Arbelos....................................176

Figure 145. Majuscule Pi 176

Figure 146. Minuscule Pi 177

Figure 147. The Egyptian Uraeus 178

Figure 148. Majuscule and Minuscule Rho. 178

Figure 149. Stau 179

Figure 150. The Dual Serpents of Minuscule Sigma 179

Figure 151. Majuscule Sigma 180

Figure 152. Majuscule Sigma Using Rotated Hexagon 180

Figure 153. Tau 182

Figure 154. Oroboros......................183

Figure 155. Majuscule and Minuscule Upsilon 183

Figure 156. About the English V 184

Figure 157. The Mysterious Phi 185

Figure 158. The Alignment of Minuscule Phi.......................................185

Figure 159. Majuscule Chi Extends Beyond the Visible 187

Figure 160. Minuscule Chi in a Graph of the Sacred Cut.......................187

Figure 161. Minuscule Psi 188

Figure 162. The Tree of Life Becomes the Phoenix Rising 188

Figure 163. Completing the Definition of Minuscule Psi..........................189

Figure 164. The Feet of Majuscule Omega . 191

Figure 165. Grafting Minuscule Omega....191

Figure 166. The Cincinnati Tablet 194

Preface

THE GREAT SERPENT MOUND HAS BEEN CLASSIFIED with a large collection of North American prehistoric earthen mounds extending from the East Coast to the Mississippi River and beyond. This particular work, however, is distinguished from the countless other mounds and earthen structures throughout the eastern United States in that its design can be dated to a period about 5,000 years ago. Only Watson Brake, a group of mounds in Louisiana discovered in the last decade of the twentieth century, can rival its antiquity. But to my knowledge, nothing in the Americas compares with the Serpent Mound in terms of the precise astronomic, arithmetic, geometric, and spiritual knowledge it embodies.

Because of the architectural skill with which the ancient animal forms and some of the geometric earthworks were constructed, in many cases they actually have outlived stoneworks built at the same time and even before. But due to their humble external appearance—they are after all little more than reinforced mounds of earth—antiquarians, not unlike today's archaeologists, did not consider them as worthy of preservation or as interesting as works of stone. Uncounted earthworks have been allowed to fall prey to artifact hunters and gold seekers, often before any responsible analysis or detailed record of their characteristics could be made. Even today, commercial interests endanger the Newark earthworks. The Ohio Serpent Mound would have been destroyed with time had it not been for the efforts of Harvard's Frederick Ward Putnam at the end of the nineteenth century.

The Great Serpent Mound is situated in southwestern Ohio's Adams County, not far from the Ohio River. It is on the western edge of an elevated plateau overlooking Brush Creek, one of the last unpolluted streams in the entire state. Owning three features, the Serpent's complete body, uncoiled and stretched out, would measure more than a quarter of a mile tip to tail. Its height varies from perhaps less than ten inches at the end of the tail's helix to several feet at the opposite end. The earthwork appears to be a serpent attempting to swallow, regurgitate, or simply be in association with an object archaeologists refer to as "the oval feature," or the Great Oval. At the very western end of the Serpent is the smallest feature, a triangular mound measuring approximately 31.6 feet along its east base.

The earthwork is aligned exactly to the north. Numerous other features show that its builders oriented it to astronomical phenomena in a startlingly rich and detailed fashion and built it in accord with precise principles of geometry and arithmetic. Many other prehistoric earthworks and stoneworks also show astronomical and mathematical connections, but it is one of the aims of this book to demonstrate how the Great Serpent Mound is unique in the sheer number and complexity of these connections. In this regard it exceeds even the Great Pyramid of ancient Egypt or the Parthenon of Greece. Truly, it is a wonder of the prehistoric world.

In spring of 1986, the odyssey of this investigation of the mysterious Serpent began, and, to date, it has not come to an end. I had been addressing the Great Serpent Mound chapter of the American Society of Dowsers at Antioch College in Yellow Springs, Ohio, in a series of talks concerning the connection of spirituality with divining practices, a subject in which I had a long-term special interest. These people, many of them my seniors by decades, impressed me with their experience in the field and their unusual insights into earth energies. One Saturday afternoon I left their company with a very nice outline of the mound—a map created by archaeologists Clark and Marjorie Hardman from an aerial photo—that one of the members thought might interest me. Another chapter member had drawn connections on the map in the form of triangles, showing positions of what the dowsers termed "blind springs"—subterranean collections of water and magnetic energy at various points on the Serpent's body. These triangles fit relatively harmoniously into each other, forming a sort of primitive gridwork along the curving body of the earthwork. The dowsers had also discovered six "energy lines" meeting at the center of the Great Oval. I was inspired to sit down and begin extrapolating on the geometry. I didn't know that the mound had a northern orientation at that time, but I came up with the first example of what later was named the "solar hexagon," called in the current parlance the "flower of life geometry." It is a continuous grid that can be superimposed very naturally upon the mound, based upon and inspired by the on-site work of the dowsers.

On the 1988 summer solstice, when all sorts of people were congregating at the mound (as in local practice at solstice time), I attended the scene equipped with the Hardman rendering of the mound. I'd hoped to find someone there receptive to the implications of the discovery of the hexagonal pattern. One of the first people who showed an interest was a Native American

shaman from Circleville, Ohio, named Little Eagle. He took a long look at it and, raising his head, faced me and asked, "Where do we go from here?" His response was similar to that of another Native American shaman, Sun Bear, to whom I later showed a copy of the pattern while he was in town promoting one of his books. In truth, I myself had only an inkling of where we were headed, feeling mostly that we were just at the beginning of a period of important discoveries. The general consensus at the mound at that time was that we should acquire as much property surrounding the park as possible in order to enable some crucial future event surrounding the mound, the exact nature of which few wished to voice. It was felt that we were about to participate in the unfolding of a mystery rite whose implication went far beyond mere antiquarian interest—that some approaching event in some way would "reactivate" the Serpent as a source of knowledge and wisdom.

Within a few weeks I was introduced to William F. Romain, an archaeologist and anthropologist who had been working at the Serpent Mound for some time, creating a more accurate map of the site. Bill was very helpful and gave me a finished copy of his now-famous ground survey. My study of the geometry of the mysterious earthwork began in earnest, for Romain's map, unlike the Hardmans', was exceedingly accurate and allowed correlation with geometrical and astronomical patterns to proceed apace.

The *mystery* of the Serpent Mound boils down to the questions of who designed it, who constructed it, and why. It is probably beyond our capacities to determine exactly what our Serpent was signifying. In the opinion of some, it is a "manitou," a Native American term for "spiritual entity." I would take this notion a step further, being now convinced that our Serpent is "Gitche Manitou," which is to say, the "Great

Spirit" and ancestral guardian of the ancient people. Yet while the Great Serpent has long been believed to be a treasure indigenous to North America, there are undeniable connections in its design to distant regions of the ancient world. The alphabet of the Greeks, while not enjoying the same antiquity of design, somehow utilized the template of the earthwork to construct its sacred system of letters. This is discussed in the last sections of this book.

In any case, it seems beyond the scope of regional archaeology to grasp the full intention of the mound's designer. However, such archaeology has helped immensely in this work, and so I am in its debt. The insights of Native Americans, coupled with the efforts of the archaeological community, have only succeeded in discerning a deeper mystery surrounding the Serpent Mound.

Our Great Serpent, showpiece of the world's ancient architectural forms, may once have been perceived as the representation of an extensive body of knowledge that could be wisely described as a philosophic masterpiece, a magnum opus. Constructed to demonstrate the highest possible esoteric concepts, our Serpent Mound is the remnant of an ancient philosophical transmission.

Though bearing some similarities to classical earth and stoneworks, the Great Serpent Mound is anthropologically distinct from the great Mystery Schools of the ancient world. These are the schools that built the Egyptian pyramids and whose knowledge and science stood behind the great Greek temples such as the Parthenon. Nevertheless, through a careful analysis of the structure of the mound, it is possible to see that it is a remnant of an ancient sacred worldview whose concerns and principles are not at all unlike those of the notably familiar monuments of antiquity. What is more, the serpent effigy is an icon that gathers in its structure knowledge from a whole series of schools of ancient wisdom. It embodies the arithmetic of the Pythagoreans, the sacred geometry behind Mediterranean architecture, the astronomical knowledge of the Babylonians, and an esoteric teaching already ancient before them all. As just noted, analysis of structure intimate to the Serpent Mound reveals that the design embodies the original template of the written alphabet that, through the Semitic scribes and the Phoenicians, the Greeks initiated the process of civilization itself through the invention of writing.

The symbolism—the image of the Serpent devouring or regurgitating the Great Oval seems to reiterate themes from world myth. It is not difficult to see its similarity to the Orphic cosmology and its snake encircling the World Egg, or the story associated with the origin of the Oracle at Delphi involving Apollo and the slaying of the giant Python. What we have here is a symbolic compendium coming from remotest antiquity, and the question is how did it come to America? What is the true source of the knowledge it contains? Did all of the ancient wisdom ultimately derive somehow from *it,* or, as seems more likely, was there a far earlier historical period or otherworldly source that communicated this knowledge through symbols that arrived both in ancient America and in the ancient Near East? For the Serpent Mound, though an earthwork, through its exact correlation with the astronomical constellation Draco, is a *celestial* serpent, and so we can truly say that it came to us from the stars!

Whatever its origin, properly understood, the symbolism of the stellar serpent contained in the Great Serpent Mound may be viewed as a *golden thread* running through all the great religious systems of the world and potentially functioning as a key to their secrets. The serpent image itself is a compacted seed of light, a bearer of all knowledge. Like the worm of the mythical phoenix, the shape of which is familiar yet forgotten, the Great Serpent's destiny is to be recognized as a harbinger of light, ultimately to be reinstated to its true fullness of form, dominating the landscape and politics of the human race. It would be the first of the apocalyptic "seals" to be opened, aptly called the Great Seal; these auguring a time when peace and prosperity will once again rule the Earth.

Though we now have begun to see that the patterns contained in some of the earthworks are actually alignments pertaining to the stars and to the paths of the sun and moon along the horizon, we are also at the dawn of a more far-reaching illumination. So profound in meaning and broad in scope is this revelation that it may very well test the general populace to the rational limits of its mental horizon. As this book attempts to disclose, because of the general and universal knowledge embodied in the Serpent's design, this little dragon may prove to be the focus of a multi-dimensional scheme of the genius of a distant golden age.

My heartfelt thanks and all love goes to the memory of my Master, Sant Kirpal Singh, without whose continuing inner guidance throughout this research, many of the insights to the mysteries herein presented would have been overlooked. The Great Master's service rendered to me has been more than a humbling experience; the methodology and explanations for the rediscovery of the first Greek alphabet were wholly dependent upon His Grace and ceaseless love from above and within.

The Great Serpent Mound chapter of the American Society of Dowsers was initially responsible for putting me on the way regarding the mysteries of the mound vicinity. Their attitude, insight, and methods in approaching ancient and sacred sites have been both an education and an inspiration. Thanks go to the Hendrixons of Montgomery, Ohio, who currently preside over the chapter, as well as the late Richie Liming, former president. A special tribute also to John Price, who literally devoted the last years of his life to ensuring the Brush Creek against future exploitation.

I am indebted to the Native American community, whose continuing love and respect for the land and its ancient sacred places—some of which must always remain concealed from the oblivious attitude of the white race—had inspired a preservation of the ancient earthworks right until the time of the pioneer movement west. I am especially pleased with the warmth and genuine interest conveyed from the members of the St. Regis Mohawk Tribe and the Mohawk Council of Akwesasne. I can only hope to be worthy of their continuing trust and respect.

Special thanks also to Drago Plĕcto, Aaron Hamilton, Fred Hamilton, Dave Duszynski, Bob Genheimer, the Bomkamps, and the many friends who helped or inspired.

Author's Cut to the Chase

A T ONE POINT IN NORTH AMERICAN PREHISTORY, a singular intelligence owning extraordinary depth of purpose designed the Great Serpent Mound. The term "designed" is chosen carefully, for the age of the physical structure is yet a matter of debate. One thing is becoming certain however: the mound serves as a focal point illustrating a number of practical operations in the sciences of antiquity. In this, its design is only *possibly* of North American origin.

"Repository" is a term rarely used in archaeology, more commonly applying to libraries and time capsules. Referring to the Serpent Mound, the word should be capitalized, for the mound is nothing less than an exemplar of the term. Currently, there is no other earth or stone work so excellently combining the "colleges" of our distant past. In this the Serpent could be termed a "multi-disciplinary" work, doubtlessly the labor of either a great organizer of scientific wisdom or an outright genius. Astronomy, arithmetic, geometry, and metrology are all wonderfully contained by it. Additionally, there are more than ample traces of the esoteric sciences of spiritual chemistry (alchemy), numerology, and kabbalistic geometry-astrology (from *qabbalah:* something received as passed down from tradition). Moreover, the creation of the first alphabet of the Greeks apparently utilized the sublime body of the serpent as the source of its numerically organized characters. There are strong indications of Egyptian, Babylonian, Etruscan, and Semitic symbolism as well, therefore the design

could date back 4,500 years or more.

Because there were virtually no artifacts discovered in the mound itself, no one in mainstream archaeology to date has successfully proven age and authorship of our "geoglyph's" design. This is the beginning of the continuing mystery, and this is where one starts to ask questions. Christian pioneers believed that it stood to explain the Edenic Serpent. Later, it was construed to be from the era of the Adena People.[1] Later still, it was argued that the mound was of Hopewell[2] origination. Charcoal samples retrieved in the early 1990s suggested yet another group having been responsible for the sculpture: the Fort Ancient People, an early branch of the Mississippi Culture.[3] On top of it all, the late 1990s brought the discovery of an extended pattern from starry Draconis nicely aligning with the most accurate map of the earthwork. As stated above, this and similar discoveries take the design so far back into prehistory that it now gathers to itself a mystique such as that surrounding the pyramids at Giza.

The Great Serpent uncannily inspires a variety of ideas and theories concerning its meaning and origins. This in itself is a clue to its true meaning and importance. The absence of artifacts may be a great blessing, for it has fueled a never-ending inquiry into Great Serpent's origins.

Earlier in U.S. history, it was popular to perceive the identity of the Mound Builders of what is the now eastern United States as a lost race of highly intelligent, well-organized, and industrious people. Speculation abounded concerning their possible Old World roots. It was rumored that a race of giants once ruled the region, and indeed many skeletons of men and women exceeding seven feet in height were discovered. Overall, an uncoordinated exploration of the uncounted tombs was enacted. This activity was accompanied by a predictable destruction of the geometric and linear pattern earthworks, the reasons for the existence of which, to this day, have not been determined. Most earthen structures were excavated long before any organized archaeological interest came onto the scene. Sometimes recorded by landowners and their amateur antiquarian comrades, their contents and whereabouts are mostly now long lost. It is odd how the mounds remained unmolested for untold centuries, becoming then obliterated with the arrival of the Christian culture in the short span of a few decades.

Early on, samples of artifacts were submitted to Thomas Jefferson who subsequently declared them "Indian." In the minds of some scholars, this commenced the collapse of the imagined possibilities including mysterious visitors from Atlantis. However, the actual fact of the matter was yet supportive of a lost race of superior accomplishments, for from first-hand excavations of their back acreage, the landowners of Pennsylvania, the Virginias, Kentucky, Ohio, Michigan, and Indiana knew of greater mysteries, and raised questions the archaeologists have never been able to answer.

Most all of the earthworks described in the Colonial and post-Revolutionary War periods are gone, and looting has taken its toll. Much has been lost not only in artifact science but in the realm of archaeoastronomy, for the original positioning of a great many structures, so necessary to determine astronomical correspondence, has been lost beyond rediscovery. So even though

the Serpent Mound was fortunately isolated from the mischief of the White Man's onslaught, it nevertheless seems an act of divine intervention that the Serpent Mound has been spared.

Now new research has begun to verify what many have mused over for generations: the design of the Serpent Mound of Adams County, Ohio, is cryptically linked to an early Eastern or pan-Indo-European influence. This is not to say that its design originated across the ocean, only that there is a link between there and here that is not understood at this time. Plato in his *Laws* inferred that the Egyptian priestcraft inherited and practiced a consolidated science of number and proportionate form expressing extraordinary harmony between the heavens and humankind. This "canon" (Greek. for "measuring rod," "rule") formed a basis for the support of civilization and culture, and was to extent adopted by the classical Greeks. The early philosopher, Pythagoras, lived in the middle of the first millennium before the Common Era, and his genius—though scattered with his faithful following his death—enlightened several successive Mystery Colleges. The Merkaba, Essene, and Gnostic Schools are well known to have contributed much to the literature and thought of the early Church. The Great Serpent Mound's design embodies so fine a focus on the essential code and cipher of these learned traditions that while they are somewhat fragmented, the earthwork offers a unifying clue to their origin. Scholars have scratched their heads for centuries, confounded by what has been termed the Pythagorean Skein: the codes and riddles of a mysterious tradition when the "gods," seen as the stars, communicated with men. The key to unraveling this may well be our unassuming Serpent Mound. Analysis of its astronomy, geometry, and measurement alone may reveal one of the greatest lost mysteries of antiquity: the

Python of Pythagoras. (See "The Pythagorean Theorem Connection.")

The Great Light Bearer

It was not until the 1980s that the first truly accurate ground survey of the giant mound was made, surpassing at least five other serious attempts spanning more than a century. The first widely known map was E. G. Squire and E. H. Davis' caricature published in their classic *Ancient Monuments of the Mississippi Valley* in 1848. This familiar drawing is still used in classroom texts in spite of its being a grotesque facsimile of the actual mound. William F. Romain, archaeologist and northern Ohio resident, with great care and in sub-freezing weather properly surveyed the entire structure. He then published this extraordinary mapping in 1987 in the periodical *Ohio Archaeologist*. Later, Romain published his classic *Solar Eclipse Hypothesis* revealing six important lunar phase alignments positioned across the Serpent's coils. But the science of archaeoastronomy took a more firm position in his long-overdue and enlightening discovery of an accurate true north line extending from the eastern apex of the hollow triangular feature (which is at the Serpent's head) down to the tip of the coiled tail. This line created a clarifying moment in the long history of the monument, for magnetic and gravitational anomalies at the site cause compasses to render unusually incorrect readings.

Shortly thereafter, Robert V. Fletcher and Terry L. Cameron added a map-coordinated contribution to the earth-and-sky aspect of archaeoastronomy, submitting that the Hardmans' and Romain's previously theorized solstice and equinox dawn events of the solar calendar could have been viewed also through alignments created by the coils.[4] Another alignment, discovered by Clark and Marjorie Hardman some years before, demonstrates the summer solstice sun setting across the Great Oval. This alignment meets at a nearly perfect 60-degree angle with the North Star alignment. All told, there are at least twelve verifiable, geo-astronomical alignments contributed by competent archaeological researches, independent of one another. In this alone is enough information on critical celestial events to fill an ephemeris on the acquired knowledge of prehistoric geo-astronomy.

In point of fact, the mound could be considered a rich synthesis of heavenly light coordinated with the intent to produce the earth body for this titan. No other effigy known in the world even suggests such a complete pantheon of meaningful celestial divinings. Thus it is at last realized that our grand old Serpent, long passed over by an international tendency to emphasize stonework over earth, is a very creative architecture resulting from a remarkably discerning mind.

A Unique Discovery

There is another legitimate expression in archaeoastronomy that does not focus on the sun and the moon directly. It is so rarely encountered that its discoveries are held as invaluable examples of the ancient genius. It looks directly to the stars themselves for further clues concerning the secret attraction of the world's most venerable sites. In the case of the Serpent Mound, we may observe hoary Draco for help in positioning the monumental earthwork back to the heavens where it enlightened the ancient stargazer's nocturnal vigils.

Over thirty points of light were translated precisely as seen in the sky to the earth, and it's only guesswork how it may have been done. Not only does it clarify the accuracy of Putnam's nineteenth century "reconstruction," but also indicates that the Serpent Mound may be viewed from nearly any direction, for its star pattern design is classically "circumpolar," meaning that its star pattern has at its center an ancient North Star. Nowhere else on our planet has such a complete expression of astral lore been found.[5] Other geo-astronomical sites are being discovered, but as for purely astral correlations, only the Angkor Wat complex[6] and of course the Egyptian pyramids corresponding to the three stars of the belt of Orion may compare, if they compare at all.

Thus, the proposed *grand* astronomical phenomenon of Serpent Mound is unparalleled. It serves as a brilliant fusion of mythological import successfully incorporating sun, moon, and stars into its leviathan form. The average observer might assume that with the uncanny ability of the designer to research and incorporate all this celestial information, he or she would have been satisfied. But the Gitche Manitou may well be the work of a genius, and genius is often very thorough in serious undertakings.

Sacred Geometry

In nearly every country of the world, schoolchildren at one time or another are familiarized with the Pythagorean Theorem. Also called the "47th Proposition of Euclid," it is the placement of three squares in such a way that a right-angle triangle is created. But if someone were to tell you that in remotely ancient times this equation was possibly taught using the visual aid of our subject, you might laugh. Yet not only the famous theorem, but several other key geometric forms may have had the dynamic likeness of our Serpent utilized in order to bring home the possible *unity of form* and *arithmetic* to the student. Coupled with their learned astronomy, geometry and measure were important areas of study

to our ancestors. This is where the understanding of the Great Serpent as a *universal template* of the ancient sciences begins to take on more substance.

But even the thought of Serpent Mound having something to do with a culture originating far away from the borders of North America is offensive to conservative archaeological and anthropological interests. Moreover, some seated academics would be displeased at the notion of their work being outdated. It is an old story with a familiar pattern. Because esoteric philosophic study never has been seriously considered an adjunct to Native American archaeological theory and practice (as dictated by the white establishment), any spiritually advanced cultural influence in the Americas is not detectable. Were all revealed however, Western archaeological interest might be stirred at the prospect of such a unique treasure in its midst. Thus much needs to be accomplished in this area, beginning with a few simple diagrams and explanations in the chapters following. It is, in part, these geometric examples that constitute a *new form* of proof—evidence not to be confused with current archaeological methods, such as digging, DNA testing, and carbon dating. For while these methods would appear to "cover the bases" for information gathering, in reality they merely reflect the materialistic bias of the conservative branch of the archaeological community.

The Great Serpent, in this "new" sense, serves as an archaeological precedent for a proper overview of the ancients' traditional integration of geometry (Greek "earth" and "measure") with astronomy to consummate the science-art of "geomancy," divination by the sacred characteristics of landscape. Such astro-geometric lore surrounding and penetrating the construction's awesome presence speaks volumes of pre-Christian sacred science, a tradition enriching the ensuing faith with the staying power of previous ages of enlightened thought. The Serpent's majestic form, nestled quietly in a very rural area of the Ohio countryside, remains a mystical reminder of a remote prehistory that we must someday regain. What is more, the park has become a place of pilgrimage for those seeking to be in touch with such a prehistory, the testimonies of visionary and dreamlike experiences are frequent. In fact, a whole book could be written on the subject. Physical and psychical phenomena in various forms have been glimpsed there. Overall, it is a hallowed place, home of a most mysterious earthwork from which the naked truth underscoring a forgotten tradition is formally revealed.

How Old Is Serpent Mound?

With the recent discovery of Louisiana's Watson Brake[7] collection of intact mounded structures, the notion of a mound being 5,000 years old or more is no longer held to be untenable. That Serpent Mound's design may be from the same era generates bright new light on the study of the antiquity of North American earth architecture.

The Serpent Mound Park receives thousands of visitors every year. It is covered with a thick, bright-green carpet in the spring, that by summer's end returns to the status of dryness as does much of the Ohio Valley flora. It stands anywhere from less than a foot at the end of its spiral tail to an impressive embankment toward the head area. Underneath the grass is a certain amount of topsoil recently placed there due to damage sustained by the Harmonic Convergence gathering in the mid-1980s. But this did nothing to alter the measure or appearance of the structure.

On average, the Serpent is about 20 feet wide on its undulating body. The head and helix are a bit more than 80 feet wide, and the Great Oval is about 124 by 64 feet. If outstretched, the total length—including the three separated features—would be 1,370 feet (by close approximation). There are variations on the linear measure of the earthwork, depending upon where the measuring stops. One will often find references to the Serpent being 1,348 feet, a figure obviously not including the small triangular feature at the west end. There are references to its being 500-plus feet, explaining the distance across the length of the earthwork.

The Serpent lies directly on the dolomite bedrock, as well as the loess that comprises the plateau, indicating that the area was found by the builders as bare stone and clay—or was *cleared* by them—an intriguing prospect![8]

At the beginning of the 1990s the sacred structure was again altered slightly, this time in the hope of uncovering evidence of the terraform's true date of birth. It was Fletcher and Cameron's idea to test-sample some small fragments of charcoal by the carbon[14] method, a very popular scientific tool. Going into a trench believed previously dug by Frederick Putnam and his late nineteenth-century Harvard team, these twentieth-century scientists retrieved good carbon and reported that the dates fell into the vicinity of the start of the second millennium of the present Christian calendar, about 1070 C.E. (930 B.P.) However, this was in strong contradiction to established belief, not to mention contradictory data, and thus the new dating quickly drew the scrutiny of the devil's advocate. That there were people at the site at that time is a well-established fact, people that burned wood for fires. It has always been an attracting magnet, and likely always will be.

A Forgotten Clue

Professor Putnam was the first professional archaeologist to spend any real time at the site, although Squier and Davis' famous journeys preceded him by about thirty-five years. He writes that at the time of his predecessors' visit a healthy forest cloaked the area, made obvious by a number of noble stumps present when he arrived for his first visit in late summer of 1883. Putnam was subtle but astute in suggesting that the mound is an important pictograph or sacred earth symbol. Perhaps predictably, succeeding archaeological interests have read his scholarship selectively.

Our professor has the added distinction of being awarded the honorable Father of American Archaeology title for his dedication and insightful methodology in approaching such significant sacred sites. He viewed the mound as a possible link to a once worldwide belief focusing its ritual import on the mercurial form of the serpent. Any number of ophidian (serpentine) earth and stone works once existed in North America alone, and Putnam describes others around the world, one even larger than our Adams County sculpture. Putnam found that such rare evidence of the serpent faith was at the mercy of simple agricultural interests: the need for a few extra acres to grow corn. Thus he purchased the Serpent Mound property in 1886 from a Mr. Lovett, yet another in a long line of would-be dragon slayers such as those who characterized the early to mid-Christian era throughout Britain.[9]

Lovett, or the one to whom he entrusted the duties of plowing, never cut deep enough with his share to disturb the special clay underlying the mound, if he plowed upon it at all. There is no indication that the head or tail was ever even disturbed by farming, and hardly any sign that

the body could have been. Besides, J. P. MacLean stated after his two surveys (1884) that although the promontory where the effigy rests was under cultivation, the earthwork itself showed no signs of having been cultivated. So if any corn planting was done, it was in the narrow space between MacLean's survey work and Putnam's second visit, a negligible amount of time. If fact, one might think the two men's paths crossed. As it was, so much topsoil had accumulated since the work was created that the original under-formation of clay was intact at the time of Putnam's purchase—safely blanketed to the uniform depth of "about a foot" by the honest professor's reckoning.

This was the clue. There is disagreement among the archaeologists, recreational and professional, concerning whether the stone-and-clay serpent was covered with topsoil after it was completed. Some believe that a thin covering was applied, perhaps to form a "skin" over the "animal." The fact is that we do not know. We *do* know, however, that topsoil will accumulate on its own, and in abundance, with time.

Putnam was careful to remark that the whole structure of the Serpent was *built to last,* a fact of his findings that is important to remember. According to Putnam, some of the yellow clay was purposely mixed with ashes, reminiscent of the Roman discovery of ash concrete—strong and water-resistant. The excavation team in the early 1990s could not interpret what Putnam meant, finding no ash. However, they may simply have not found what Putnam found, for the limited number of trenches they permitted themselves handicapped them.[10] It should be clearly established that our dedicated Harvard man is the only reliable source we have today for this kind of history. With this understanding, the following information casts a new light on the possible age of the Serpent Mound's design. Has his emphasis on Putnam's soil depth been over-looked? Is the location of the mound conducive to longevity?

Intentionally walked upon and well baked in the hot summer sun, the great meandering form may have been an attempt to create what could be a *titanic ceramic*. This would not be a "fired" ceramic as we think of it today, or even as the Adena People may have fashioned in their as-yet-undiscovered early kilns.[11] The Mandan people are reported to have packed clay to an extremely hard consistency to play a certain field game. The floors of their houses were of clay hardened and polished like a ceramic. It is known that certain African villages packed the earth to the hardness of concrete, polishing it with the natural oil from their feet. Although he redistributed the topsoil in his reconstruction, Putnam did not alter the shape of the clay effigy, and thereby the original under-design remained intact. That figure is the one we view today, and was first mapped, with minor inaccuracies, under the auspices of the Ohio Historical Society around the beginning of the twentieth century by Clinton Cowan.

Putnam intimated that the Serpent and the Adena were coeval, meaning that when the Adena (1000 B.C.E. to 100–200 C.E.) were there, the mound was as well. Perhaps the abundance of clay helped him to form the opinion that the Serpent Mound may have been an Adena creation. This is not known. In this reasoning however, the Great Serpent would have been a project that went right along with the development of these very early ceramics.[12] The sun-drying technique would have been replaced by controlled fire even as the art evolved. As logical as this may sound, it may as easily not be the case, for the mound may well be pre-Adena. To understand why, we have to make special note of Putnam's soil depth and then look a little farther.

Standing on Putnam's Shoulders

Between the years 1987 and 1996, a distinguished Ph.D. in archaeology, Robert Connolly, worked at nearby Fort Ancient. Just off Interstate 71 north of Cincinnati, Fort Ancient is also a frequently visited structure, attributed to the hand labor of the Hopewell Culture. It is very large, with great walls thrown up in a painstaking effort that must have taken many decades to complete. Early settlers thought it to have been a fortification, hence the name. It is now believed to have been more ceremonial, harboring a number of large notches interrupting the continuity of the great wall. Each opening is being examined for possible astronomical alignments, and some have already shown strong indications of yearly and cyclical horizon events, especially in the northeast corner of the enclosure. It was Jack Blosser, archaeologist with the Ohio Historical Society, who suggested consulting Dr. Connolly on the subject of soil accumulation termed *pedogenesis* (Greek: *pedo*, "soil" plus *genesis*, "creation").

Serpent Mound is about 43 miles from Fort Ancient on a beeline. Both sites have received about the same amount of moisture over the centuries, and both hosted healthy highland forests. Carbon dating at Fort Ancient has been consistent and solid, as a dig to a certain level yields artifacts and carbon enough to date the structure to the time of the Hopewell, even early Hopewell (100 B.C.E.).

In the course of his researches, Dr. Connolly observed that in areas where the pioneers had raised no buildings and made no gardens, an average amount of earth had naturally accumulated. This process of pedogenesis yielded an interesting fact: about ten centimeters (nearly four inches) of new soil had been generated over a 2,000-year span. Flood plains, such as exist just below Fort Ancient and Serpent Mound, may easily acquire yards of material in a similar time period. Thus these two sites are known as "highland enclosures," and therefore serve as ideal acreage for the study of soil accumulation.

Putnam candidly stated in his 1889 *Century Magazine* article that in his time, science had no way of telling how long it takes for a foot of "vegetable mold" to accumulate. But thanks to Dr. Connolly, we are at least beginning to get a ballpark idea. Ten centimeters over 2000 years is a little less than one-quarter inch per century, about the thickness of 100 pages or leaves from an average dictionary. One could look at it like a tree dropping *its* leaves once a year, ideally falling into a protected enclosure to be gradually degraded by the subtle chemistry and tiny microbial appetites of nature.

The professor found about a foot within and on the embankment of the oval, the head's triangular area, and the tail. The whole park showed between five inches and two feet, averaging to something better than a foot—information made more pertinent in light of the probability of the builders having cleared the entire area of surface soil before proceeding with their work. The floor of the oval (by definition the most ideal area to determine soil accumulation) was specially prepared to be flat and smooth. Would it be correct to think that after their trouble the builders would have added topsoil to the floor of the oval? Wouldn't that be like throwing dirt on your sanctuary floor? Since it is not a mounded structure, it would have needed no "protection" from rains. So Putnam was not only asking the right question, but he may have wittingly solved a great mystery through wise observation. Soil depth would place the age of the Great Serpent Mound somewhere in the vicinity of 4,500 to 5,000 years.[13] This is not an unrea-

sonable hypothesis, given the facts.

This would place the Serpent Mound into the prehistoric period called the *Archaic*, and quite possibly constructed by the people called the *Alli*, *Alleghan*, or *Allegewi*, after whom the beautiful Allegheny Mountains were given their name. It is written in the old accounts that they were a mighty people, and workers of wonders. In spite of this, the knowledge of how unyielding established theory can be prompted the search for further evidence of such age. But first the new carbon dates had to be put into perspective.

If a foot of soil accumulated all over the Serpent Mound, and recalling that it was constructed right on the dolomite and loess bedrock, what have the carbon samples from 1070 C.E. to do with accurate dating? We don't know—except that *someone* was spending some time at the site less than 1,000 years ago. It has been shown that the early Mississippi Culture had a small village nearby.

Associate professor of anthropology at Ohio State University, William Dancy, mentions that although radiocarbon is regarded as reliable, the charcoal found in the Serpent Mound could have found its way in into the structure long after it was built. Was carbon dating appropriate procedure for an accurate determination of age for the Serpent Mound? Fletcher and Cameron had created an interesting controversy worthy of further investigation.

Nevertheless, one might be lulled into thinking that parts of the earthwork were made of wood or something organic originally. If such organic material *was* an intimate part of the architectural structuring, that would certainly be solid evidence for age determination through carbon dating. But this was not the case, for the Serpent Mound is unanimously declared to be strictly of earth, clay, and stone construction. It was just carbon that was found—carbon possibly from campfires.

Could the earthen serpent have been reclaimed for ceremonial purposes within the last 1,000 years? Were these possible inheritors seeking to reclaim its powerful presence and rediscover its mysteries? Could signal fires have been lit for some purpose we do not understand? Shouldn't the question be raised as to *how* the fragments of charcoal found their way into the earthwork instead of assuming that they were deposited there as the earthwork was constructed?

A Tip of the Hat to Dr. C

Anthropologists and geologists sometimes use the term "formation processes" to describe how what once lay above ground can end up below through the tunneling and burrowing activities of small rodents and larger mammals. Dr. Connolly described an excavation he once undertook wherein he passed the level of cultural modification into earth or clay never disturbed by man, and yet the artifacts kept appearing. There is something almost humorous about it, as though Nature had decided to play a trick on the scientists. The carbon pieces retrieved by the 1991 excavation team are believed to have been very near an area that Putnam had aerated, conceivably making it easier for the invasion of groundhogs and mice. Added to this, a piece of flint was found intruded below the level of cultural modification in that same excavation. Thus it is not out of the question to suggest that fires could have been lighted atop an already well-established earthwork. In this, the formation processes theory tends to considerably narrow the spectrum of carbon dating acceptance attempting to specifically date the Serpent Mound.

From the Earth to the Stars

Again, to really *prove* something in archaeology, there should be supporting evidence to corroborate the theory. For this, the constellation Draco coupled with simple geometry awarded the theory of age its second proof. Bringing in a variety of reliable star charts, and using a transparency of the mound properly reduced to eliminate incorrect proportions, research revealed that virtually every possible star and light-source of the constellation in the vicinity of the matching map fell upon or by the edge the Great Serpent. Very quickly though it became clear that one lonely-looking star did not fit the outline of the Serpent. It was disarming at first, for here were more than thirty stars and galactic lights falling precisely on the survey map.[14] Yet this one star did not fit in. Instead it rested dead center beneath the seventh coil from the tail—the first below the head area. This irregularity, as it turned out, was to be my second proof.

The luminary was shortly thereafter identified as Draconis-*alpha*. What is remarkable about this star is that at the time topsoil would have begun accumulating at the site of Serpent Mound, **it** was the pole star. What is a pole star? It is a star that sits directly over the planetary pole, apparently not moving even as all the other objects in the night sky move. Because of the effect of precession, one pole star may replace another over a span of time encompassing the clockwork movement of the zodiacal constellations. The star was long ago named *Thuban*,[15] and it is generally accepted that it was used to align certain monuments, such as the Great Pyramid, to true north. Because of its stationary status, Thuban was highly regarded and was reported to have been viewable even during daylight hours.

On an intuition, the "renegade" star was used as a pinpoint for a good compass, and the ink end extended to the northwest tip of the Serpent survey, i.e., the tip of the small triangle mound. An arc was taken to a circle, and the swing touched nearly perfectly on the base of the Serpent's tailing. The distance across the circle corresponded to a measure already found in two of the geometries hosted by the Serpent template, approximately 680 feet. Thuban was the pole star in and around 2750 B.C.E. (4750 B.P.), and so there was a match with the topsoil chronology theory.

To say this in another way, since the pin of the compass touched on Thuban, and the top and bottom of the Serpent were neatly encompassed by the circle, the Serpent could theoretically be viewed as Thuban-centric, i.e., Thuban marked the exact halfway point of the earthwork's design. Thus the so-divided Great Serpent, imagined as a mythological constellation, would have rotated with precision around the highest point of the northern sky, like clock hands sweeping the dome. A clever design like this would only have had real meaning when Thuban was the North Star. (See Figure 7 in the section "Archaeoastronomy.")

One more piece of evidence, and a very good case for this new theory of age would present itself. It came incidentally. In constructing a line parallel to the Polaris line downward from the representation of Thuban (beneath the seventh coil from the tail), the western edge of two of the snake's coils touched so neatly that the alignment appeared intentional. This naturally did not negate the vertical positioning of Romain's true north line (which connects the tip of the tail to the east apex of the concave triangular feature), but rather served to illustrate the subtlety and complexity of the designer's vision. Polaris of course is the present pole star, located at the end of the handle of the Little Dipper, Ursa Minor. (See Figure 9 in "Archaeoastronomy.")

Here then were *three* pieces of evidence. Thus it is that our serpentine masterpiece is possibly of a design and construction considerably older than previously thought—as old as the pyramids of Egypt, perhaps older.

The Draconian Serpent and Stonehenge

When determining geo-astronomical alignments, certain rules are necessary to achieve success. Theoretically, the ancient astronomers of Stonehenge and Serpent Mound knew well the variables of viewing horizon lights, coming and going. A science would have naturally arisen when the challenge of building a single structure to compute and incorporate everything worthy on the horizon was met. Britain's Stonehenge is believed to be the most remarkable sighting computer known from the ancient world. This finding on Stonehenge is in large part the result of research by Gerald Hawkins. And although not everyone agrees that Stonehenge was used as such an astronomical calculator, the size, shape, and position of Serpent Mound seems to back up Hawkins's theories. A replica of the dimensions and size of Stonehenge was placed at the point where the lunar and solar alignments of the Great Serpent fall closest together from the coils, slightly west of the central portion of the structure.

Then the asterism of Draco was compounded to the illustration.[16] The result was enlightening. Not only was the size of Stonehenge relative to Serpent Mound in terms of geo-astronomical alignments, but the addition of Draco clearly indicated something of special significance: the twin rings of Stonehenge nicely touched the four points of light on the "dipper" part of the Little Dipper. It was as though a message from the past sprang up suddenly, revealing the inspiration for the ground plan of Stonehenge. (See Figure 10 in "Archaeoastronomy.")

It deserves mention that Stonehenge is believed to have been an early temple of the Sun god, Apollo, brought to the Celtic Region in prehistoric times. This is also noted in *Stonehenge Decoded*. So began to emerge a pattern of sacred geometry, astronomy, and architecture coincidentally joining the two monuments. But there is more.

The Egyptian Connection

Not a few students of the earthwork mysteries have remarked that the oval and head of the serpent effigy strongly remind them of the Eye of Horus, an ancient Egyptian icon, illustrated under "The Theta Symbol" later in this work. But there are other apparent Egyptian connections, not the least being the ankh or crux ansata, illustrated in "The Traditional Tree and the Great Serpent."

Using the figure of the sacred hexagon, and extending its sides to form twin triangles, the special figure of the *vesica piscis* is created. This figure demonstrates the "fusion" of the twin circles and the offspring of this pair of opposites embodied as the Great Serpent. The diameter of either circle is so near the base side measure of the Great Pyramid, that the difference is negligible. (See "The Vesica Piscis" and "The Great Serpent and the Great Pyramid.")

The Lost Oracle of Delphi?

If Stonehenge is in juxtaposition with the Great Serpent through a certain type of astronomical connection, what school originated the system underscoring these monuments?

Commencing with "The Serpent and the Mysteries," the bulk of this book deals with the preservation of the Mysteries with the serpent as focal point. As *Logos* or *Word*, the Great Serpent is used to reintroduce the first known numerically oriented alphabetical system. The alphabetical theory as presented begins with the mythology of the slaying of Python by Apollo, the subsequent skinning and dismembering of the dragon, and the discharging of the corpse down a certain shaft in the earth. The lost Oracle of Delphi, now more myth than mention in circles of scholarship, is in theory as intimate to the Serpent and Stonehenge as was the Voice of the Temple intimate to the spirit of Python. Much of this theory should rest on the probability of Pythagoras[17] having put together this first alphabet, though it does not necessarily. Originating in Greece around the time of mid-first millennium before the Christian era, each symbol, from alpha through omega, majuscule and minuscule, is described and discussed with some detail. The presentation of the collection of letters emphasizes in nearly each case a certain part of the serpentine form in conjunction with previously cited geometry and astronomy. In this, *the book is designed to be read from cover to cover.*

In addition, some personal observations regarding the significance of the Serpent Mound effigy are included. From time to time, I write in the first person. As an *initiate philosopher*, this author has been made to see a pattern in the landscape indicating the possibility that our *Gitche Manitou* is part of a grander picture. This picture, which came in the form of a visionary experience while working on this project, is with humility submitted for the reader. All in all, this is not an ordinary work, and I am grateful to my publisher for taking the distinct risk of providing it for the public.

Ross Hamilton, January, 1999

The Mystery of the Serpent Mound

A Vision Beyond Politics: Frederick Ward Putnam

IT IS UNKNOWN WHO DESIGNED AND CONSTRUCTED the Great Serpent. We know that its locale has been visited and inhabited by any number of groups of people from antiquity. It is written that Native Americans had settlements at the Serpent Mound site as late as the early 1800s. The times were changing though, and men with political or military ambitions sought to remove all the indigenous people to make the land "safe" for the hordes of settlers moving west from post-Revolutionary New England, the Virginias, and the Carolinas. Names like "Mad" Anthony Wayne, William Henry Harrison, Simon Kenton and Daniel Boone yet resonate in the greater Ohio Valley, while those of Tecumseh and Blue Jacket are now celebrated in annual outdoor stage events. There is a growing detachment and sense of deep regret among some descendents of those early European settlers for the actions of the Colonial and post-Colonial American government. I met a young couple one afternoon by the Brush Creek at Serpent Mound who live on a huge 600-acre farm near Cincinnati. They admitted it was literally stolen from the "Indians" by the husband's forebears. While they have legally inherited the land and it has become their traditional family homestead, they yet harbor the sense that the property is not really theirs.

But was it not the site of Serpent Mound that the native people were most reluctant to concede? For this was not an area of military or agricultural value, but a sacred place—an ancient religious shrine—evinced by numbers of specialized burials and living sites from different periods of prehistory. In Great Britain, Stonehenge is a comparable site—a place so revered that generations of the gentry felt comfortable in the thought of its vicinity being their final resting-place. But for all the mystery and accolades surrounding England's most famous landmark of antiquity, there is potentially a greater enigma and unsung honors due our earth-treasure here in Ohio.

F. W. Putnam's legacy is the Serpent Mound itself, he having carefully recorded his thoughts on the subject. He was associated with Harvard and the Peabody Museum, and virtually all artifacts recovered from the site of the Serpent Mound Park are still locked up in Boston. In spite of requests, the trustees there today will not relinquish these important works of art even though Native American interests would be better served if they were returned to Ohio. The problem stems back to the time of Putnam. He was instrumental in donating the park to what is the present-day Ohio Historical Society so its preservation would be ensured. But the recovered artifacts, so valuable in the research of the time, were considered as spoils, and to this day, the fact of possession overrides ethical considerations. For this, Putnam is not so much to be blamed, for his work here was magnanimous in its future implications. Besides, at that time (post-Civil War), the East Coast was still very much the country's center of learning and international exchange. But times have changed, and the day is approaching for those examples of Ohio's pre-history to be returned to their home ground.

Putnam's Story

The most singular sensation of awe and admiration overwhelmed me as this sudden realization of my long-cherished desire, for here before me was the mysterious work of an unknown people, whose seemingly most sacred place we had invaded.

In the company of four fellow archaeologists, Putnam toured a number of ancient sites in the early 1880s. With the enthusiasm of an adventurer—having explored the natural waterways and primitive roadways—he describes the rigors of getting to the Serpent site. This man was no ordinary archaeologist, as proven over time by his accomplishments. He describes reclining on one of the engulfing folds of the titan serpent even as the sun began casting its deep shadow from the west. In his diary he relates acquiring a certain excellent state of mind that comes with carrying out one's noble ambitions. As I pored through his letters at the Cincinnati Historical Society Library, it was moving to note that he had less than a shoestring budget, and that on occasion his work was barely able to continue.

Putnam writes that in 1859 a tornado ripped directly upon the Serpent's hill, destroying most everything above ground except the saplings. The holocaust led to the land being cleared for primitive farming, and crops were planted for a very short period in the area of the earthwork. But the place shortly thereafter grew over with briars, sumac and redbud. While it was time-consuming, he and his associates cleared all this away on their first visit.

… and the view thus obtained … led to a still stronger desire to know more, and a

resolve to do all in my power to preserve this singular structure, which seemed so strangely transplanted from the mythology of the East.

FWP had the heart of an adventurer and the soul of a poet. Above all else he was insightful. With his encompassing love for earth antiquities, and with a self-imposed responsibility for them, a certain veil was taken away, the same veil that confounds men given to more worldly goals. But this man's words have been selectively overlooked by the wave of material seeking that for well over a century has tainted the essential spirit of archaeological discovery across the globe. His inward vision has at best been interpreted as stimulating, and at worst a capitulation to the romantic whims of his supporters in order to raise further funds.[18]

To describe the Great Serpent as "strangely transplanted from the mythology of the East" intimates not only the subtlety of Putnam's overview, but also an almost supernatural gift of insight into the nativity of the figure's design. He saw something comfortably situated yet somehow out of place. Something spoke to his sensibility of an eminent and celebrated work of art which, while of earth, yet echoed a quality of intelligence not commonly associated with such a primitive setting. This is why his words have been passed over: not out of disrespect, but because it has only been of late that we have garnered the implementation to lend substance to his most personal vision, a vision beyond politics.

Science and the Horse of Reason

One of these implementations is accurate astronomy. This is not telescopic astronomy as it is commonly perceived, but the naked-eye observation of solar, lunar, and astral luminaries as they relate to ancient works. As though breaking new ground, Putnam writes in this wisdom:

> ... *as the last rays of the sun ... cast their long shadows ... I mused on the probabilities of the past; and there seemed to come to me a picture as of a distant time, of a people with strange customs, and with it came the demand for an interpretation of this mystery....*

With the instincts of a natural philosopher, the professor began his work that summer in the 1880s. Not until the second half of the twentieth century have astronomical alignments been enthusiastically sought in North American archaeology. But they were scheduled by logic to become a focus, albeit logic steeped in tragic irony. A looter's cart was put before the horse of reason. During this same period throughout the Ohio Valley, many of the structures possibly displaying the ancients' selective astronomical expressions were reduced to ground level, leaving little trace of their ever having existed.

In spite of all the destruction, there is slowly accumulating evidence that an earth-sky coalition may have been painstakingly laid out in pockets of the Ohio Valley region. One of the best examples of the prehistoric astronomy is embodied in our Great Serpent, physically central to the ancient moundworks of the region. But there is a great mystery here, a mystery that may ultimately have world-class ramifications. Possibly subconsciously, Frederick Putnam intuited the presence of such an enigma: "the unknown must become known!" he exclaimed.

It is not unreasonable to suggest a stellar-oriented estate, a virtual paradise wherein the rule of the natural deities of light would rationally structure a grand theater-temple for the human drama to be played out at its best. Yet there are elements clouding this overview, and problems that must be addressed.

Post-Putnam, the earthwork seems to have been relegated to a narrower point of view—one forced on the general public for generations. This view concludes the Serpent Mound to be a serpentine form made of earth and stones, constructed by people portrayed as technologically primitive in comparison to some other ancient cultures. Thus the questions posed to schoolchildren have been *what motivated these Stone Age Indians; and how many baskets of earth did it take?*

Putnam, on the other hand, was ingenuous in his approach, being intellectually free of the typical restraints associated today with such field work. He outlined a great challenge for future generations of archaeologists, amateur and professional. It seems that each generation has become a little smarter and a little more insightful, until now we are just coming up to the standards set forth by our wise professor from Boston. If we consider the serpentine mound of Adams County to be a thing of remarkable beauty, then we are just beginning to realize this man's inner vision.

> *That the serpent was prominent in the religious faiths of the Americas is beyond question, and that, to a certain extent, in combination with phallic and solar worship, it extended from Central America to Peru and Mexico, cannot be doubted, whatever its origin.*

Putnam here strongly suggests that the Serpent has the characteristics of a classic solar temple or shrine, the resonance of which being widespread. In one of his footnotes he tells of the writer Posidonius having witnessed a great serpent in Syria. It had scales the size of shields, and two people on horseback riding on opposite sides of the body could not see each other.

Putnam draws attention to the fact of the setting sun's rays touching upon the center of the Serpent's oval feature, where a small stone structure like an altar stood. It was not until recently that the Hardmans noticed that the summer solstice setting sun creates an excellent alignment through the central axis of this oval feature. Putnam's inference was that the sun was at the center of a fertility rite. Thus he asks the rhetorical question of whether or not Serpent Mound provides evidence for an ancient faith having its origins arising in the East. This in spite of the fact that the artifacts he unearthed in nearby burial mounds were apparently not from anywhere else but the Americas. Putnam considered that this serpent's background was rooted in an ancient world history, perhaps in the religious heartland of the mystic East. Now new evidence to support his contention has been found.

The Work of the Worm

This idea of an Eastern (pan-Indo-European) connection (which, incidentally, Squier and Davis also touted as feasible) opens up a proverbial can of worms. For what it's worth, those who are in the vanguard of scientific discovery often seem to get the "true" first impression of their discoveries. After that, their findings are analyzed, taken apart, and reformed, sadly losing the spirit of the original interpretation. There is a "film" of opinions settled over the Serpent Mound— like an intellectual fog prohibiting this first pristine, unadulterated, and enlightened view to continue on. Certain archaeological interests have suggested that the Serpent Mound may be only a little more than 900 years in age. This finding is based on questionably applicable carbon dating (see "Author's Cut to the Chase") and a comprehensively researched iconography.[19] This

study suggested that a few serpent image glyphs found in post-1000 C.E. Ohio Valley art indicated a source of inspiration for the Serpent Mound design. To be fair however, the Great Serpent could as easily have inspired the little glyphs, none of which demonstrate the specific shape of the monument.

Carbon dating is one of the technological breakthroughs of the twentieth century, but like a great toy, it is sometimes a bit overplayed, and even inappropriately applied. In the Adena and Hopewell excavations of Snow, Dragoo, and Connolly for example, carbon dating was usually employed with items suitable for testing, such as pottery, flint, pearls, and copper. Unfortunately, there were no artifacts and nothing but carbon was found in the structure of Serpent Mound, making such dating a departure from the more rigorous standards of the leading exponents in the field. Were the entire serpentine structure made up of carbon like the small piece reported in the early 1990s, there would be a solid case for the establishment of age, for then the serpent form itself would be an artifact that could be tested. If the carbon-dateable material could be shown as necessary for the Serpent's construction, that would be adequate proof for the claim of the archaeologists. But here again, the voice of Frederick Putnam offers a better clue, and his insight is extends into our time.

Upon removing the sod within the oval, the dark soil in the central portion was found to be nearly a foot in depth, where it must have formed after the oval work was built. How many centuries are required for the formation of a foot of vegetable mold we do not know; but here on the hard gray clay forming the floor of the oval was about the same depth of soil as on the level ground near the tail of the serpent, where it has been

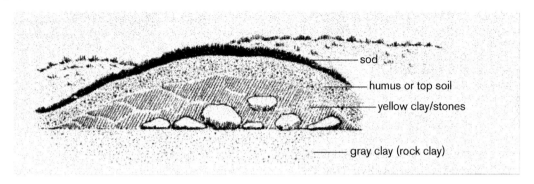

forming ever since vegetation began to grow on the spot.

With frank honesty, our friend Putnam states that the science of the late nineteenth century knew little of such matters as the elapsed time for soil accumulation. In this statement he gives no indication that there was any pioneer gardening on these two important points of the Serpent's body. Added to MacLean's observation that to his knowledge no farming took place specifically on the body of earthwork, and given the understanding that it would have been illogical to farm at these points, the professor made an astute analysis. Thus it was Putnam's careful notation of the depth of soil at the site that again makes his diaries invaluable in the reexamination of the mound now, well over a hundred years later. Putnam assumes that the builders added nothing to the gray floor of the oval, and who would refute his opinion? Because of this single observation of soil depth, we now are able to extrapolate the age of the Serpent at around 5,000 years.

One of the main reasons that Native American earthworks have not received as much attention as the stoneworks of Britain, Egypt, and Mexico is simply because the *perception* of earth architecture differs dramatically from that of stone. Stone may be constructed to sharp angles

Figure 1. Putnam's Diagram Showing a Cross-section of the Serpent Mound

Putnam's diagram showing the constitution of the mound through a cross-section. Putnam did not excavate the entire structure, rather cutting a few strategic trenches.

and heights, whereas earth seems limited by comparison. The use of stone in ancient Egypt, Greece, Britain, Europe, Southeast Asia, India, and Central America has occupied the attentions of archaeologists so much that the earthworks of North America have been placed in another category.

… and it is evident that the whole structure was most carefully planned, and thoroughly built of lasting material.

What Putnam observed and what is now being proven out is this: under the correct conditions, earth structures may stand the test of the elements as well or considerably better than stone structures. This fact coupled with his theory that the Serpent is actually a solar temple of specialized design leads to the irresistible thought that the Serpent may have been a central figure in a broader picture. With the discoveries of lunar and solar alignments to the coils and head of the creature, its importance has been strengthened, and the clues to its greatest mysteries are finally unfolding now.

The Fire and Stone Mystery

Due to its height, the area of interest was unaffected as the glaciers crept slowly down from the north in the last Ice Age. The Serpent Mound rests on an "island" of sorts, an unusual geological feature around which the ice packs moved. The glacial epoch, suddenly over about 12,000 years ago in the region, left much alluvium as sand and gravel deposited (and now mined) in southern Ohio. The watershed for the Ohio River extends about one hundred miles to the north, a result of the melting ice fields.

One of the main problems overshadowing acceptance of Serpent Mound as the expression of a scientifically evolving intelligence has been the fragmented prehistory of North America. In nearly all other ancient sites around the globe where astronomical and geometric principles have been demonstrated as logical and probable, the tendency to control fire well enough to melt and amalgamate copper has also been shown. It is simply puzzling that the Adena and Hopewell cultures lagged so significantly behind the rest of the world in this area of fire control and manipulation, for we know they were not of low intelligence.

The introduction of the bellows in some form was associated with these other civilizations, the dating of which coincides with the new dating of the Serpent Mound's design. The clear star and soil-depth dating of the Great Serpent would, coincidentally, place it into this older period of technological knowledge. It is somewhat tempting therefore to associate the traditions of the more ancient Copper Age with the ancient folk of the Ohio Valley—especially in view of the abundance of copper in Michigan to the north. Both the prehistoric Adena and Hope-

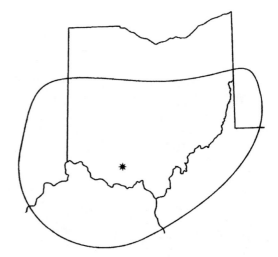

Figure 2. Heartland of the Prehistoric Adena-Hopewell People

The heartland of the prehistoric Native American culture, termed the Adena-Hopewell People, was quite large. The Adena are believed to have inhabited the area from around 1000 B.C.E. slightly into the Common Era, and followed, according to the legends, the Allegheny People. The Hopewell then immediately followed the Adena in an actual overlapping of cultures starting shortly before the first millennium of the current calendar. This area covers five states, including Indiana, Kentucky, West Virginia, and Pennsylvania as well as Ohio. As seen, the Serpent Mound is a centrally located structure within the ancient scheme.

well people used the metal to some extent in their art. Feasibly the original religious shrine in eastern North America, was the Serpent Mound's tradition a powerful influence on the indigenous people, "dictating" a conservative and preservationist Copper Age tradition, in spite of the lack of evidence for the bellows, on the soon-to-arrive mound building culture?

Similarly, the ability and tendency to create lasting stone structures seems to be a common denominator around the rest of the ancient world. Yet this is not the case in the Ohio Valley. Only a bare mention of walls made of rough sandstone slabs can be found in the Ohio county histories written in the nineteenth century. These rough stoneworks quickly disappeared as people used the stone to build houses, roads, and canals during the early 1800s. There are some exceptions, such as the Glenford Fort in Perry County, Ohio, which still stands. It is interesting to note, however, that there was certainly no shortage of stone for construction in southern Ohio. Many of the creeks of the great Ohio Valley watershed bear an enormous resource of easy-to-manage, flat stone. The Hopewell People made earthen walls fortified by such stone. There are some small boulders in Serpent Mound. But overall these prehistoric people seemed to prefer to express in simple earth— at least on the surface. For this reason, and not forgetting the lack of evidence for the annealing of copper (in spite of its availability from the Michigan area to the immediate north), eastern North American archaeology has not received the same sort of glamorous attention as other regions around the globe.

Putnam's contribution to North American archaeology has likewise not received the same kind of attention as the great exploitation of Egyptian antiquities by nineteenth-century archaeologists. Yet now, in light of advances in science and philosophy regarding such ancient sites all over the Earth, it has become obvious that his contributions are absolutely priceless. Men such as Putnam often do not receive the honors due them in the short span of their human lives, and yet their legacy guides and molds our future courses of action as though with superhuman sagacity, based upon reason and a desire to know the truth. This book is thus much in the professor's debt, for without his instincts and insights, we would not today know nearly as much as we do about the Great Serpent.

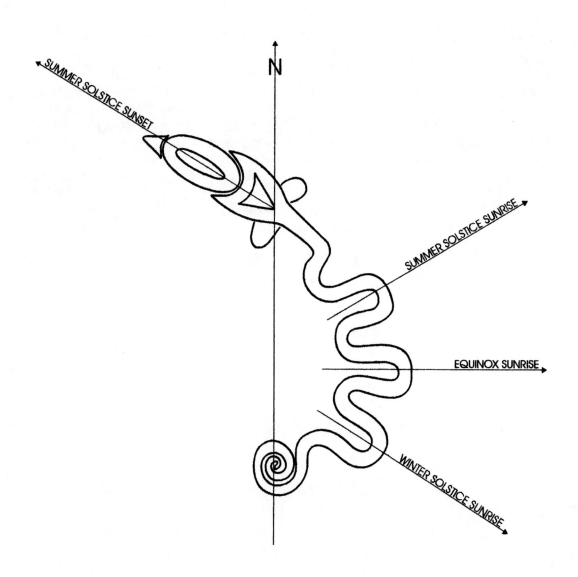

Figure 3. Solar Alignments at the Serpent Mound

Archaeoastronomy

The Sun and the Moon

WHEN NIGHT CAME TO THE ANCIENT WORLD'S people, they lit their campfires and lamps, happy for the illumination provided. But on clear nights, especially when it was warm, they bathed in the light of the moon and the stars. We now understand that they, unlike us, comprehended the sky with a religious regard. Some thought the stars were small openings in the dark vault of heaven, allowing the light to stream through. Others revered the stars as the estates of gods. We know they constructed artificial caverns and rooms, carefully engineering the architecture so that only the light from a particular star would illuminate the darkness of the sanctuary chamber. In this science, they could aptly distinguish and even "bathe" in their particular god or goddess's celestial light, actually communing with that deity's *house*. Truly, they believed in the magic of the night heaven, and the great timepiece she was to her closest allies, the astronomers. Since they did not have our electric lights, they could see everything without the glaring light-fog our cities produce.

It is logical to assume that, just like today's dedicated astronomers, the old ones had a different sleep schedule. Today we know but a scant trace of their methods though, knowing better the result of their calculating arts in extant astronomically oriented structures. Very often it would appear that they chose to conjunct heavenly rays with earth and stone monuments. At times certain shadows would be cast, perhaps giving rise to the "modern" understanding of the sundial. Another aspect of their art was to sympathetically reflect or "capture" the mirror image of a star grouping as an effigy or pattern on the landscape. But great dedication *must* have been required to thoroughly assess the grand assembly of the celestial dome. For now, untold centuries later, our best researchers are held nearly spellbound by the sheer imagination and grandeur of the ancient star science's secrets—secrets that, like rare fine wine, are being rediscovered and tasted only gradually.

It is not very difficult to understand the way in which the first observatories evolved. What should first be understood is the passion the astronomers must have had, as well as the devotion. To them stargazing may not have been a science so much as a religion—not as objective as we consider external things today. Thus perhaps *their* astronomy was very much both astronomy and astrology so unified that little could be placed between them. It would have offered knowledge of past, present, and future, enabling them to plan, predict, prosper, and perform in the way of their forebears. We know little about their coming to predict eclipses of the sun and moon, but there are hints that they developed a painstaking process over many years. Today such prediction is nearly flawless, for we know the angles, shadows, cones, and passages of the moon.

An ability to accurately predict such events would have awarded the shaman great prestige and even power in other areas of village life. So it is believed that it was the seekers and keepers of knowledge who founded the first observatories.

The sun has an easily predictable series of annual rising and setting points on the horizon, but the moon is not so regular. Because of the relationship of the moon's orbit to the Earth's orbit, the "maximum" and "minimum" aspects displaying the rising and setting positions of the moon on the horizon take considerably longer to reveal themselves than the sun's maximum and minimum points. Our moon has a tilted orbit about us, encompassing what is termed a "nodal precession" that requires approximately 18.61 years to complete. We have lived by its movements for so long that our bodies fluctuate by its magnetic effects, evidenced in the menstrual cycle, the period of the waxing moon.

Perhaps the greatest challenge to the early astronomers was the tracking of these phases of the moon to establish some definite repeating pattern. Lunar tracking would have been most time-consuming considering the variables. Given the short life expectancy of many ancient people (30–50 years average), it may necessarily have been a science-art transmitted immediately to younger adherents. We know from tradition that native people in the Ohio Valley used the cycles of the moon for planting, harvesting, and celebrating. However, such tracking only scratches the surface of lunar observation, for the full moon appears regularly. Far more sophisticated lunar alignment chronologies have been shown incorporated into larger works not considered pure observatories. These alignments hint of a complete knowledge of the 18.6-year cycle. If this is so, and if these people had a firm comprehension of this cycle, they probably had at least a cursory knowledge of eclipses, for such information is based upon an advanced tracking of the lunar cycle.

We now know that certain of these earthworks seem to align with sun and moon at specific events of the solar and lunar year. What is remarkable about some of these alignments is that they appear to be "cut and pasted" from knowledge of a very sophisticated, computer-like observatory such as Newark or High Bank. In other words, some of these alignments are seamlessly joined to geometric works, and so cleverly that they were not even found out until the last part of the twentieth century of the Common Era. To put this another way, the ancients of the sacred Ohio Valley evidently fashioned astronomy and geometry into one expression. Such a craft evokes the term "fusion."

But because such fusion is not indicated in many of the later mounds, it has been suggested that a select few of these earthworks were authored by inspired thought not fitting to the usual mold of theory. The 1700s of Jefferson speculated on an exotic race, the evidence for which was found in abundance by the early settlers when they began digging up the mounds. Those Colonial days gave us the oral testimony of the Delaware, who claim that the territory all about Serpent Mound was populated by an ancient and mysterious race called the Allegewi, and that the Ohio River was called the Allegheny or *Allegewi Sipu*, river of the Alleghans. Are we coming full circle in considering a mysterious, unknown race to have designed and constructed the Great Serpent?

Purportedly having gone to generations of record keeping, and having substantial intelligence and imagination born among them, could these forgotten people have put their cumulative wealth into the creation of effigies? Surely such endeavors would have been a fine medium to embody several aspects of knowledge. Was

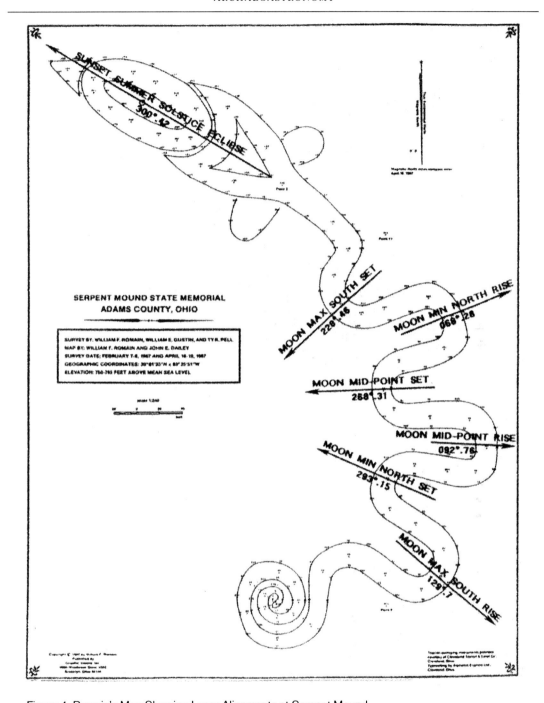

Figure 4. Romain's Map Showing Lunar Alignments at Serpent Mound

Romain's map as it first appeared in *Ohio Archaeologist* showing the lunar alignments.

this their purpose, to consolidate all their learning into a single symbol?

Because Serpent Mound shows the creature in the act of attaching to, swallowing, or spewing forth a large object, one of the possible interpretations of the whole structure is that it is an indicator of a great eclipse event or a desire to predict eclipses. There are other interpretations, but given the distinct probability that the Serpent Mound is a multi-disciplinary expression, the eclipse theory deserves some attention. But could the Serpent Mound have been used to *predict* eclipses? If so, there is less evidence for what current science would consider logical steps leading up to such a computer-like machinery. Stonehenge, with all its postholes and apparently astronomical calculating stones, would be a better candidate. Yet it is important to keep an open mind on the subject, for we don't know what kind of science these people may have possessed. We only make educated, logical guesses. We dig and look for tools, bones, artwork, and plain carbon, any of which may be temporally misinterpreted, according to how they are associated.

We know that the native shaman had sublime knowledge of nature, both above his head and below his feet. But who started the geometric and effigy earthwork tradition? Who designed the Serpent Mound and similar mysterious sites such as Circleville and Newark in Ohio with the authority of a master of astronomy and geometry?

The shaman culture of the pre-Columbian, Colonial, and post-Colonial periods did have some deep knowledge of astronomy. It was the solar eclipse of 1451 that urged the Seneca to join the League of Iroquois, and a solar eclipse in 1806 that helped the Shawnee prophet Tenskwatwa establish credibility. So the possibility exists that knowledge of how to predict a solar eclipse was a part of Native American spiritual science. Even going by the most fundamental calculating methods, an observant shaman could be correct at lunar or solar eclipse prediction one-half the time, for partial blockages of sunlight seem to come in groups counting six to twelve to eighteen full moons.[20]

Romain's research also found that among Native American people north of Mexico, there were various explanations for the phenomenon of eclipse. Usually, a large beast or monster was believed to swallow the sun. In the table contained in his article, more than twenty separate nations or tribes are mentioned. The creatures include a dog, a frog, a toad, a cod, a bear, a lizard, a coyote, and a rattlesnake. Evil *manito*s are also given notice.

The map showing the various lunar alignments to six of the seven coils of the Great Serpent has proven to be unique among effigies worldwide. In fact, it demonstrates an aptitude for advanced lunar phase sighting which up until the time of its discovery was not seriously considered an avenue of research. Part of the problem has been the over-emphasis placed upon grave-artifact science. Archaeoastronomy has been refreshing for archaeology, bringing the bright sky to shine upon the dark earth. The advocates of archaeoastronomy opened the floodgates of possibility, at once casting strong new light on the accomplishments of prehistoric science.

Among these advocates were Clark and Marjorie Hardman. They discovered the summer solstice setting sun alignment bisecting the great oval feature at the head of the Serpent. As may be recalled, Putnam either consciously or unconsciously hinted at this more than a century earlier. After the efforts of the Hardmans and Romain to make known the possible solar and lunar alignments to the serpentine design, Robert Fletcher and Terry Cameron published an informed map demonstrating four possible solar

..

alignments. Roughly corresponding to Romain's maximum south rising position of the moon, the second coil from the tail also serves as a comfortable area from which the winter solstice sunrise may have been viewed. Similarly, the fourth coil from the tail likely hosts the spring and autumnal equinox sunrises; and the second coil from the head may have established a *coin of vantage* from which the summer solstice sunrise was seen.

How ingenious to use the same coils for completely different celestial body alignments! Did these people worship the sun as Putnam suggested, or did they have a broader wisdom? Is the Great Serpent in part a tribute to the phenomenon of eclipse, both lunar and solar? Could it be that the designer simply wished to cement the greater part of an astronomical encyclopedia into one spectacular image, including all important astronomical aspects?

The North Star

In addition to solar and lunar connections, there are other possible alignments. Chief among them, and perhaps the most important of all, is the North Star or "Polaris" alignment discovered by Romain. As cited, this line extends from the head area to the tail area and is very specific, no doubt for reference. This alignment is of unusual interest, for no one previously had sighted true north to be in accord with an accurate astronomical mark. It is fairly well understood that there are other ways to find true north. But previous maps have never demonstrated anyone taking the time to show it. Instead, tools such as compasses coupled with guesswork were used. Because there are magnetic anomalies at the park, the North Star Line has lifted a long-standing obscurity preventing a correct analysis of the earthwork's complete possible plan and purpose. For exam-

Figure 5. The Hardman Summer Solstice Setting Sun Alignment Crossing Romain's Polaris Alignment

The designer of the Great Serpent utilized sacred geometry in direct conjunction with astronomical alignments. The Hardman alignment of the summer solstice setting sun meeting with Romain's Polaris alignment creates a nearly perfect 60° angle. Continuing the Hardman alignment to the southeast, the asterisks of the hexagon are passed through while the Polaris alignment is perpendicular to the top of the geometry. (Hamilton 1993, after Hardman and Romain)

ple, the Hardman alignment of the summer solstice sunset neatly meets with it to form a virtually perfect 60-degree angle. Subsequently, the correct interpretation of several geometric forms is made possible, as will be illustrated in the section concerned with geometry, measurement, and numbers.

Just one thought. Polaris has only been the exact North Star in recent history, viz. midway through the twentieth century. If the northern pole star was used to align the Great Serpent, wouldn't it likely have been the one in position before Polaris?

The Draconis Mystery

With vast convolutions Draco holds
Th' ecliptic axis in his scaly folds.
O'er half the skies his neck enormous rears,
And with immense meanders parts the Bears.

Erasmus Darwin's
Economy of Vegetation

There are a number of stories and myths from around the world entertaining the slaying or subjugation of dragons, serpents, and related creatures. Most have been lost due to changes in interpretation or relegation to children's tales, though modern psychology, in its flirtation with classical myth, interprets the dragon as an aspect of the ancients' superstition. In reality, the suppression of astronomical tradition at the hands of such institutions as the early Church has effectively consigned the priceless heavenly jewels of antiquity to either the occult or keyless metaphor, leaving us to wander in a labyrinth of intentionally proffered misinformation. It required the discovery of the Rosetta Stone to realize the methodical drive of the Church to obliterate the hieroglyphic idiom.[21] The later genocide of the gentle Cathars was another little project of the Holy See; and then there was the problem of Galileo, astronomer and physicist, with whom a hapless papal court had to deal. These are but a few examples of how and why the highly symbolic dragon or serpent is now perceived as either a negative influence or an outright fantasy. In short, such celestial knowledge's editing and suppression has successfully validated the agenda of a once-heedless cult which, preaching a glorious solution on one hand, yet equivocated for generations in order

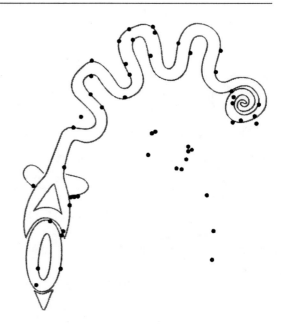

Figure 6. Romain's Serpent Mound Map Superimposed Over Draconis

The accuracy of Romain's 1987 survey is demonstrated by the overlay of the many-starred asterism of Draconis. Each point of light was given equal size in order to demonstrate the accuracy of the original designer's vision. (Hamilton 1997, after Cambridge and Romain, graphic by Mason)

to consolidate political power. Do we yet look down upon the Mayan and Aztec method of fear-mongering and wholesale murder when such an elitist and imperialist doctrine was, in principle, doing the same?

Yet while the post-325 C.E. "Church Fathers" —inheritors of a rich tradition of number, geometry, and measure—were actively shrouding the cumulative wisdom of former ages, the slow wobble of precession continued. This singular phenomenon's influence has effectively cast more light on the accomplishments of the past than all the tallow and oil Rome has burned in her sanctuaries for centuries.[22]

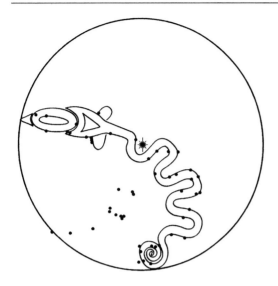

Figure 7. The Thuban Circle

The ancient north star Thuban which preceded the present pole star Polaris (the dot touching the outside of the circle) is used as the center of this geometry. Both ends of the Serpent are equal in distance from the center point, Thuban. (Hamilton 1997, after Romain)

The Great Serpent Mound has been matched with a large *asterism* of Draconis.[23] I was fiddling around with a transparency of the earthwork one morning over the constellation's likeness in a small astronomical guidebook. Making a little headway, I went to a bookstore nearby and got more astronomical charts. Things got more interesting, and so I petitioned an astronomer friend for more star charts, and she willingly helped. Each chart got a little better, a little more detailed, and a little more specific. Finally, I settled on one produced in the late 1990s by a prominent university. *That was it.* At least thirty stars and other points of light fell right on the edges of the survey map. I was careful to reduce the serpent image proportionally. After many days of work coordinating the map with the star chart, I presented my finding to the head of astronomy at the local Museum Center. He regarded it with some interest and noted that the asterism of Draco was accurate.

Knowing that the map of the Great Serpent was accurate as well, I felt like I was the first to see again and share an ancient "blueprint" from which was designed one of the world's most remarkable works of art.

The Grand Dragon

In accord with astronomical lore, Draco has been relatively close to or a part of the northern heavenly axis for about 7,000 years. The Great Dragon has thus been "circumpolar," i.e., within 30 astronomical degrees of true north for that time. This minimum of 5000 B.C.E. would place Draco in a favorable position for selective viewing and the creation of mythological archetypes. Time is allotted to develop a broadly accepted cosmology, including variations on a single theme. Such characters as the antediluvian oracle of Gaia, Python, or the Edenic serpent, tempter of Adam's spouse, could be included within such a chronological envelope. One poet suggests that constellations were like trees and the stars their fruits, possibly giving credit to our Old Serpent as one and the same as Ladon, guardian of the Garden of the Hesperides with a tree bearing golden apples. That Draco was the reference in Revelation 12:4 describing the tail of the serpent casting one-third of the stars of heaven to earth is acceptable to some scholars. This is shown later with a detailed illustration.

Caesius considered it to be the Great Dragon that Babylon held in reverence with Bel. The Persian Magi called Draco *Azhdeha (Hashteher),* the Man-eating Serpent. The Hindus thought of it as a sea-going alligator or porpoise, naming it (for worship) *Shi-shu-mara.* It may also have been the Egyptian *Hes-mut,* Raging Mother.

It was Drakon Δρακων with the Greeks, although Eratosthenes along with Hipparchos called it Ophis Οφις, the latter being valued at 582 or 770, according to the interpreter's background in Greek (Pythagorean) alphabet science. The two bears (Ursa Major and Minor) are said to have once been seen as Draco's wings, though Thales is held to have "lopped them off" around 600 B.C.E. By this action he is thought to have encouraged the ensuing asterisms to the ranks of a grand, emerging cosmology. The mythology of Cadmus and Europa is associated with the constellation Draco as well, leading into the "twisted" serpent being thrown into the sky by the great goddess Athena. The Egyptians considered it the Crocodile, while the Chinese celebrated it as *Tsi Kung,* "Heavenly Emperor's Palace." This designation was doubtless due to its most high position in the ancient night sky. Indeed, as already stated, the astral dome was once known as the home dwelling of gods or some similar angelic designation, each point of light a potential house. The creation myth of the Babylonian *Tiamut* possibly was enjoined as early as 2750 B.C.E., the nativity of that civiliza-

Figure 8. Comparison of the Two Depictions of Draconis

Two identical representations of the full constellation consisting of its main stars as recognized by modern astronomers. The figure on the right demonstrates the current allusion to the Dragon, while the Serpent Mound figure on the left has the head area of the effigy in a reversed position. This comparison aptly reveals a possible gap in the way in which constellations have been viewed between prehistoric times and the present. (Hamilton, 1999, after Romain; dragon illustration correspondence to Draco discovered by Pat Mason, dragon after a 17th century French doorway)

tion as well as the period of Thuban's tenure as the celebrated pole star.[24]

But of special interest is one Babylonian account telling of a celestial serpent with a "snail" attached or "drawn" on its tail. It should be noted here that the Adams County serpent, replete with snail shell-like tail, is located on the constellation in *reverse position* to the currently familiar allusions of Draco. In other words, where we today envision the tail of Draco through the imagination of artists, the head of Serpent Mound appears on Draconis. This suggests a

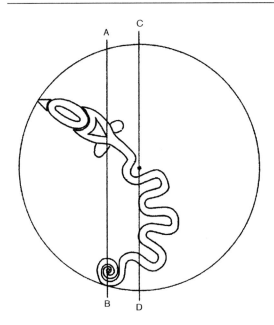

Figure 9. Polaris and Thuban Alignments

A parallel line (CD) to Romain's true north alignment (AB), demonstrates how the ancient pole star, Thuban (seen beneath the first coil), could have been used to align the Great Serpent's design as early as 5,000 years ago. (Hamilton 1997, after Romain)

view our celestial beauty in juxtaposition with another famous monument of antiquity.

The Serpent and Stonehenge

As noted in the introductory section, when the map of the Serpent Mound is placed in conjunction with the constellation Draco, and including the Little Dipper (Ursa Minor), the already cited possible lunar and solar alignments of Serpent Mound point to the "dipper" part of the Little Dipper.

It might be of some interest to state clearly that the knowledge of Draco's association with Serpent Mound came a full ten years after

problem with lost or broken tradition, for the constellations as now viewed may or may not offer clues to prehistoric earthwork design. So currently, though the tail stars of Draco include Thuban (just barely fourth magnitude in brightness), the name derives from an old Arabic phrase that refers to "the Serpent's Head." Interestingly, if you hypothetically unravel the Serpent Mound tail, it nicely completes a covering of the remaining stars in Draco—stars now considered the head of the dragon.

Was anchoring the ground plan of Serpent Mound in the highest visible stars prerequisite for the incorporation of other things such as the solar and lunar geo-astronomical lore? To answer this question properly, it may be of interest to

Figure 10. Serpent Mound with Big and Little Dippers

The Draconian Serpent Mound with the Big and Little Dippers, showing the way in which the Little Dipper's four lights touch upon the inner and outer rings of Stonehenge.

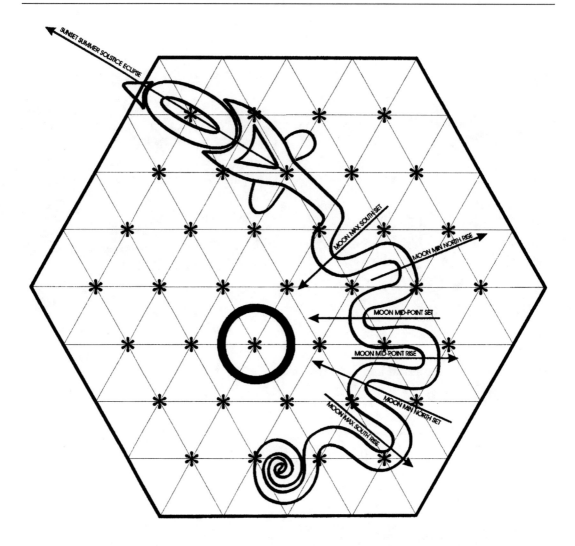

Figure 11. The Arrows of Artemis

The Arrows of Artemis: shafts of the moon finding the perimeters of Britain's most revered ancient structure. This shows the rings of Stonehenge in proper proportion with the Great Serpent, included within the sacred hexagon. Romain's discovery of six important lunar phase alignments with the effigy indicates a possible familiarity with the 18.6-year lunar cycle. (Hamilton 1993, after Romain)

Romain, Fletcher, and Cameron made their maps. Both the 1993 and 1995 editions of *The Mystery of the Serpent Mound* placed a scale of Stonehenge's rings with the Serpent Mound to demonstrate how the lunar and solar alignments fall into an area about the size of the famous British landmark. It looked interesting and was intended simply to point out that Stonehenge and Serpent Mound may have been built on the same approximate scale. You can imagine my

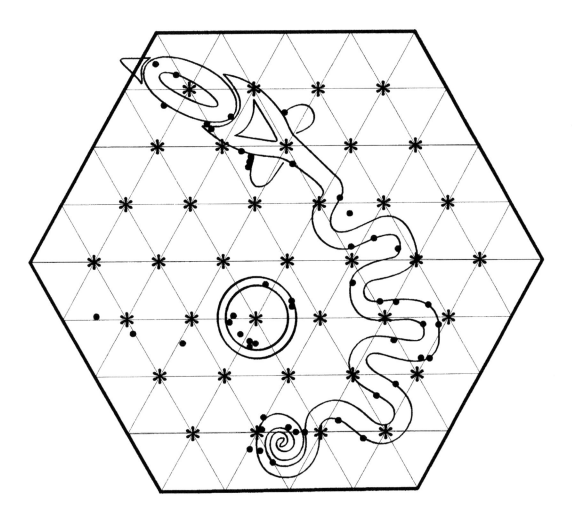

astonishment at noticing how, when adding the star chart ten years later as an overlay, the Little Dipper's four corners fell upon the inner and outer rings of where I'd placed the Stonehenge circles. To say this in a different way, it required *virtually no change* of my original graphic's position. So not only did Serpent Mound appear to be based upon Draco, but also now Stonehenge *appeared* to be based upon Ursa Minor!

After placing the Serpent Mound Map (with

Figure 12. Stonehenge and Serpent Mound– A Sky Map

The twin rings of Stonehenge are shown here to scale with the Serpent Mound along with their associated constellations in a composite rendering. (Hamilton 1997, after Romain, graphic by Mason)

lunar alignments) to position with Draco-Ursa Minor and then adding the likeness of Stonehenge, the addition of a certain geometric form enclosing everything was overlaid. It is referred to as the Solar Hexagon and has in itself remarkable measurement and proportion. This hexagonal figure is also described, though encoded, in the *Revelation to John*, as will be reviewed in detail later in this book. Currently, one school of thought calls it "the Flower of Life geometry." (See also "The Xi Symbol.")

Then the wheels in my head began to turn around, and it was not long before my thoughts came to this conclusion: Serpent Mound and Stonehenge appear as two elements comprising a larger picture pointing possibly to a highly evolved school of astro-architecture, the origin of which is not known. Another element or piece to this puzzle would be the Great Pyramid at Giza, as will be illustrated. It was no longer satisfying to work from the assumption that Native Americans, as we think of them, designed Serpent Mound. It is of a design that seems to have no home base—no specific country or culture responsible for its phenomenon. In addition it

is silently making a unique statement. There is an independent nature about it that makes the Serpent Mound, for lack of any better description, an anomaly.

One thing was very obvious, however. Without the correct map, there would be a continuing controversy regarding the reliability of Putnam's "restoration" over a century ago, i.e., when he re-emphasized the clay understructure to be the original shape of the mound. With the large number of celestial lights falling directly upon or on the thin outline of this technologically astute survey, little doubt can linger regarding Putnam's intent and quality of labor on those summery days after the Civil War. The stars also reveal the possible fullness of the helix having been interrupted by the walkway, as well as giving us today some notion of how the Great Oval was approached by the designer. The reasoning behind the width of the serpentine meandering is also indicated through a study of the stars in conjunction with the map.

The Great Serpent and the Mysteries of Geometry

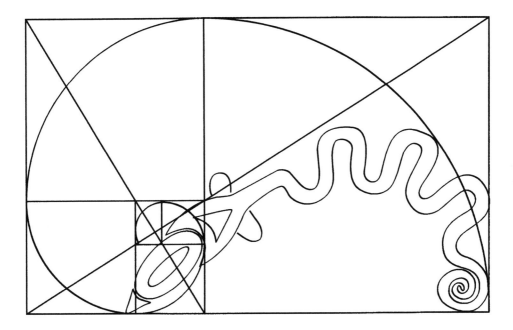

Figure 13. Serpent Mound Relative to a Golden Mean Spiral

Sacred geometry was of prime interest to the ancient schools of architecture. This one consists of five sacred-cut boxes, intimately joined, graduating smaller. It demonstrates the flexibility of the earthwork to embody the golden mean. Of special interest is the fact that the long axis of the large box is 718.2 feet by approximation, a figure achieved through multiplication of two key units of ancient measure, the 264-foot unit (Marshall) and the 2.72-foot unit (Thom). (Mason 1999, after Romain).

Come, I shall show you the Logos, and the mysteries of the Logos, and I shall explain them to you in images that are known to you.

Clement of Alexandria

IN CHRISTIAN THEOLOGY THE SERPENT ENTERS WITH Moses, growing from a tempter to a terrible dragon in John the Revelator. Thus it is a focus of the first and last chapters of the Christian scripture. It is the beginning and the end of the mystery studies as well, for its illustration stands as perhaps the most profound of all symbols in religious and esoteric mysticism.

*I am the Alpha and Omega, says the Lord God,
Who is, who was, and who is to come …*
Revelation 1:8

From ancient Egypt, we find that a reference to the Great Serpent was in association with *Nun,* the "Outflow" (putting into motion) "of the Primeval Water" (the True Substance). The creature of this formless void was known as *Nehebkau,* serpent of many coils, perhaps comparable to the lines of force of the mysterious field produced by the lodestone. From out of this primordial atmosphere of the Creator came this Serpent, i.e. the Will stirring things into comprehension. He roiled the Divine Water, creating the energetic life energies. Later, *Atum* makes his appearance, and he is as the soul of Man, the original Cosmos, surrounded by the coils of *Nehebkau.*[25]

Similarly, in John we find that "In the beginning was the Word …" and the statement that the "darkness (the void) comprehended it not." This is followed in due course with a reference to the coming of the Man, in this case, the messiah. The Christian savior is the embodiment of the Word, the Power of God, and the Water of Life. There are many analogies to the sameness of Atum and Adam and the Atom. The similarities are discussed with some detail in this section.

In modern times, the mysteries of the science of spirituality are enjoying a decent revival, and the serpent as metaphor is once again being viewed as a possible link to understanding the nature of divinity. Over the millennia, the tapestry woven in the wake of the hallowed creature's swath is one attempting to describe that which mediates form out of formlessness, and life out of that which is only potentially animate. Thus the serpent is sometimes associated with death and rebirth. The familiar serpent of the countryside sheds its skin once a year or so and is outfitted with fresh new scales. It dies and yet does not die. It glides with mercurial movement across the floor of the forest and is gone. If aroused and challenged, it is as formidable as nearly any creature. Yet it stands apart, made worthy by poetic prose of a higher description.

*Heaven and earth were as one thing in
 the beginning.
Nothing had separated or drawn apart in
 any way.
The forces of the cosmos were one in the
 Great Egg
Which the Serpent had regurgitated
 before itself.*
R. H.

Figure 14. Serpent in Association with an Egg

That the Great Serpent was the pre-Creation Deity to the Orphic College is beyond doubt. It is an axiom of that school's persuasion that the Serpent preceded anything of the two worlds, i.e., the principle of duality. Thus may be understood the allusion to the serpent as God or as the willful instrument of the Divine for creativity's concern. In this wisdom, the Serpent is the unific tool-aspect that stirs things into comprehension. Ultimately, it gives rise to the creation of Man—he contained within the Cosmic Egg or Oversoul. In this the Serpent is honorable, for it becomes the essential spirit, *pneuma,* or breath emanating from the subtle and primal Consciousness. This is the Great Serpent: projected and manipulable. It was this Serpent that gave rhythm and animation to the dark pool of Primeval Substance. It was the Creator's magic wand by which light and firmament was achieved. It was the pen of the Creator's measure and form.

It was the *Ruler.*

The Philosophy of Geometry

If there was a Big Bang, where did the matter and energy come from to support it? Call it an oversight, but it seems that there is a bit of a gray area here, one that physical science evades by searching for smaller and smaller particles. So philosophy and mysticism are enjoined for those souls who are not satisfied with a strictly objective approach to matter. Here is an important departure point of the Spiritual Science as proffered in the Mystery Colleges from the popularly supported science of today. The creation of the Proto-Atom from an imperceptible Spiritual Essence[26] could be grossly compared to freezing hydrogen so that from an invisible state it becomes visible. The Primal Consciousness has Will Power, and the concept of this Primal Lord (That which preceded everything material or not) was to the sages of the ancient wisdom in sympathy with the subjective consideration of a simple circle or sphere. To the wise

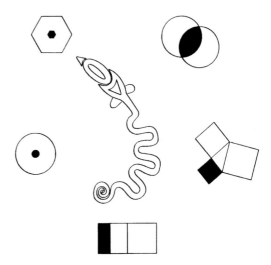

cosmologist, the circle regarded contemplatively lent certain knowledge of the soul itself. Contemporary science considers the proton possibly a sort of spherical thing, a form building on which various atoms come into existence. The sages assumed that Spirit and Matter were directly connected, even as a part of Adam was integrated to create Eve. "Matter" is a term believed to be derived from the Latin *mater,* mother. If the Primal Consciousness (proto-God) was (or is) as a circle or sphere, then the soul as well as the ensuing atoms would also carry those traits.

Since the laboratory of the human mind is fundamentally composed of subtle material itself, it is as difficult to comprehend the ever-existent Spiritual Essence as for the eye to see ultraviolet or the ear to hear a high-pitched dog whistle. Even initiates of the College's highest order were human, and thus required some special training for the mind at the beginning.

The sages by logic assumed first the use of number and then geometric form to gently structure the mind of the student to receive the inevitable revelation of the spiritual reality from

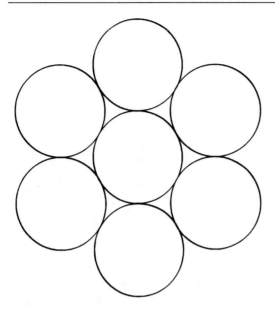

Figure 15. Seven Circles—The Foundation of the Hexagon

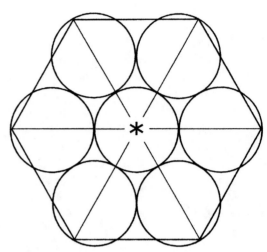

Figure 16. The Hexagon of the Wise (Hamilton 1999)

above the level of the senses. Once the student became receptive to the theory, it was a matter of practice to become established in its wisdom. It is this *practice* that formed the basis for the authority of the Mystery College down through time, and it is known by various names or disciplines in accord with the country or climate in which it was permitted to proceed. While symbols and geometry played their part, overall it was enjoined as the internalized comprehension of the principles of Light and Sound, the *bread and water of life,* provisions for the mystical journey back to the Reality.

As shown in the accompanying figure, a single circle surrounded by six others of equal diameter is a geometrically perfect axiom. For a reason that must be put forth as self-explanatory, the numbers six and one are relative in terms of the circle.[27] St. Augustine mentions that six is a sacred figure.[28] Pythagoras cited six as a *perfect*

number, because its factors of division (1, 2, and 3), added make six. It is notable that the Christian messiah had 12 disciples, and that 24 elders or *prakritas* contribute to the external and internal makeup of creation, as described below. As explained in the following section, souls as spirits were ideally considered to be little orbs or spiritual suns and moons in their native and heavenly environs. The lofty imagery of the *Revelation to John* emphasizes the seven spirits in front of or before the *throne* (Rev. 4:5), referring in code to the seven circles necessary to establish the sacred hexagon.

The Spirit of Geometry

Geometry existed before the Creation. It is co-eternal with the mind of God ... Geometry is God Himself.

Johannes Kepler

What is God? He is length, width, height, and depth.

St. Bernard of Clairvaux

Even putting aside the testimony of the mystics, the incorporeal soul is understood to be essentially "spherical" in its native environment. As freed souls, we are "sun-like" in nature. By way of analogy, musket balls were formed of molten lead dropped in weighed portions from a tower into water, and a similar process is performed today for buckshot. Molten lead naturally forms a sphere because its own mass finds a center of gravity once temporarily released from the effects of planetary gravity during the fall. It is not unlike water drops in a weightless state.

Similarly, such internal magnetism is an intimate condition of the created soul or spiritual entity in that each and every individual spirit owns a "mass" which, united with its native homeland, essentially becomes the spherical shape. In the body, however, the spiritual currents of the little soul become plastic in order to fit the mold of the human being by way of the nerve fibers. At the time of death or initiation at the hands of a competent Mastersoul, the *microsoul* undergoes the return, however temporar-ily, to its original shape, experiencing great relief and high joy.

It is for this reason that the sphere and the circle, and subsequently the hexagon, are particularly interesting to the mind of the incarnate soul. There is a substantial resonance in sympathy between the geometry and the underlying Reality. The ancient cultures worshipped the sun for the reason that the Sun was within. It is little different with the moon. Certainly the grasping of this fact in a conscious sense has been inhibited over time due to restrictions in education regarding the subject of Spiritual Science. Nevertheless, there are and will always be advanced and insightful mystics who remind us of the connection. Jelaludin Rumi, the Persian Adept and founder of the order of Sufis, wrote centuries ago:

Catch hold of the Music
That lasts throughout eternity;
Search for the sun
That never sets.

The Serpent as Universal Template

The Hexagon

HAVING EXAMINED THE ASTRONOMICAL ASPECTS of the Great Serpent, the lore logically moves toward understanding any possible associated geometry. While the Great Serpent, as we have seen, is not strictly expressed through sacred geometry, it is nevertheless a very necessary part of its understanding. Astronomical study precedes the geometrical, for it is by the natural association of the stars and moon and sun that the notion of geometry enters—especially in the case of our subject. For example, it was not until after the Hardmans published their summer solstice setting sun alignment that the work of the dowsers and the rudiments of the hexagon came along. As discussed more completely below, the size of the creature is determined by the spread of the solar and lunar alignments, while the shape is figured to a greater or lesser degree by the star correspondence. Yet a bit of each goes into the other, for the in-and-out undulations of the Serpent are to an extent determined by the solar and lunar alignments.

The Great Serpent is therefore a virtually indivisible joining of this triune of astronomy—sun, moon, and stars. It stands to reason that modern science, with its self-limiting approach to archaeology, would not have suspected this any more than it would have seen a connection between astrology and astronomy. I had and still

have to bear this in mind, for the geometric forms you are preparing to see and read about are as intimate to the Serpent's meaning as are the stars, sun, and moon. In fact, I must leave judgment to the reader concerning the plausibility of this figure of a snake additionally fitting to and explaining several classical geometric forms. To put this into the way of an inquiry: once the stars, sun, and moon had been consulted for the design of the Serpent, how could anyone have simultaneously allowed for the earthwork's inclusion of the following forms of the hexagon, vesica piscis, Pythagorean Theorem, golden spiral, and sacred cut?

I can't really say, but it is a *great* mystery, and perhaps it is equivalent to discovering the hidden diary of an ancient genius. Needless to say, it gives me great delight to present it to the public. So let's begin with the geometry, measurement, and numbers associated with our subject, the Great Serpent.

If you are like many intelligent people, you may have had an aversion to geometry and number your entire life, and could do just as well without it. If this rings true, consider this: you are not alone. Geometry, like mathematics, is an acquired taste. Once you get your feet wet, however, it can be fun—even exhilarating.

It was the American Society of Dowsers local Great Serpent Mound chapter that formulated the groundwork for this particular geometry, the first produced here. It was through their years of returning to the Serpent Mound Park, season after season, and their careful comparison of notes and experiences, that their unusual discoveries were mapped and properly plotted for everyone to see.

Anyone who takes the time to read this chapter looking for an exclusively Native American connection may be in for a surprise. This is part of the enigma that is Serpent Mound. No one really knows who designed or constructed it. Native Americans have known it since long before the first contact with European men. But one should judge for oneself. Are these geometric forms complementing the serpent image of Native American origin?

Before making a decision, consider that a good part of this chapter is devoted to understanding how the figure of this hexagon neatly corresponds to the visionary phrasings of the Revelation to John. It is apparent to some lovers of sacred geometry that the Revelation is literally loaded with specialized geometric lore. Two of these specific geometric classics—the hexagon and its vesica piscis—along with others are discussed and highlighted in the following pages. The purpose is not only to introduce these forms as time-honored to the antique Mystery College, but also to show how they meaningfully relate to our Old Serpent. Ideally, this discussion will convey how the design of Serpent Mound is very much pre-Christian, and was in point of fact borrowed from earlier schools of thought. Most noted among these schools was the Pythagorean.

> *... and in front of the throne there were seven flaming lamps burning, the seven Spirits of God.*
>
> Revelation 4:5

The grouping of the seven circles is a grand mystical axiom of geometry. As explained in the introduction to this section, spirits were consid-

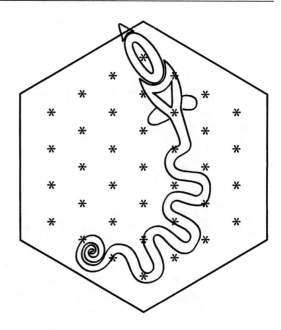

Figure 17. Great Solar Hexagon: Throne of the One

ered to be little suns or moons by the ancient cosmologists. The seven "spirits" were "in front of" or "before" the sacred throne of God.

This is the bench or laboratory from which God as Creator is believed to have accomplished the work of the Universe. Thus six circles of like dimension irresistibly surround a single circle (perhaps "pinpointing" the original whereabouts of the one God). Then the creation, or rather the crea*tive* part, begins for God.

With a straight-edge rule, lines are cast through the centers of the circles in the cluster of seven.[29] In doing this, the central circle has an extended asterisk-like formation in its center, signifying the primal Spirit radiating forth from the "Central Universe." In this action, the true "throne" is made, for then a border or perimeter is fashioned about the sacred cluster.

The Design of the Hexagon

Satisfied with the perfect workability of the circle-conceived hexagon, it was then a matter of the internal modifications of geometry and finally measure that challenged the designer. These modifications were 24 marks about the hexagonal configuration, even as they would appear at 15° intervals on a circle surrounding the throne. Transferred to the perimeter of the hexagon, lines were drawn in a certain fashion (see Figure 18) so that 96 equilateral triangles ensued. Subsequently, 37 internal points of reference became visible.

Forming the archetypal focus wherefrom the entire Creation has its origin, the *seat of Spirit* was considered unique in design as in application. It contains a wonderful union of proportion, measure, and geometric features. It is as though conceived as the formula of the Invisible taking a form for the purpose of continuing expression. Having made the form, the Creator (Pure Spirit) shines upon and from within it, fashioning it to be the departure point of all creative endeavor. It is literally the *throne of spiritual intelligence* wherefrom the Eternal One may be contacted. For those who like sacred geometry, this is a smorgasbord.

There is an excellent indication of the importance of this form preserved in the Book of Revelation. While it's true that this last section of the scripture has been somewhat tampered with and interpolated more than biblical literalists would care to entertain, this particular section seems to have remained undamaged over nearly two millennia. Purportedly concealing this information from those considered unworthy (the uninitiated), the author carefully outlines the basic premise of the esoteric college:

Anyone who proves victorious I will allow to share my throne, just as I have myself overcome and have taken my seat with my Father on his throne.

3:21

Let anyone who can hear, listen to what the Spirit is saying....

3:22

Then, in my vision, I saw a door open in heaven and heard the same voice speaking to me, the voice like a trumpet, saying, "Come up here: I will show you what is to take place...."

4:1

With that, I fell into ecstasy and saw a throne standing in heaven, and the One who was sitting on the throne....

4:2

Emphasis upon rising above the realm of death through practice of Sound Principle (the Voice of God) was first and foremost to the initiate of the Mysteries. It offered a real connection with the Spirit, one beyond mere scriptural reading and ethical social life (Rev. 3:22, 23; 4:1).

With the door opened, the writer's beautifully couched language is timeless in its import, capturing the imagination of countless people down through the centuries. Rooted in the formalities of carefully conceived geometric expression, the adepts and prophets exercised their right to promote their most noble ideals in the language of true philosophers and poets. Moreover, they brought it home with the authority behind the attainment of Spirituality (4:2).

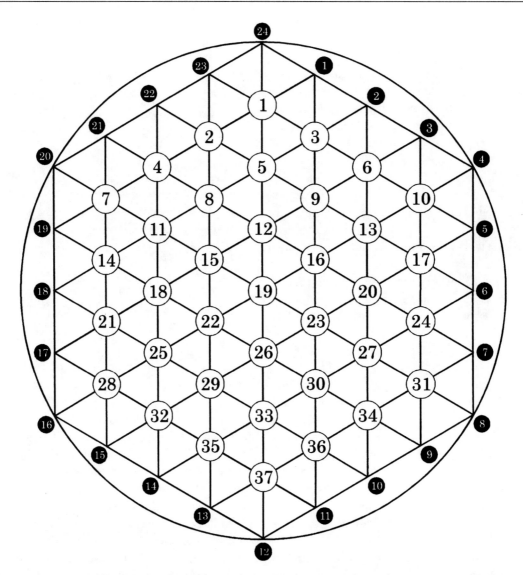

Figure 18. The Numbering of the Sacred Hexagon

The Seven Spirits and the Twenty-four Elders

Round the throne in a circle were twenty-four thrones, and on them twenty-four elders sitting....

Revelation 4:4

Flashes of lightning were coming from the throne, and the sound of peals of thunder, and in front of the throne there were ... the seven Spirits of God.

Revelation 4:5

The knowledge of sacred geometry and arithmetic was requisite for the novitiate, for like the Seven Spirits of God before the throne, it required seven circles before the hexagon could be established. The novice, yet under the influence of the senses, is at first unable to comprehend the spiritual content of life and considers the knowledge of the throne a sacred mystery, ultimately a revelation once properly understood.

Flashes of lightning coupled with peals of thunder reveal the two primary expressions of Spirit. For the beginning student, this was *God-into-expression,* the Spirit making itself both visible and audible.

The twenty-four elders are the principal constituents of the throne. With their presence, the throne is later seen as the Primal Atom made by God. From the ancient records of Spiritual Science, we read of the 24 *prakritas* (Sanskrit). These designate the specific parts lending real character to the throne of the Divine, subsequently becoming the Atom and then Man (Adam, the human). To the ancient College of the Mysteries, the Atom was the soul of the human being, as will be discussed in detail.

The comparison of the Atom to Man was logical and natural as well as practical to those advancing in this sacred science, for the Atom contained the code from which the human form was figured, ultimately manifest as its familiar appearance. *"The body is the manifest of the soul"* is an axiom of philosophical logic as well as a verity of the immortal arts, proven upon the development of spirituality (learning to rise above the narrow limits of the senses). This Primal Atom is no less than the described throne, revealed to the beginning student through knowledge of several geometric forms in order to lend the mind some imagery to relate to. The most obvious of these is the "solar" hexagon derived from the seven circles.

For reference, these elders, with Sanskrit equivalents,[30] include the following:

the seed mind or *Chitta*

4 the ego or *Ahamkara*

the intellect or *Buddhi*

the lower mind or *Manas*

and

the five organs of sense or *Jnanendriyas*

the five objects of the senses or *Tanmantras*

20 the five organs of action or *Karmendriyas*

the five conditions of matter (solid, liquid, gaseous, fiery, and ethereal)

The Elders as the Human Form

Initiates of the highest attainment sometimes speak of the human body as a curious and strangely shaped creature. The design carefully follows the dictates of not only Nature, but physics, metaphysics, geometry, and mathematics. It is the product of natural selection in the highest meaning of the term. The schools of thought termed *anthropocosmic* and *anthroposophic* are both ongoing efforts to maintain this supreme understanding of Man's relationship to the Creator. This is in spite of the effects of daily life and social problems casting darkness over this enlightened knowledge. Basically, the human form is held by the Master-Saints and Adepts of Spiritual Science as the foremost creation of God, the individual being a *microcosm* (miniature version of the Cosmos). The soul as well is a microscopic form of the Creator's Oversoul, compared to a "drop" in the ocean of All-Conscious Spirit.

The intellect *(Buddhi)* and the lower mind *(Manas)* have been compared to the opposing poles of a magnet. The positive pole of intellect has the function of pointing out (directing the attention of the incarnate soul, *jiva*) to that which is true or *truth*. It causes the attention to be raised up—back to its Source. The lower mind rules over the lower twenty principles, its chief function being the observation and regulation of the creation beneath itself.

Aiding the lower mind in this regulation are the three *gunas*—positive, negative, and neutralizing governors—created by the seed mind *(Chitta)* itself and passed on through the lower mind. The *gunas* help to polarize and temper the fifteen principles having to do with desires-in-action within the arena of Time and Space where the human being dwells. The positive *guna (sattwa)* includes the five organs of sense; the negative *(tamas)* includes the five objects of the senses; and the neutralizing *(rajas)* includes the five organs of action.

For example, the desire to touch causes the hand (organ of action, neutralizing) to feel, activating the skin (organ of sense, positive) so that the object (touching, negative polarity) is fulfilled, satisfying the desire.[31]

The Four Beasts as the Four Ideas

The four beasts (Rev. 4:6, 7) as the four ideas complete the knowledge of the throne. From this throne then descends a rational advancement of order for the Creation. It becomes an encoded blueprint for the creation of the Proto-Atom, the sphere of the Oversoul, the Son of God, the spiritual entity, and finally the basis for a logical progression of forms culminating in the human being.

From time to time a Master of Spiritual Science (sometimes referred to as a "Cosmic Master") will admit that most planets contain Man in some form and in some dimension, generally having the apertures and appendages as does the human species. Man is the general shape of the Grand Universe containing many sub-universes, in which all things live and have their existence, from humans to gods and angels. Thus, an indeterminable variety of life forms, all based upon the anthropocosmic shape, dominates the worlds. It is not a matter of debate in spiritual circles as to whether Man is at the apex of the hierarchy of life, but rather how the soul best learns the lessons to gain an appointment to the Man-body, in whatever sphere of existence.

The already mentioned twenty-four principles take form around four classic *ideas* having their nativity in the Intelligence of the Creator. The Atom is interpenetrated by these ideas, and composed in them. However, as these are merely ideas in the thought of the Creator, the Atom is essentially an illusion. This is only to say that *Chitta* or seed mind is not *Chit*, Universal Love. So without the continuing Will of the Divine supporting and coordinating these four ideas, the spiritual entity never inhabits lower forms, never learning the lessons that material existence may have in store. The four ideas are:

The Word or Vibratory Principle

Time

Space

The Vibratory Structure (the shell of the atom)

Due to the abstract nature of these concepts, the Mystery College of necessity created similes to lend them substance. When one is attempting to appeal to a physically situated audience, physically oriented symbolism fills the proverbial need. Such metaphor can be the greatest vehicle for getting across the hypothetical or theoretical axiom, although without a teacher who is well aware of the symbolism's basis in reality, such descriptive analogues can become literal.

So in essence, these four ideas compose the possible existence of the Atom and are essentially interdependent, i.e., one does not exist in its familiar way without the other three. The twenty-four elders owe their continuing existence to these four ideas. It is Love *(Chit)* that causes the unique integration of the four. Divine love quickens and sustains their union, bringing about *Chitta,* the seed mind. Subsequently, every individual atom of creation is sustained in the image of the seed mind. In this, there is a subtle sympathy existing between the spirit and soul of man and all material creation. The connecting link is held to be the Sound Principle or Voice or Word.

Translated to the mystical poetry of scripture, we find in the Revelation:

In front of the throne was a sea as transparent as crystal. In the middle of the throne and all around it were four living creatures all studded with eyes, in front and behind.

4:6

The first living creature was like a lion, the second like a bull, the third living creature had a human face, and the fourth living creature was like a flying eagle.

4:7

Each of the four living creatures had six wings and was studded with eyes all the way round as well as inside; and day and night they never stopped singing: Holy, Holy, Holy is the Lord God, the Almighty; who was, and is, and is to come.

4:8

Every time the living creatures glorified and honoured and gave thanks to the One sitting on the throne, who lives for ever and ever,

4:9

the twenty-four elders prostrated themselves before him to worship the One who lives

for ever and ever, and threw down their crowns in front of the throne saying:

4:10

You are worthy, our Lord and God, to receive glory and honour and power, for you made the whole universe; by your will, when it did not exist, it was created.

4:11

Telling of a crystal sea before the throne, 4:6 emphasizes the clarity of vision. Like clear quartz crystal forming neatly to hexagonal columns, the understanding of the throne's possible shape is quietly revealed to the reader. When considering the previous stanza (4:5), which speaks of the seven spirits also *before* the throne, the connection between the seven circles and the crystal-like throne is covertly revealed to the initiate.

Then in the second portion of 4:6, the four creatures are introduced. In the accompanying illustration, this is shown as lines carefully graphed over the hexagon. This is further described in 4:10 wherein the elders throw down or *cast* their crowns. In geometric terms this means *the casting of lines* to create a sort of net in which they hope to catch their "fish." Thus the four living creatures, interpenetrating the throne and crossing over each other to show their cooperative interdependence, form multiple (37) asterisk conjunctions. Thus is created the illusion of so many "eyes" studding the throne all the way around as well as inside, i.e., *"in front and behind."*

Stanza 4:7 figuratively describes the characteristics of these four ideas as the mystic comprehends them. The first and last creatures, the lion and the flying eagle, stand for *Time* and *Space*—the ideas forming the basis for the fabric of illusion. The second creature, a bull (sometimes translated as a calf), is the Vibratory Structure, the idea for the natural shape of the Atom, strong and resilient. Mentioned third is the mysterious creature with a human face, appearing humanlike in its features. This is the Vibratory Principle or *Word*, as few other things could symbolize it. This is evidenced in John 1:14 when the disciple wrote:

The Word became flesh.

The interpretation of the Atom (the throne of the One) is given greater clarity in Revelation 4:8 as we read that each of the living creatures has six wings. The sacred hexagon, having six sides, is divided **on** and **at** the angle of each of these sides four times, creating the appearance, as noted above, of a studding around and inside the throne. Once this happens, the life of the living creatures permeates the throne, creating a wonderful music called singing. Thus the four ideas cohere, working together to sustain the Atom or throne of God. This maintains a holy place of dwelling for the unific Spirit.

Revelation 4:9 and 4:10 suggest that after the aspirant has comprehended these ideas, then the possible existence of the twenty-four elders becomes obvious. In other words, the four ideas precede the elders. Geometrically, the casting of the thirty-seven eyelets or asterisks gives rise to the twenty-four exterior points. Since the Proto-Atom necessarily precedes the human form with its twenty-four constituent parts, this is a fine point of philosophy.

So it is written that the four living creatures are studded with eyes, indicating an all-seeing, perhaps all-knowing consciousness. In this wisdom, the substantiality of the throne is as a wonderful fabric, the warp and weave of which are determined by the cooperation of the four living creatures. However, were they to work independently of one another, they would only be four *ideas*, and the throne a mere fabrication.

Stanza 4:11 is sometimes translated to indicate the pleasure taken by the Creator, especially after the fact of the twenty-four elders becoming recognizable entities subsequent to the glorification of the throne by the four living creatures. As more thoroughly discussed in the next section featuring the *vesica piscis*, the duel factors of Force and Feeling (Will Power and Consciousness) originate the Vibratory Principle, sustaining the Atom. In this, the essential nature of the Eternal is one of joy arising from the pleasure of the One.

Because human beings consider Time, Space, the Material Atom, and the Vibratory Principle to be separate or separable concepts, the understanding of the unific Creator is unclear to most. The Mystic Adepts or Saints say that this lack of a bond between God and humankind is the result of ignorance, and that this ignorance is the result of not rising to the level of the throne (as the Revelator writes), i.e., the Atom that is the human soul. This Primal Atom, composed of the four ideas, gives rise to the twenty-four crowned principles or elders, the virtual temple of the One, the human form. A twenty-fifth principle, rarely mentioned but by savvy esoteric scholars, is the spirit-primal, spark of Atman, the individualized Son. Descending from the eternal regions above the creation of darkness (the region of the material atom), this spirit arrives by the action of Universal Love, *Chit*. This action may be compared to the gentle hand of a child relocating a firefly to a crystal jar.

The status of the Atomic incarnation, which applies to all human beings, is termed *jiva* (jeeva) in Eastern terminology. The best equivalent to this in Western terms is *sinner*, for until the soul is freed of the complex tentacles holding it in the human form, it is yet under the influence of mind and related matters, termed Satan and his angels in the biblical terminology. (See also the section: "The Symbolism of the Serpent: Alpha through Omega.")

The Vibratory Principle

All the mentioned qualities, conditions, principles and ideas depend fully upon the continued outpouring of the Vibratory Principle, mentioned as one of the original four ideas but serving as the mainstay of all: the omnipotent bonding and integrating Power. The greatest mystics affirm that this Word is the whirring motor power of the entire Creation; that it brings all things into manifestation and sustains all things, ultimately removing itself, returning to the pre-creation state. Thus it is an intimate part of the material atom, yet precedes all material creation. It is called the quickening will of the Divine and was known down through the ages by the founders of various religious orders who were thoroughly familiar with it. As discussed in the introductory section, the Word was imagined as the Great Serpent. The great philosophers refer to it as the *music of the spheres* or octaves of life. It is likened to waves or ripples on the great Ocean of Love. Theosophists call it the Voice of the Silence, and the saints of all the various religions have testified that it is the voice of the one God, saying his Name. Thus it is that we read:

> *Then I heard all the living things in Creation—everything that lives in heaven, and on earth, and under the earth, and in the sea, crying: To the One seated on the throne and to the Lamb, be all praise, honour, glory, and power for ever and ever.*
>
> *And the four living creatures said, "Amen"; and the elders prostrated themselves to worship.*
>
> Revelation 5: 13,14

Αμεν: 96

Figure 19. Αμεν: 96

The word "Amen" is valued at 96 by the ancient Pythagorean Greek method of symbol-number correspondence, alpha = 1, mu = 40, epsilon = 5, and nu = 50. The New Testament, originally written in the Greek, is believed to have used this system throughout, its initiate scholarship carefully conceiving words and phrases to embody specific numerical value. There are 96 triangles contained in the hexagon, and they combine to produce this sacred figure. The hexagon is believed to be a geometrical analogy to the Atom or soul of the human being. The term Amen therefore is intended to bring in the understanding of the True Word or Vibratory Principle enlivening the entire Creation, as well as the soul itself.

The Timeless Wisdom

An appropriate understanding of the Great Serpent Mound and, as shall be seen, the mysteries of a pre-Christian College, is contingent upon the careful study of such schools as the Pythagorean, which with some success encapsulated much of the prehistoric wisdom pertaining to Divine knowledge. Other cults and cultures, stemming from Egypt and the Mediterranean, the ancient European and Celt, and the Maya-Aztec in the West, have turned up parts of the esoteric Tradition. These parts, fully reassembled and properly assimilated, will doubtless serve to rekindle the science and philosophy of a distant era when human beings understood not only themselves with considerable insight, but their God as well.

The College of the Mysteries, no matter where it was located or who its Headmaster was at the time (or you could say at any given time), always flourished as a center of higher learning in the true sense of the word. The "graduates" of such institutions were entrusted with the noble work of linking the general populace with information that would normally be out of reach. They did it through art, architecture, literature, and even through influencing politics. As stated later, these initiates were, from the outset, the prophets, sages, and sainted advocates of the Divine. Throughout time, the one unifying factor of all these great individuals has been the principle of Sounding Light, the veritable Word of God. There are no boundaries of religion, social standing, or race separating them.

Though not realized by us today, the main religious systems of ancient times were founded by men and women who knew the same God, the same Inspiration. Even in the isolation of Australia, there is a belief in a Creator who made their ancestors. In this instance it was as a reward for the cooperation and goodness of the first animals. Their Creator happens to have been a great serpent. Yet it is only the rare shaman, rabbi, imam, priest, or minister who successfully pierces the veil of universal "dream-time" and rises above their own system to reconnect with the same God—the same "throne."

It is due to the condition of ignorance *(Avidya)* that the souls taking up the human form are generally not happy in their life on Earth. The Primal Atom multiplied by the Creator and made mundane constitutes the countless material atoms of the universe. As long as human beings fail to understand themselves as the Proto-Atom, all of Creation, including the body itself, only creates a stumbling block on the way to the higher discernment and the sacred discrimination of *self-realization.*

The Jewish tradition of mysticism offers further insight into this long-forgotten realm of timeless wisdom, carrying several keys to the doors of time-honored philosophic science.

But the Semitic culture has not stood alone, for each and every one of the seven great world religions offers a part of what has become a great puzzle. Each is integrated in a grand picture revealing humankind as one race in a meaningful relationship with the Universal Spirit. Prominently displaying the principles of light and sound, a proposed effigy-temple after the design of Serpent Mound conceivably operated at some date in remote prehistory.

As described in detail later, such a temple could conceivably have been powered and made animate by the *ark of the testimony*, a potentially rich source of electrical energy. There is some strong evidence that the Serpent Mound design and the box were associated. The working knowledge of this powerhouse would have been part of a great religious-philosophic experiment having its roots deep in the prehistoric world. The sacred hexagon under other geometric applications reveals the ark's perfect dimensions (see "The Serpent and the Ark"), utilizing confirming measure and a deliberate incorporation of a true north alignment diagonally across the box. Someone may have laid the groundwork in the Great Serpent's design for a future purpose that of necessity is not given to the general populace to know at this time.

For this reason and others, a great deal of care has been taken to present this material in a certain order. Comprehending the true lore and meaning of this most sacred hexagon is the beginning of a strange journey—an odyssey of sorts—that step by step prepares the reader for a proper revelation of an alternative archaeological meaning behind the Great Serpent Mound of Adams County.

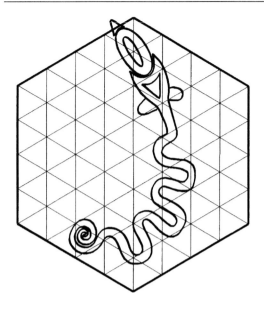

Building the Hexagon: The Redoubtable Foot

As a purely geometric figure, the hexagon would of necessity have been construed after the fact of the aforementioned six circles forming around a single circle. The alternative method of creating a hexagon using the radius of a single circle repeated six times would not logically apply in this instance. As discussed in the section "Archaeoastronomy," the size of the Draconis-inspired Serpent would have been determined from the geo-astronomical spacing of the sun and moon. Any unit of measure would logically be back-figured from that. The size of the first circle underscoring the hexagon would thereby have been the invention-ground of a precise and fundamental unit of measure, a building block of sorts. Interestingly, this unit would not of itself be given precedence for display, but rather be utilized in a service capacity. It would thus *serve* to emphasize other units in terms of itself. Some of these units are featured in "The Measure of the Stars."

This mercurial unit was in theory thus con-

ceived as the result of the multiplication of the cardinal figure of 6(0) by the ratio of π (3.141). This was not to create a circumference measure, but rather to create a lawful or most sacred standard underscoring the hexagonal figure, i.e., the Throne. The designer may have had intimate knowledge of the mysterious π ratio, and for practical reasons.[32]

I was able to sort this out by figuring backwards after the fact of rediscovering the hexagon with the Serpent lying over it. Curiously enough, the hexagon may have been originally figured using numbers derived from the square of six in terms of the 10-part or decimalized foot. Through subsequent back-figuring, each circle underscoring the hexagon was found to be 188.46 feet in diameter.[33] Out of curiosity, I divided it by 60 feet, and the figure of π revealed itself as an accurate 3.141. (See "The Measure of the Stars.")

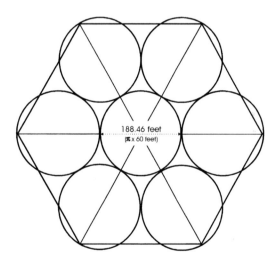

Figure 20. Pi and the Geometry of the Hexagon

Π: A very accurate version of the universal figure may have been used to create the geometry of the hexagon giving rise to the concept of the decimalized foot as a mercurial, mediating measurement.

Figure 21. Vesica with Double Serpents from the Middle Ages

The Vesica Piscis

There was a rainbow encircling the throne, and this looked like an emerald....

Revelation 4:3

In his original classic *The View Over Atlantis*, John Michell quotes a certain Dr. Oliver:

This mysterious figure Vesica Piscis possessed an unbounded influence on the de-

tails of sacred architecture; and it constituted the great and enduring secret of our ancient brethren. The plans of religious buildings were determined by its use; and the proportions of length and height were dependent on it alone.

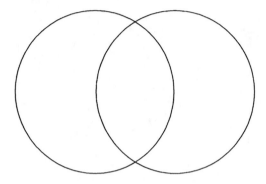

From the Latin, *vesica piscis* figuratively refers to the "swim bladder," which is responsible for the balance and grace of a fish in motion. I've kept plenty of fish, and some of the more exotic Japanese goldfish really depend upon this bladder—centered in their backs—to maintain any semblance of being upright. As a geometric figure, the vesica piscis is a very important description of symmetry, harmony, and proportion in art and architecture. Who discovered it and where it originated are long forgotten. However, the *figure of the fish* is considerably more antique than any artifact removed from the tombs of the dead in the century-long ransacking of the Ohio and Mississippi Valleys.

In the pre-Church era, the catacombs of Rome were known to harbor many secret pictures and signs of the mystical faith of the Fish, Ιχθος. Today, a modest revival is fairly widespread, the figure and the Greek symbols being commonplace on the bumpers of many cars. It's a small, partial vesica piscis, turned on its side. Unfortunately, the majority of these little signs spell out in the way of the later Roman style, substituting an *upsilon*, valued at 400 in the Greek, for the more logical *omicron,* valued at 70. Thus we see on the back of uncounted commuter vehicles ΙΧΘΥΣ, clearly missing the point.

What *was* the point? The *numbers* were the reason for many words and phrases being constructed as they were throughout the entire New Testament. Numbers dictated the spelling of things. It is a long story and a lost art. Suffice to say, however, if the original Greek spelling of the name of the messiah was Ιησους (Jesus, they had no "J") and was therefore valued at 888 (10 + 8 + 200 + 70 + 400 + 200), wouldn't an alternate title for the Christian *Lord of Hosts* reflect the same numerology? The rule was that your word had to be within 2 of the correct value. Thus Ιχθος is 888 + 1. Contrarily, the Roman Church, having properly lost the initiate mysticism after the Council of Nicea around 325 C.E., lost as well the correct comprehension of the earlier Greek genius. Perhaps because there was an upsilon in ΙΗΣΟΥΣ (the capital spelling of Jesus), the mistake crept in for the spelling of the Fish as well. Unfortunately, this particular type of ignorance was the hallmark of the new take-over culture at the time of Constantine.

In any case, the vesica has been used down through time to successfully produce the ideal field of divine order in geometry. Perhaps the initiate philosophers as geomants saw the vesica subject symbolic of the *magnesia of the wise.* Put in simpler terms, it is the royal magnetic field. But like the other geometric forms associated with the Serpent in the pages following, the vesica is not confined to one interpretation.

Within its sacred central area have been depicted mother and child in art, for the vesica also has the most important interpretation of *womb.* It has been likened to archetypal eclipse imagery, with sun and moon elucidated as clear orbs inundating one another. It suggests the bringing together of two complementary qualities which, conjoining, give rise to their principal expression. In short, the vesica piscis brings together the positive and negative attributes of life, and the result is the rediscovery of their unific Source, or at the very least, their commonality.

With all its possible interpretations, it is wise to lay this sort of premise than to attempt an explanation after the fact of the Serpent's positioning within the vesica. Besides, considering how well such high philosophical verities may be conveyed through such a visual aid, it is easy to see why this geometry has been used so extensively and for so long. All told, it is among the more aesthetically pleasing geometric forms known, for it seems so be trying to speak to its admirer of things profoundly beautiful.

To the esoteric student of bygone eras, the ultimate interpretation of the twin circles joined was the equating or commingling of Repulsion and Attraction, which, interacting with radical harmony, gave birth to the offspring called the *Word* (Amen, *Aum*), Vibratory Principle of all creation: the Inspiriting Essence. In this, the Serpent as effigy becomes the created or manifested form of the esoteric *Word.*

To paraphrase the *Holy Science,* encapsulating much of the ancient tradition of the Indian Masters, Word or Sound Principle is at the outset of creation. The coming into expression of Omnipotent Power is Vibration, beginning as a pleasant sound heard on the right side by the initiate. As the enlivening Spiritual Power sustaining the Atom, the Word is nothing less than *Time* as the idea of change existing within That which is changeless; and *Space* as the idea of division existing in That which is indivisible.

Taking the form of the Great Serpent, this holy Sound Current is virtually irrepressible and is indispensable in the creation of the Atom itself.

As the Primal Principle of Sound, it was in the beginning, the first expression. Thus it subsequently gave rise to all light, the second primal expression, evident in the Serpent's embodying a generous array of solar, lunar, and astral light, unique to the ancient or modern world.

The Sages knew of the four primary ideas—the Word, Time, Space, and the Vibratory Structure (the body or shape of the Atom)—as resulting from the duel uncreated qualities of Feeling and Force. The great poet Hesiod uses these principal ideas as Eros (Word), Chaos (Time), Tartaros (Space), and Gaia (the Vibratory Structure) in his classic *Theogeny, the Generation of the Gods*. Further, there are twenty-four principle elders in the form of twelve Titans and twelve Olympians.

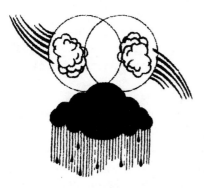

Like a warm air mass meeting a cold front and instantly producing moisture in the form of rain, Force (the Omnipotent Repulsion) meets with Feeling (the Omniscient Attraction, Love), producing Vibration, the Water of Life, and the Word of the Divine. Since Time, Space, and Vibration may all have measure applied to them (chronological, linear, and rhythmic or musical measure), the hexagon, the vesica, and the Serpent itself all offer important figures of measure, as will be described.

The great vesica piscis was apparently cre-
ated in a symbolic wisdom, and after the geometric creation of the throne of God. But this order could be argued among philosophers for a very long time, for these figures contain visible keys to the door unlocking the mysteries of the Logos itself.

Construction of the Vesica Piscis

The vesica piscis is formed by the touching of the perimeter of a circle to the center point of another having the same diameter. The figure is easily recreated by starting with a circle and joining a second circle with it at the point of the first's radial anchor. For our purpose, however, a different technique is used. As shown in Figure 23, an equilateral triangle is constructed, taking care that one side is down and horizontal as a base.

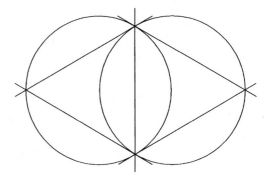

Figure 22. Womb of the Creative Forces

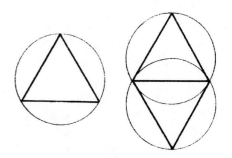

Figure 23. Construction of the Vesica Piscis Using Equilateral Triangles

The triangle is then circled. In the next figure, a second triangle, also circled, shares the first's base, creating the classic vesica figure.

Going by this information, the hexagon housing the serpent has four of its sides extended, creating twin equilateral triangles. When the circles are drawn about the two triangles, an apparent link between the Serpent and the vesica piscis is revealed.

Designated as depicting the hallowing womb of creative forces as well as the mysteries of life itself, the vesica proper is the area wherein the twin circles have their commonality, i.e., the area where the two forces commingle, creating the powerful agency of life. As can be seen, the Serpent's tip as well as part of the tail exceeds the vesica slightly. This could be interpreted as the insufficiency of the creative matrix to contain the power-principle of creation, that which moves easily in and out of the visible world, similar to that which underscores all electrical and magnetic forces.

However, there are other cogent interpretations, including the Serpent *waiting before the womb,* and conversely, the Serpent serving as umbilical cord between Heaven and Earth.

These and other mysteries are addressed in the final sections.

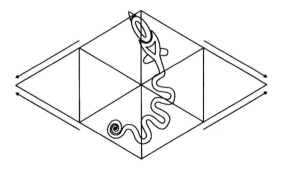

Figure 24. Link Between Serpent Mound and the Vesica Piscis

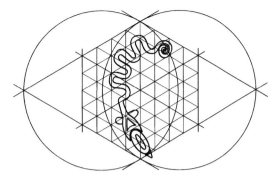

Figure 25. The Great Serpent as the Word or Logos

As the mediator between the twin circles, representing the extremes of Nature, the Great Serpent becomes the Vibratory Principle, or Word of the Creator.

The Pythagorean Theorem Connection

It is conceivable that the proto-philosopher Pythagoras conveyed the knowledge of the sacred serpent, Python, to his trusted disciples. Unlike an architect's "serpent"—a flexible, elongated template used to trace difficult curvatures—his template would have been a fixed version of an ancient axiom in general science. Unfortunately, there is little historical evidence for much of what the great teacher accomplished, for his life was believed taken by sinister forces, and his work scattered with his disciples to the four directions.

However, the fact of the Great Serpent's image fitting cunningly into the sage's famous 3–4–5 theorem, introduced more than two thousand years ago, has further altered the way our earth Serpent is perceived. Serpent Mound's design *seems* to have been made specifically for the geometry of the Pythagorean Theorem. This is in spite of the fact that it may easily predate Pythagoras himself by a very long time. So given the previous two figures of the hexagon and its vesica piscis also vying for identity with the serpent's form, how should this mystery be approached? Here again is the hint of the possible grand unity of the ancient sciences and arts through our Serpent's science-art. We have seen how it possibly unifies the ancient concept of astronomy through bringing together sun, moon, and stars—a complete astronomical expression. This in itself is a considerable accomplishment. But now the serpent is saying something else as well. It's saying that it is fully astronomical *and* geometrical.

During the period of several years that I studied other writings connected to the Great Serpent as well as other important antique sites, these geometric formulas were discovered only at intervals. It was like each was a separate entity to itself. Each in its turn offered a complete explanation *in itself* regarding the intent of the designer. For this reason it has been an uphill walk to attempt to present them together in one collection.

But to make it all seem more complex, the designer of our sculpture-in-earth added the dimension of *measurement* by the numbers we now refer to as "Pythagorean." *Pythagorean* means *whole numbers* were used to form ratio relationships in the geometry—like the Pythagorean Theorem's triangle, 3–4–5. Further, after the fact of the rays of sun and moon dictating the structure's size, a basic unit of measure would possibly have been born demonstrating these whole number ratios. In other words, the Serpent may also be the source for a widely applied antique unit of measure. This concept of unifying geometry, number and measurement makes up the latter part of this section.

So when this multidimensional Serpent began to present itself, the question arose: *why didn't they construct such an insightful masterpiece in the more fitting medium of stone?* There were literally tons of readily available rock, and some stone boulders were used to lay out the basic pattern underlying the mostly clay base.

The most obvious answer comes to us from Professor Putnam. He noted and emphasized that the whole earthwork was solidly constructed and built to stand the test of time. It could be added that the great Greek temples, the pyramids of Egypt and Mexico, as well as Stonehenge might not boast of such marvelous preservation through the millennia. The problem, of course, has been man himself. Stone is a tempting target for vandals, religious reformers, and builders in need of materials. Serpent Mound was (and is) fairly isolated. This additional factor worked in favor of its preservation as well.

But there has always been the question of how accurate Putnam's reconstruction was. Putnam is really the only authority we have for in-depth nineteenth century analysis of the Serpent Mound. Did he alter the mound to suit his own taste—his own creative ideal? Fortunately, and thanks to Fletcher, Cameron, and Romain's maps, this question has finally been answered. Putnam apparently did not alter or change the mound, but restored it to its original appearance (taking into consideration the extra topsoil added by the passage of many centuries). As mentioned, we know this from a count of the many stars that fall with almost uncanny precision upon the general outline of these survey maps. Putnam *really did good work.*

Anyone who has visited Serpent Mound will notice immediately that it is not on a flat, level plain like the Egyptian pyramids or Stonehenge. It appears intentionally placed on a piece of land, shaped roughly like itself, as though to parody John Donne, saying: "I am an island unto myself."[34] So finding the astronomy as well as the geometries took looking a little harder, digging a little deeper. A man once questioned the hexagonal configuration about the Serpent, for

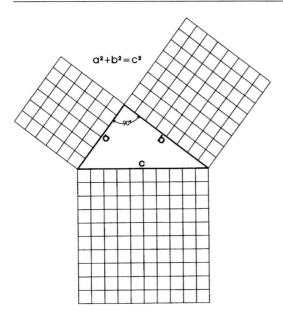

$a^2+b^2=c^2$

Figure 26. The Pythagorean Theorem

there wasn't any flat land around to lay it out. At that point it began to become clear that the serpent image was, with some purposeful intent, isolated. This idea of it deliberately being made "solitary" made sense, for in this way, no single geometrical association would dominate its interpretation. The Great Serpent was becoming a most sacred exemplar as the research progressed, possibly created to satisfy anyone's interests in science and art. But this geometry of the Pythagorean Theorem was particularly solid and interesting for the following reasons.

For those who aren't familiar with this theorem, it reads:

In a triangle owning a 90° angle, the square of the hypotenuse is equal to the sum of the squares of the other two sides.

The hypotenuse is the longest side of the triangle. To square one of the sides, simply make a square using one of the triangle sides as the first of a square's side. Ideally, the squares are graphed off to be able to calculate and multiply their units. In the classic 3–4–5, the number of units in the two smaller squares (9 + 16) is equal to the numbers of units in the largest square (25). This underscores the Pythagorean tendency toward whole numbers, and subsequently units of measurement corresponding to such whole numbers.

Because this famous theorem is a geometric law, its influence, like that of Pythagoras, goes beyond the flat page of the book it may be imprinted on. It reveals an order balancing three things as though they were actually one owning different aspects. Overall, this little classic has been outstanding in demonstrating the relation that exists between number and form, in its time creating a new element of reason for geomants as well as mathematicians. The theory and practice of alchemy also was likely influenced by the equation causing the three parts to become unified.

But there seems to be something missing from the famous equation, something unseen that has carried the mysterious fragrance of the secret philosophy of Pythagoras down through the centuries. To this day a sensitive person may view the riddle of the theorem and detect the presence of a certain inexplicable *spirit* in the figure of the equation—a residue or trace hinting at the knowledge jealously possessed by the elite of the last golden age.

This "spirit," I believe, is the image of the celestial serpent, template of heavenly Draconis. The *Python of Pythagoras* (a pet name—no pun intended—I like to use for this geometry) utilizes the North Star alignment as the line separating the squares forming the right angle of the central triangle.

Since the geometric star chronology of Serpent Mound predates Pythagoras considerably, one is caused to consider what seems unthinkable: not only did Pythagoras inherit the priceless theorem from a far more ancient source, but our illustrious Serpent is none other than the image of *Python* after which Pythagoras took his name. Since we know that the philosopher was a great mathematical and geometric innovator, it stands to reason that he may somehow have come across this equation intact with its original tool-ruler, i.e., the Great Serpent. In fact, he may have somehow inherited a very rich tradition of astronomy, geometry, metrology, and mathematics in general from a resource as yet unknown, evident in the present collection before the reader. What's more, he successfully encapsulated it all, with few suspecting that he was a link in the golden chain of the ancient wisdom. What was the first philosopher's source of information?

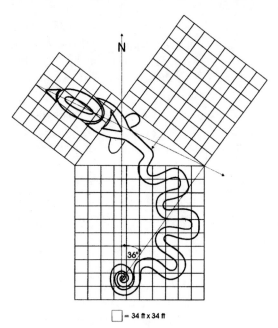

= 34 ft x 34 ft

Figure 27. The Python of Pythagoras

The 3–4–5 sides of the famous theorem's triangle are doubled in this example to lend relevance to the Serpent overlay. The square of 6, known as the "Square of the Sun," occupies the upper left of the equation. Since one of the interpretations of the Serpent's position is its possibly swallowing or regurgitating the sun, this is an important key. The square of 8, known as the "Square of Mercury," is on the upper right. Mercury carries the message of the light, and thus the neck parallels the square. The square of 10, called the Square of the Earth, assimilates all.

The Python of Pythagoras is exceptional in that it combines astronomy with geometry and measure to a

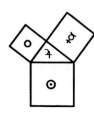

Figure 28. Astrological Symbols Associated with the Pythagorean Theorem

This figure shows the astrological symbols identifying the three squares. The square of 6 on the upper left stands for the Sun; the square of 8 on the right is holding the symbol for Mercury; and the lower square holds the symbol for the Earth. In the center is the symbol for Jupiter, which, although not depicted in its square form, governs the numerical attributes of the three sides as they join to form the central triangle. Considered by some to be the three most important divinities in support of Jupiter (Zeus), Apollo, Mercury (Hermes), and Ceres (Demeter), represent three stable principles of Olympian philosophy.

very high degree of didactic art. It is extraordinarily sophisticated, yet deceptively simple. The North Star line, running from the tip of the tail to the eastern apex of the hollow triangular feature, perfectly separates the 6 and 8 squares. The small triangular feature, long a mystery in that it does not point to any known geo-astronomical or earthbound phenomenon, appears to point out the center of the west side of the six square—the "Square of the Sun." A line extended from the southeast side of the square of 8 meets the tip of the Serpent's tail, forming a perfect 36° angle. There are other interesting "proofs" of the Serpent-theorem association as well, some perhaps yet undiscovered.

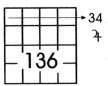

Figure 29. Magic Square of Four

This illustration describes the magic square of 4, sacred to Jupiter, epithetically known as Cosmetas, the Orderer. As the king of the gods, Jupiter (Zeus) became the binding principle of all the divinities so that they would work as a single power. The sum of the square, i.e., the sum of the numbers 1 through 16, is 136, and virtually the same figure represents the germ of the solar square, 1.36, divine sulfur. Note that each block (Figure 27) is equivalent to 34 feet, one-quarter the value of the illustrated square of 4. The sum of the three sides of the theorem is 24 x 34 feet, again exalting the figure of 816.

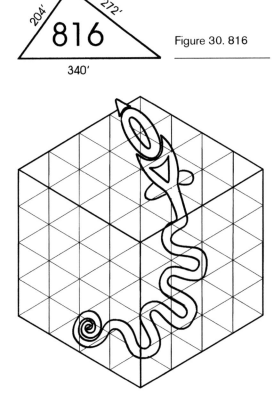

Figure 30. 816

Figure 31. The Enigma of the Cube

Among the geometric forms passed down to us as Pythagorean, the idea of the hexagon giving rise to the cube has been given special notice. In the figure, the Serpent form is shown on its hexagonal field with the embellishment necessary to give rise to the illusion of the cube. Some believe this was Pythagoras' method of bringing the student out of plane geometry into three-dimensional geometry. As seen before, the Great Serpent serves as intermediary. Note that the cube contains 64 smaller cubes, the square of 8. The Serpent passes through every dimension of the cube, width, height and depth, ending with its tip beyond the confinement of the sacred geometry.

The cube is often regarded as a form of potential, the sphere a form of dynamism. In this way of viewing the Serpent, it can be seen as extending its into four dimensions. This it is like a caterpillar aspiring to become a butterfly.

The overall significance of the 64-unit cube is full of potential in a mystic-chemical sense as well. Oriental asceticism declares the vital procreative energy, sacred to Mercury, to be abundant with both the solar and mercurial essences working together to produce a great harmony. Ancient alchemic texts from India and China suggest the amalgamation of mercury with gold believing the vitality of the gold is made protracted if accomplished in correct proportions. Gold was associated with the sun. Reckoning such an amalgam to the standards of the periodic table, the atomic numbers of gold and mercury (79 and 80) are themselves protracted by adding their numerical constituents together. In this, 79 becomes 3160 and 80 becomes 3240. The two then added produce 6400, the great mercury (the square of 8) or carrier of the solar-mercurial essence.

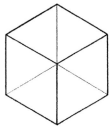

Figure 32. The Twenty-four Sides of the Cube

Since the cube is composed of six faces, they may be construed as six bases for six pyramids seamlessly fused. In this there are 24 sides within the cube. In any case, the 8 corners form the tips of pyramids that also become each other. In this the mercurial 8 and the solar 6 are perfectly conjoined, like cinnabar.

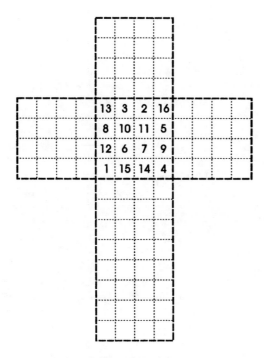

Figure 33. The Cube and the Magic Square of Four

Were all six faces of the cube construed as the magic square of 4, the sum of all the numbers would be 136 x 6 or 816.

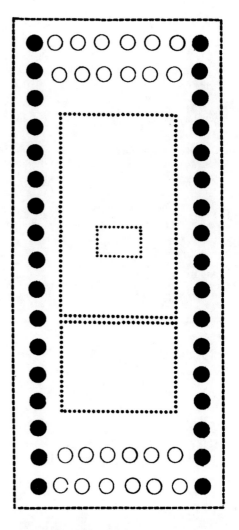

Figure 34. The Figures 34 by 24
Discovered in the Parthenon

The ground plan for the Greek Parthenon reveals two long rows of pillars totaling 34. Between them on opposite ends are two groups of 12 pillars, making 24. In this we see the 34 x 24, noted first above in the foot measure of the Serpent Mound contained within the Pythagorean theorem. Through careful examination, instances of the golden mean (phi or 1.618) can be discovered in the Parthenon, although some architects believe that the ancients could not have discovered it, only sensed it. [Modified after Dinsmoor, 1950]

The Serpent and the Golden Ratio

In his book *Liber Abaci* published in 1202, Leonardo Fibonacci ("Leonardo of Pisa") introduced a problem that translates:

How many rabbits can be produced from a single pair which from the second month produce offspring, and no deaths occurring to any?

The answer is the now-famous "series of Fibonacci," reading like this:

0, 1, 1, 2, 3, 5, 8, 13, 21, 34, 55, 89, 144 …

Excluding the rabbit factor, it is a matter of simple addition to produce the series. Any number in the pattern is the product of the two preceding it. By the time the series grows to 4181 preceded by 2584, the well-known 1.6180339 is discovered as a result of dividing the greater number by the lesser.

Though it would be convenient to credit Fibonacci with the invention of what is now popularly referred to as the *phi ratio* (ϕ, φ), in reality Mother Nature invented and applied it long before. Leonardo placed the ratio into the hands of geometricians, mathematicians, and architects with excellent results. However, since the ratio a logical progression of natural growth, we find the *golden thread* winding its way through spiraling shells and starfish, endless varieties of flowers, and even the trunks and limbs of higher animals.

The Serpent Mound exhibits a number of instances of the golden mean, and doubtlessly there are many more as yet undiscovered. Because of the earthwork's shape and perfect natural proportion, the sacred ratio reveals itself the same as it would in any living thing. How-

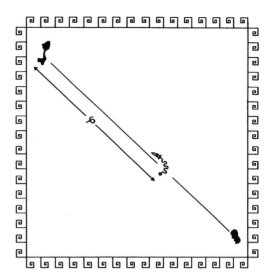

Figure 35. Ophi—the Ancient Greek Name for Draconis and Serpent

Dividing the distance from Fort Ancient to Tremper Mound by the golden mean (1.618), the Great Serpent is found to lie upon the divine ratio. While current science would be reluctant to explain this as anymore than sheer coincidence, the two Hopewell structures determining the length of the line also indicate a certain philosophical range. The fact of the Great Serpent arbitrating the Land of Light (the Fort Ancient observatory) unto the Land of Shadows (the cremation house of the very early Hopewell) illustrates an intangible mystery that may one day be proven more than coincidental. The distance of this line, approximately 70 miles, if represented as the Greek omicron (valued at 70) and divided by ϕ (the golden mean, 1.618), yields *ophi*, the ancient Greek name for both Draconis and serpent. Could we have the remnant of a timeless message intentionally encrypted on the landscape in the form of a ley line? Such tantalizing clues beckon us to seek alternative methods of archaeology to peer yet deeper into the veil of prehistory.

ever, there are some rather telling instances of the figure that are apparently deliberately conceived on the part of man. Thus the originality of Fibonacci's discoveries can be questioned.

Geometry experts, as architects, have argued for a long time that in the front and parts of the interior of the Greek Parthenon, the golden section is intentionally applied. Parts of the Great Pyramid, notably the King's Chamber, also were composed from its sacred rule. So to those who have some savvy in this area of study, it should come as no surprise that our Serpent was composed in light of such an aesthetically pleasing proportion. In fact, it may embody it from several directions.

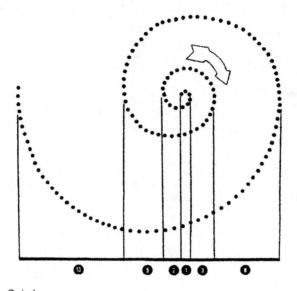

Figure 36. The Golden Spiral

The unfolding of spiraling shells, many flowers, tendrils, leaves, and even the growth of a fetus within the body of the mother all take on the expression of the phi series. It is believed to be found everywhere in nature, if we only have the time to discover the universal growth pattern. Turning a clockwise direction, the segmentation of the above figure is a good demonstration of a shell's gradual growth. The phi series begins with 1. 1 is added to itself to produce 2, and then 2 is added to 1, making 3. 3 is then added to 2, making 5, and then 5 to 3 to produce 8. Adding 8 to 5, 13 is produced, and so forth.

This arithmetic, inherently a part of natural growth, is considered a deliberate methodology, for the last number in the series is always "consulted" before the next stage of increase. The way of nature, mysterious and beautiful, produces a variety of wonders far too numerous to catalog.

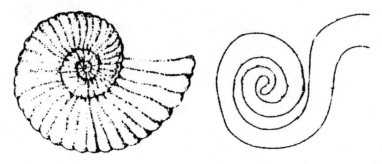

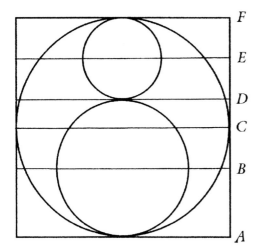

Figure 37. The Arbelos

The *Arbelos* (Greek: "a strong shoe") of Archimedes displays the phi in several different instances. Taking AC as half the side of the square, the golden mean can be seen.

if AC = 1
    AE = 1.618
if AB = 1
    AC = 1.618
if AD = 1
    AF = 1.6

As will be shown in the section on alphabetical construction, the Great Serpent is related to the Arbelos by way of the Delphi Circle.

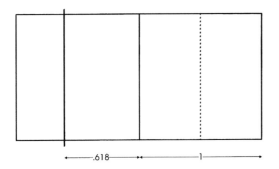

Figure 38. The Sacred Cut

Possibly the most graphic among all the ways in which the phi proportion might be illustrated, the sacred cut

uses the very simple form of the square to reveal the true phi ratio of 1.618.

The right square is considered one unit. A dotted line serves to bisect the square perpendicularly, i.e., from top to bottom. At the bottom of this dotted line the sharp pivot of a compass is anchored, and an arc is created by touching the upper right and left corners of the same square. Continuing the arc down to the left, the base of the right square is met. A solid line then is drawn to the top of the square. Using careful measure, it can be seen that the square on the left has been divided at .618 of its length from the centerline between the two squares. This .618 is called lesser phi, φ, and is distinguished from its counterpart minuscule phi, ϕ, for the sake of philosophy.

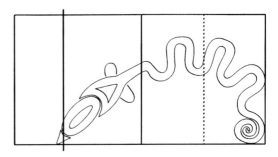

Figure 39. Serpent in the Sacred Cut

Like Figure 40, the above includes the Serpent shape within the double square matrix. The length of the twin squares is 676 feet, 26^2. The number 26 is a key to the square of 8, called in esoteric tradition Mercury. The figure 260 is one-eighth the sum of that square's 2080. Being 10 greater than the ceremonial 666, 676 conveys the idea of controlling and taming the fiery influence of the sun by the cool artifice of Mercury: the Serpent swallowing the sun.

Note that the triangular tip of the Serpent exceeds the line of the sacred cut. Like the Serpent laid over the hexagon and the cube, the extension mound at the head end of the creature does not easily become included when proper measurement is applied.

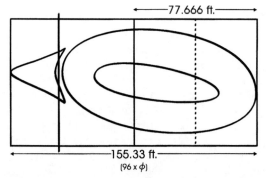

Figure 40. Use of Sacred Number at the Serpent's Head

Again using the sacred cut, this figure shows the distance from the west tip of the small triangular mound to the east end of the ellipse as the number 96 multiplied by 1.618034, phi. In terms of the foot, this is 155.3312 feet. Dividing this figure in half to determine either square's side, the foot measure comes to approximately 77.666 feet. Taking the sacred cut from east to west, the resulting geometry is significant in that it demonstrates the use of sacred number in combination with like geometry. Note again the separation of the triangular feature from the oval bowl, signifying the premises of the golden mean.

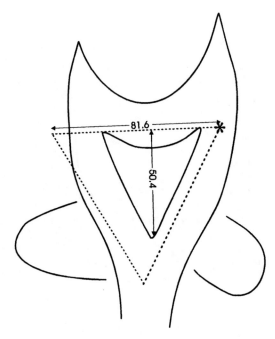

Figure 42. A Further Example of the Phi Ratio at the Serpent's Head

The measurements of both the triangular mound and the hexagon's triangles reflect the essentials of the Universal Law in ancient architecture. The figure 50.4 feet is the result of dividing 81.6 by the golden mean, 1.618.

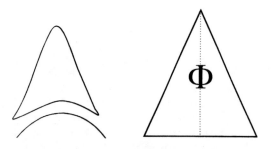

Figure 41. Phi Ratio at the Tip of the Serpent

The three side lengths of the triangle on the right, when added and then divided by the length of its perpendicular bisector, equals twice the golden mean or 3.236. These same dimensions characterize the small triangular feature at the west-most extremity of the effigy.

The illustrations show several outstanding and sophisticated instances of phi. Explanations of the ratio's philosophy are included later in this section. It is conceivable that our Python is of a design that has been proportioned to embody the *golden rule* itself. Even as it complements many figures of geometry in its association with them, so it is complemented. Used in both number and formation of the Great Serpent, consciously or not the golden mean has proven itself an integral companion to the architect of our earthen masterpiece.

The Philosophy of Phi

In mathematics, the nature of a relationship between two numbers is called *reciprocal* if their multiplication produces unity (1). An example of this is as follows: if 2 divided by 1 is 2, and 1 divided by 2 is .5, so 2 times .5 is 1.

When one is divided by phi (1.618034), the cursive form, called "lesser" phi (φ), .618034, is the result. Similarly, when 1 is divided by φ, phi is the result. Thus:

$$\phi \, x \, \varphi = 1$$

Named the *divine reciprocal,* ϕ and its counterpart φ are philosophically responsible for the preeminence of the base-10 system, for it is their mirror-like image of each other that produces 1, and the figure of unity gives rise to the base-10 system [1(0)]. Keeping in mind that this is the philosophic approach, it is easy to grasp. In fact, the term **phi**losop**hic** contains "phi" twice in its construction. That the word for serpent was *ophi* in the ancient Greek is no mere coincidence.

Some Names for Phi

Phi's expression has other names, and surely there are terms for it that are yet to be invented. As the *golden section* or *golden mean,* it has served the science of geometry and architecture for centuries, if not millennia. "A perfect course or position avoiding extremes," is a definition of the *golden mean*, metaphor of the *golden section*. It is also known as the *sacred cut* (Figure 39), the *divine ratio* or *proportion* (Figures 37 and 40), as well as the *golden thread* (Figure 36). This last term attempts to express the ability of phi to weave its way through all nature and knowledgeable artifice.

For the amateur mathematician at the breakfast table, phi has many fascinating and seem-ingly inexplicable applications, forming results delightful to ponder. The mathematics of phi have been used to usher the mind of the mystic into the ways of deeply integrated harmonies characterizing the secrets of Nature. Like the arcane *alkahest* of the initiate philosophers, its explanations are physical as well as spiritual. Being both analogous to the alkahest and the phi ratio, our Great Serpent, stands as a grand key to the study of the Mysteries.

The Great Serpent and the Great Pyramid

In late summer of 1793, William Henry Harrison, later to become the ninth president of the United States, examined the ancient necropolis-in-earth of what was soon to become downtown Cincinnati, Ohio.`

When I first saw the upper plain on which the city stands, it was literally covered with low lines of embankments. I had the honor to attend General Wayne, two years afterwards, in an excursion to examine them. We were employed the greater part of a day in August, 1793, in doing so. The number and variety of figures in which these lines were drawn, was almost endless, and as I have said, almost covered the plain. Many so faint, indeed, as scarcely to be followed, and often for a considerable distance entirely obliterated, but by careful examination, and following the direction, they could be found again.

Huge perfect circles, titanic elliptical works, squares hundreds of feet across, and all complemented by mounds rising over forty feet into the air, dotted the surrounding region as well as the Cincinnati plain. The very next year excavations were carried out, and many of the artifacts shipped off to the east. Among those who

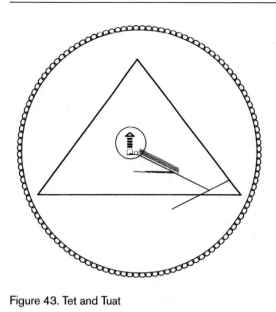

Figure 43. Tet and Tuat

The circled area, showing the famous granite piling above the King's Chamber, resembles the Egyptian *tet,* believed to be a mystical transforming device surrounded by the *tuat,* the sacred space of heaven. The height of the missing capstone area is 31.6 feet, the same measure as the small triangular feature at the head end of the Serpent.

their own, new evidence coupled with the old may begin to support the theories of the pioneers. Now, after over 200 years, we are beginning to understand the original intent of both the function and mysterious placement of the earthworks.

Part of the problem has been the methodology of the white man. Organized archaeological science did not take a firm foothold until sometime after the Civil War era. Because of the late-blooming antiquarian authority, landowners and fortune seekers had already thoroughly excavated the mounds noted for their anomalous appearance or suspected of owning the greatest antiquity. In most all cases, the precious grave goods have been haplessly scattered, many objects lost forever. In Cincinnati, nearly every earthwork has been destroyed. There are, however, a few noteworthy exceptions, such as the

studied them, Thomas Jefferson concluded that these were "Indian" works, and thus commenced disbelief in a theory of a lost or exotic race having once dwelt in the Ohio Valley.

In the decades to follow, many private citizens entertained the romantic notion of an advanced culture having inhabited the region—for very strange skeletal remains as well as inexplicable artifacts were found throughout the new frontier of the Ohio Territory. Numbers of skeletons exceeding seven feet in length lent the newcomers a belief in a race of giants. These long-departed men and women of such large stature were thought to have authored the giant earthworks. Though this notion was summarily dismissed by the academic archaeologists who arrived far too late to make the discoveries on

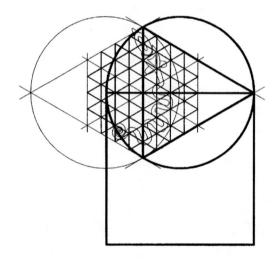

Figure 44. Rediscovering the Base of the Great Pyramid

The vesica piscis of the Great Serpent possibly relates to the Great Pyramid. Did a single school of architecture dictate the design of both monuments? (Hamilton 1993)

never-violated Great Norwood Mound, occupying the highest point in the area of the present day city. Through similar good fortune and strategic placement, the Serpent Mound, with a handful of other ancient works, was not so in the way of "progress" that it could not be preserved. Serpent Mound is to Cincinnati's east.

Harrison's noting of the protracted linear mounds is important, for it hints at an understanding of an as-yet unrecognized form of stewardship practiced by these misunderstood and very mysterious people. Due to its subtle expressions, the belief in the "serpent" was far more widespread than we may even detect now. The white man destroyed these beautiful moundworks in main part because he had no clues as to what their function was beyond "ceremonial." In Cincinnati, some of their shapes and positions were recorded, though not as rigorously as we today would have liked.

In fact, our modern, technology-driven world has all but obliterated the remnants of what Michell refers to as "a great scientific instrument [which] lies sprawled over the entire surface of the globe."

Indeed, our present civilization has viewed ancient structures worldwide through the eyes of an education smugly assured of our being the first in the long history of the planet to have achieved any significant culture. But in reality, we may be relatively barbarous to our distant ancestry once we are made aware of their *spiritual* technology. Theorized to once have encompassed the entire globe, a well-aligned system of terrestrial and solar energy collection and distribution scientifically unified the planetary entity. It is thought that this system may have successfully eliminated deserts, controlling weather patterns effectively over land and sea. The flowing fingers of the magnetic current, serpent-like, run over the surface of the globe, accumulating here and there in coils, always meandering in search of consummation.

Apart from the obvious symbolism contained in the Great Serpent, the most practical indication of whole planetary regeneration and climate control is in the location and geometry of the Great Pyramid. The megalithic masterpiece of the Middle East is located at a place having closest accessibility to the great landmasses of the planet. The magnetic field of the Earth loses parts of its flux as it combines with matter, creating a "positive" charge, tending to accumulate in areas of heavier gravity, such as the Great Pyramid's massive build-up of stone. Subsequently, this grand pyramidal structure is theorized to have once avidly attracted the charged cloud groupings and moisture patterns, inducing low-pressure movement across the face of areas usually dry. Meteorologists might agree except that modern weather science is not connected with the ancient science, lacking the benefit of its more enlightened point of view. Along with the Great Serpent, the Great Pyramid may have served as a powerful; spiritual-magnetic center, a place where high cooperation with nature created a vacuum-like pull, beckoning water-laden and electrically charged airs to the vicinity of a relatively arid clime.

Did the "serpent power" coil and create a "flux" beneath the Great Pyramid?

In light of present-day knowledge concerning the ancients, it is now considered feasible that some of the old temples, such as the Tower of Babel and the Temple of Solomon, were naturally designed to attract and accumulate electrical forces. Theoretically boosted by the spirited power of the ark, such edifices would have been intentionally created to glorify the God of all-nature, especially under certain atmospheric conditions. Like the high mountain where Moses found holy ground in view of the burning bush, the mountain of Giza may once have glorified the desert with a sounding fire before any known records.

That the same school of architecture designed both the Great Pyramid and the Great Serpent is a compelling thought. Certainly the timeline is there, if not an obvious Egyptian connection to the Serpent form. The time of Khufu was extraordinary for architectural achievement, as was the time immediately following with his sons as rulers. This period marked the beginning of dynasties, though of the time before very little is known. The Serpent Mound is apparently designed under the influence of the same Pole Star that inspired and directed the first great Egyptian builder. Similarly, very little is known of the time preceding the Great Serpent. At one point in that prehistory, these two monuments may have been viewed together, like two parts of a great puzzle. Was there a single planetary system oriented to the grand scheme of an enlightened religious science, the parts of which were carried to various key positions of the known globe? If so, was it ancient even before the time of Khufu's genius—was his era inspired to revitalize an already-weakened and desiccated system stemming from the collapse of the last Ice Age? Is the Great Serpent's design rooted in an architectural school that was once responsible for maintaining an entire planet's ecological well-being? If this is the case, did the fabulous ark resonate beneath the reasoning of some the higher expressions of this school?

From the often-quoted Revelation to John, we find a clue that the Mystery College had knowledge of the occult fire of electrical energy. Later, in The Serpent and the Ark, it will be shown how passages 11 and 12 of chapter 13 refer to the familiar ankh or symbol of Mercury as carrier of the messages of heaven. Stanza 13 states:

And it worked great miracles, even to calling down fire from heaven onto earth while people watched.

Scientists today tell us that it usually requires an attracting charge concentrated on the earth to cause lightning to be discharged from the clouds. With what was termed "knowledge of Mercury," the ancient architects may have been enabled to draw down from the sky a virtually constant stream of *fire* from the heavens in plain view. Through consummation with the positive charge of the magnetic *earth-spirit,* this power was suitable to transform their temples into living capacitor/resonators of a type inconceivable to today's science. The ancient halls of remote ages may have been truly resonant and hallowed through such spiritual science. But in order to ensure this contracting of celestial power, a very specialized generating device—one perforce "controlled" by the Divine—would have to have a permanent niche somewhere in the architecture. Such a charge would attract the mythical *sky-spirit,* often shown as a bird symbol, though sometimes referred to as a serpent taking the form of a dragon. Our own Serpent Mound, created after a design of the highest stars in the heavens over the northern magnetic pole, may have been "tapped" in a powerful and poetically brilliant expression of sympathetic magic in those days long ago.

The Great Pyramid would apparently epitomize architecture specifically designed to house an ark. Both occultist and archaeologist agree that the celebrated King's Chamber was intended to hold someone's body. This is correct, but probably not in a literal sense. Rather, it is correct in a figurative and mythological sense. While it was pointed out years ago that the King's Chamber had a stone sarcophagus fit to hold an ark-like box with its carrying poles, such an insight was dismissed on the grounds of the question of the instrument's possible purpose.

From ancient Egyptian mythology we read of Osiris who, murdered and cut into so many pieces, was resurrected by his sister from a box wherein all the body parts were placed. Surely it was that long ago that the Sun indeed came forth from the seat of the "King's Chamber," ruling all Egypt and the world from beyond death. The Great Pyramid at Giza stands today as an empty house, a pharaoh's tomb that may once have hosted the most sublime and powerful of the ancient science's secrets, the transformation of matter into spiritual energy. As the immortalizing cycle of the phoenix, were the skies and the earth perfectly consummated in those days, the desert itself blooming through the perennial "sacrifice" of the Son?

The term "pyramid" is rooted in the Greek *pyros,* which means "fire." As a geometrical form, it has caught the imagination of geometry lovers for thousands of years. Electrical current, like fire, seems to find its way upward, especially if the upward path gives it less resistance.[35]

Through information provided by tradition and passed on through Egyptian, Greek and Jewish scholars, the solar hexagon, as the Great Serpent, may have inspired the Great Pyramid. Prior to the reign and rule of the grand monument of Egypt, another masterpiece, now reduced to the mere trace of its original splendor, may have been the architectural crown jewel of a great civilization in the western continent. This is not to say that the Great Serpent was constructed before the Great Pyramid, only that if the two were designed together, the Great Serpent would have been the first on the drawing table.

Serving as the tomb covering over the hallowed throne of God, and perhaps capturing metaphorically the exalted power of the celebrated *worm* of the timeless phoenix, the Great

Pyramid possesses an important link of measure and proportion to the Great Serpent's hexagonal lair.

By way of a long-forgotten comparison involving a circle, a square, and a triangle intimately joined to one another, a possible link between the two inscrutable monuments may be observed. Perhaps coincidentally, the kabbalist doctrine enjoins the use of these three primary forms as an ingress to its wisdom, for with them may be discerned all pertinent knowledge with time and patience.

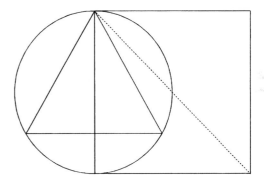

Figure 45. Using Circle, Square and Triangle to Divine the Golden Mean

Figure 45 shows an equilateral triangle circled. The circle is then bisected, and the diameter length applied to create the square from center to right of the circle. The square's long axis, seen from the apex of the triangle downward to the lower right corner of the square, when divided by the length of the triangle's side, closely approximates the golden mean, viz. 1.633 as compared to 1.618.

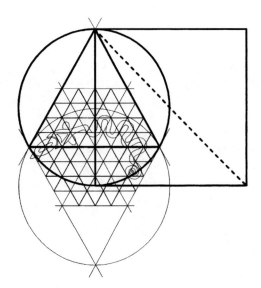

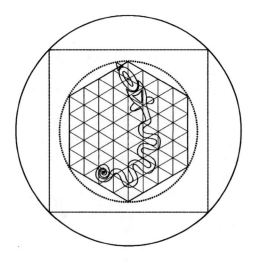

Figure 47. Serpent as Center of the Great Pyramid's Geometry

Figure 46. Geometry of the Great Pyramid United with the Solar Hexagon

This figure duplicates Figure 45, though with a different perspective. The same triangle is used to create the serpentine vesica piscis. The diameter of the vesica circle is 10.666666 (10 and 2/3) units of the bisected equilateral triangle (96 of which characterize the hexagon with sides of 81.60882 feet). The result is 70.67531 (the square root of 4995) multiplied by 10.666666 or 753.9 feet approximately, very near to the average length of the four base sides of the Great Pyramid now. With little imagination, the large square very comfortably becomes the base of that largest pyramid at Giza.[36]

The question of whether the arcane school created the Great Pyramid in view of the hexagon may never be proven to the satisfaction of all investigators. However, the relationship of the triangle, circle, and square may illuminate the mind of the mystic geometrician even like a shining key to a tradition perhaps more ancient than Egypt itself.

Figure 48. The Great Pyramid and the Measure of 777

The vesica piscis owning circles of 777 feet in diameter can be shown to complement the side of the Great Pyramid at Giza. With a little imagination, the sacred scarab of the ancient Egyptian myth can be seen. The scarab, like certain accounts of the legendary phoenix, laboriously rolls together a large ball of earthy resin in order to continue its process of life.

The twin circles are enclosed within the twin squares with the upper circle equaling 1.5 of the 777-foot sides of the squares. The pyramid's height is the golden section of the circle-square, in this diagram between 480 and 481 feet.

Figure 47 simplifies the foregoing geometries by surrounding the solar hexagon with the proposed square representing the Great Pyramid's base, subsequently circling both geometries. The foot diameter of the square's circle, 1068.72, divided by the foot diameter of the hexagon's circle, 652.87, is very close to true phi, closer in fact than the dimensions of the ark of the covenant, which has the ratio of 1.666 i.e., 5 divided by 3.

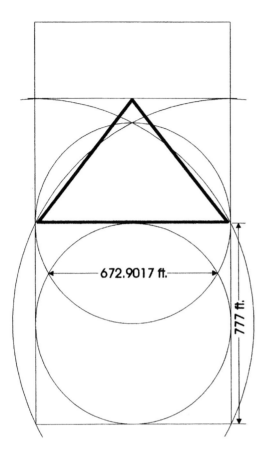

672.9017 ft.

777 ft.

The numbers 666, 777, and 888 represent the idea of primal Spiritual Power evolving into the form of a perfect angelic being. Over the centuries the philosophical approach to this mystery has been lost. Attempts to reconstruct the true meanings of the symbolic numerical relationships have been partial, and as a result, the numbers 666, 777, and 888 have had their meanings separated from each other and are now touted as either good or evil.

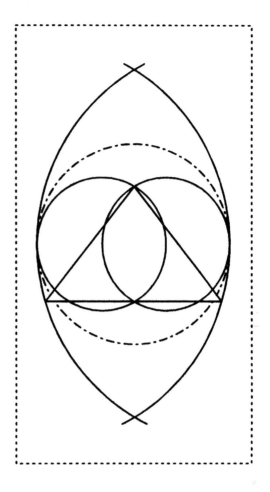

Figure 49. Geometrical Reasoning behind the Architecture of the Great Pyramid

This figure offers an explanation for the geometrical reasoning behind the architecture of the Great Pyramid. However, taking into consideration the foregoing illustrations, a more complete understanding of the architect's mind comes into view.

The Traditional Tree and the Great Serpent

In the year 1902 the Reverend Landon West published an inspired article declaring the Great Serpent as identical to the one of notoriety in Moses' Genesis. He said the earthwork was created directly by God to remind humanity of their proverbial fall from grace, intimating that this Land of the West was where the first people struggled and prospered—an ancient and similar belief held by Native Americans. Interestingly, Reverend West, of Pleasant Hill, Ohio, believed the Serpent to be in the act of swallowing a fruit from the Tree of Life. Perhaps the good minister didn't realize the full implications of his prophetic message, for harder evidence linking Adam's Garden to Adams County has become curiously apparent, especially in light of a powerful connection to the Revelation to John.

Introduction

WHEN I DISCOVERED A POSSIBLE ARCHITECTURAL connection with the Great Pyramid, the Serpent at once began to become a little overwhelming in my mind. So many answers seemed to be given before the questions were asked. The earthwork was becoming "bigger" than it was supposed to be. I was brought up with the notion of Serpent Mound being merely an exceptional earthwork, nothing more. Further, overemphasis on the Great Pyramid over the years by a number of writers and investigators tended to crowd the earthen serpent (among other ancient works) out of recognition. At the time of this discovery it would have been easier on my mind to just dismiss the connection between the two ancient giants as "interesting coincidence." But the connection was there, and I knew it intuitively. The real problem was how to go about explaining this sort of connection to people whose minds were oriented completely differently.

Love. That's all I could come up with. I knew then that the design and purpose of this little dragon was conceived out of this most important essence. Nothing else could explain its exceptionally well integrated and multiple expressions. So to explain it would require more of it. In this, I had very good luck.

I was initiated by a perfect Master of Spiritual Science in 1969 and have spent the majority of my adult life enjoying the meditations provided through my Master's instructions.[37] I have met a few living saints and enjoyed their company. The local gentles[38] have been kind, aiding me in several instances with difficult problems.

Under the Master's guidance, I had my first real visionary experience in Vermont. Since then, my life has been pleasantly interrupted from time to time with insights and visions, as my Initiator had provided the technique for going deep enough on a regular basis to prepare for regular inner experience. The Master's protection allows one to strive and attain genuine spirituality, such as described by the Apostle Paul,

Rumi, and others. He was very clear from the beginning that we need not give up our religious beliefs to take up the spiritual path, for its universal message only crowns the mainstream faith systems. Like the *Tree of Life*, which nearly every faith refers to in some form, the *human form* is the true temple—the true mosque, church, and sacred site. Without the form of man or woman, the soul does not have the organ of the inner eye[39] with which to see beyond.

Some believe that like the Old Testament story of Joseph and the Pharaoh, one needs someone else to interpret dreams or visions. Over the years, I've found that real visionary experience can be understood directly by the one having the vision if a well-integrated method of self-analysis is employed. My Master provided this and much more. It was the helping hand of the inner Master that gave the insight to retrieve much of the information on the Serpent Mound. But this knowledge contained in Serpent Mound has been so well concealed that a massive veil hinders its ready assimilation.[40] This work will not be fully understood by the general public for some time into the future. In fact, there is a resistance to it in the archaeological community due to their almost strictly material bias. Nevertheless, there are those key people who require this information at this time. The Serpent Mound experience should be taken as an adventure into a well-hidden mystical realm concerned with stars, sun, moon, geometry, numbers—and *love*.

From the beginning, the understanding of geometry was a primary focus for this work. So when it came to the discovery of the Tree of Life, it wasn't purely dumb luck. First, this effort is only a *re*discovery of how the Tree was originally conceived.[41] Someone in the Egyptian *and* some similar later college knew of it,[42] for without the hexagon to serve as its modifier, it would have twelve spheres—i.e., the beast would have eight

"heads" instead of seven. Second, it required at least two years of studying and creating "magic" squares before it even occurred to me to try the formula for this one using the square of eight.[43]

In any event, what follows is the way this chapter was presented, with few changes, from the earlier edition. The Tree of Life, brought forth by the Jews, apparently was an inherited version of the most famous religious symbol attributed to the ancient Egyptians, the ankh. Evidently, the Egyptian (or pre-Egyptian) craft knew the use of numerical squares.

I cannot emphasize enough the crucial turning point this discovery was in this research. To state it simply, the virtual "core and kernel" of the Mystery College, and its link to a distantly ancient tradition, is embodied in this finding.

The Ank as Tree

It is this ank (ankh), a symbol traditionally associated with the ancient Egyptian religious culture, which may further illustrate the deep underlying sophistication encoded in the design of the serpent earthwork. Used as a sign of enduring life and regeneration, the ank is noticeable in a majority of the images depicting the Egyptian pantheon. It evidently is a literal key to the vault of the Mysteries and is still popularly used today, however little understood, as an amulet or charm expressing a belief in continuing life much as the cross is worn by Christians to signify everlasting life. There may in fact be a direct symbolical relationship between the two crosses, though Christendom must, out of necessity, deny it.[44]

But the evidence of the ank or *crux ansata* only deepens and widens the mystery of the Serpent. It underscores a rather advanced system of theological science and literate form thriving prior to historical reference. The powerful influence of what could rightly be termed an *Edenic*

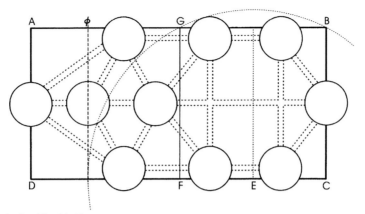

Figure 50. Kircher's Sephirothic Tree

An analysis of Athanasius Kircher's Sephirothic Tree appearing in his *Oedipus Aegypitacus* (1652) reveals the artist's careful use of the phi ratio for the purpose of communicating the distinct levels of created and spiritual regions for the Kabbalists. It is denuded yet geometrically intact.

The following explanation uses the considerably more ancient Theosophy of the Indian Spiritual Adepts in conjunction with Kircher's diagram to demonstrate the obvious connection the Sophic-Kabbalistic tradition holds with the Path of the Great Saints, *Sant Mat*. With an understanding of the origin of the Sophic-Kabbalistic Tree, the sacred wisdom of Egyptians, Jews, and Arabs, underlying the mystical Christian tradition, is more easily traced.

The three highest orbs in the figure stand for the sixth and seventh regions, *Tapoloka* (sixth) and *Satyaloka* (seventh). *Satyaloka* is the region of the True Substance beyond any subsequent comparison, and *Tapoloka* is called the Sphere of the Holy Spirit and Eternal Patience. Separated by lines BC and E in the figure, they are *Agama*, the Inaccessible (sixth), and *Anama*, the Nameless (seventh).

The next level, including two orbs (lines GF and E), is the fifth sphere or *Janaloka*, region of Spiritual Reflection wherein the idea of a separate existence (spiritual ego) originates. It is called *Alakshya* (*Alakh*), a realm that is nonetheless higher than the Causal, Astral and physical worlds. Thus it is called Incomprehensible, home to the Son(s) of God. The next sphere, touched by line FG, is the beginning of the region of the Primal Atom, the creation of Darkness or Maya. It is called *Maharloka* and is the connecting link between the purely spiritual regions and the lower creation. Referred to also as "the Door," it is familiarly called *Dasamadwara* in the catalogs of the Masters.

The next level, containing two spheres, is called *Swarloka* or *Mahasunya*, the Great Vacuum. It is the region of the magnetic aura surrounding the great Atom, and electrical powers stemming from it. It is the Causal Region as compared to the *Maharloka* above, which is Super-causal.

The next sphere is called *Bhuvarloka*, region of *Sunya*, Vacuum Ordinary. Here the subtle matters as electrical attributes form the body as it is familiar to us, though bright and readily adaptable to the will. Here, by the diagram, the phi intersects, signifying the repository or seat of the visible form (man, woman), free of its gross attributes. Ascribed to the square and influence of Mercury, it directly influences the last sphere, *Bhuloka*, that of gross material, called by the Kabbalists Sephiroth 10, Kingdom, line AD.

In all fairness to the supreme Spiritual Science of the Indian subcontinent, the Kabbalistic tradition appears to be a disconnected fragment of a greater school of Initiation that long ago had contact with empowered Godmen. The Tree of Life, as it is called, is a universal symbol and can be made to fit virtually any school of thought, however pertinent or lacking in substance. The following sections of this book ideally cast more light on the far-reaching implications inherent in the symbol, showing how it was originally presented in association with the Serpent long before it was removed and isolated for use by various segregated schools of influence.

This seemingly poorly-shaped sphere atop the cross is a representation of the heaven beyond the material universe. This strange orb could at times be found resting atop the heads of certain Egyptian deities, perhaps most notably the falcon-headed Horus.

Figure 51. Strange Orb

school of esoteric wisdom, anchored in a superior knowledge linking humankind with the divine nature, would be indelibly marked in the spiritual-mental makeup of the human race. Such a deeply seated memory would be difficult to erase from the collective humanity. It would, by its nature, arise from age to age through some good circumstance, inundating our historical cultures with its timeless and classically conceived truth. Just as seeds with viable germs may lie hidden unnoticed in the earth throughout the cold months, so a divinely conceived, perfectly constructed symbol of the Mysteries may return

by way of a perennial urge of those fortunate spirits desiring a return to the *garden*.

But the secret of the ank has never been made mundane any more than the other sacred symbols of our most antique cultures. In part, the "gods" were elaborated numbers, for a strict code of Monotheism was the rule and law of the Mystery College. Without a Unity or One, mathematics and astronomy as well as geometry would have been unreasonable to perform. The Masters indeed endeavored to be as this Unifying Principle, and as such formed the fundamental core of all the philosophic systems, even as we know them today. The *god* of the ank and tree would have been the equivalent of Mercury (Greco-Roman), Hermod (Teutonic), or Thoth (Egyptian), and for the following reasons.

Numbers and the Divine

It was for the purpose of science and social convenience, as well as for the establishment of a definite code of communication, that the idea of lending divine disguises to numbers was instituted. So well did the idea work that today we continue to use the systems laboriously created by an ancestry that is countless generations removed from us. All matter is derived from number as evidenced in the periodic table of the elements. The entire Creation is literally and figuratively composed of numbers. Held by the Sages as an illusion, matter itself is merely a dense version of the Eternal Substance. Following the geometric and numerical creation of the protonic atom, it was only a matter of duplicating and multiplying it with infinite variation. Complementing this atom itself, the Great Serpent embodies specific measure to ensure harmonic proportion. This, in subsequent comparison, was intended to ensure a connection with the Creator's intelligence.

7	58	56	9	48	17	31	34
57	8	10	55	18	47	33	32
6	59	53	12	45	20	30	35
60	5	11	54	19	46	36	29
3	62	52	13	44	21	27	38
61	4	14	51	22	43	37	28
2	63	49	16	41	24	26	39
64	1	15	50	23	42	40	25

31	40	25	34	27	36	29	38
42	17	48	23	46	21	44	19
39	32	33	26	35	28	37	30
18	41	24	47	22	45	20	43
55	16	49	10	51	12	53	14
2	57	8	63	6	61	4	59
15	56	9	50	11	52	13	54
58	1	64	7	62	5	60	3

25	34	30	37	36	27	39	32
24	47	19	44	45	22	42	17
49	10	54	13	12	51	15	56
64	7	59	4	5	62	2	57
1	58	6	61	60	3	63	8
16	55	11	52	53	14	50	9
41	18	46	21	20	43	23	48
40	31	35	28	29	38	26	33

12	5	60	53	44	37	28	21
54	59	6	11	22	27	38	43
13	4	61	52	45	36	29	20
51	62	3	14	19	30	35	46
15	2	63	50	47	34	31	18
49	64	1	16	17	32	33	48
10	7	58	55	42	39	26	23
56	57	8	9	24	25	40	41

Called the Square of Mercury, the magic square of eight is the best working example of a numerical "god," for it promotes harmony and interaction. This magic square, unlike the others in the basic premise of seven squares, can be internally arranged in a variety of ways, making it the most plastic and workable of these primary seven. Due to its multiple harmonic expressions, the square reveals in part the reasoning

Figure 52. Magic Squares Sacred to Mercury

These magic squares, having their numbers connected on a blank 64-square field, conceal unusual geometric forms. Considered to be sacred to Mercury, these figures, like the one following, may have been used to put across the understanding of the union between number and form.

8	58	59	5	4	62	63	1
49	15	14	52	53	11	10	56
41	23	22	44	45	19	18	48
32	34	35	29	28	38	39	25
40	26	27	37	36	30	31	33
17	47	46	20	21	43	42	24
9	55	54	12	13	51	50	16
64	2	3	61	60	6	7	57

Figure 54. Solar Hexagon and the Tree of Life

When the square (divided thus by eight) is conjoined with the hexagonal figure, being sure to touch its top and bottom with the points of the hexagon's top and bottom, the mathematically conceived crescents fall directly upon the asterisk-like conjunctions of the hexagon. Note that the hexagon cuts off the bottom two crescents. Note also the fact that some crescents turn up, indicating the ability to hold the heavenly gift, while others turn down, indicating the lower worlds of the atom.

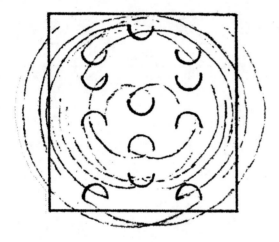

Figure 53. Magic Square of Eight as Building Block for the Tree of Life

The ank, as well as the Kabbalistic Tree, may have been derived from this particular version of the magic square of eight. Once joined with the sacred hexagon in a certain fashion, the familiar ank and tree reveal themselves clearly.

behind the venerable musical concept of the octave. Eight proves itself to be a pillar of support lending great power to nine, subsequently attributing a consummate dignity and authority to ten. Because of its mercurial combinations, the magic square of eight is associated with life-force energy, i.e., the covert carrier of nature's most vital messages. Due to this, eight is considered the greatest of servants among the "gods," respected by all and revered by many. In this selfless capacity, Mercury's square earns the epithet of "dragon-master," harbinger of the qualities originating the concept of the divine creature which guards the Treasure House of the Gods: literally *Thesaurus* or Word-giving agent. This is important to note.

This great dragon of the Bible[45] is portrayed

with the ank. The technique for isolating this timeless symbol involves the construction of the magic square in its most common way, subsequently connecting the numbers as they are correctly arranged in a prescribed fashion, in this case using a good compass after a measuring rule.[46]

The interrelationship of the hexagon and the ank-kabbalistic tree provides a basis for decoding much of the ancient mysteries, including enough of the Revelation to John to take its interpretation out of the immature ideologies of politically inclined Churchmen. The hexagon alone provides much of this information. In this sense of balancing pairs of opposites[47], the Serpent appears as an intermediary designed to draw together and blend opposing forces of nature.

Spirit and Matter

The power of the sun has been compared with that of the soul. As the soul is cleansed of its various mental impressions and stains on the journey back to God, it begins to shine with the light of many suns. The old enemy, mind, takes the attention of the conscious soul and runs it into matter. The body of course requires this attention to sustain life, for the soul currents are conducted along the complicated nervous system. But how much is too much? When should one begin to reverse the attention to focus on things of a less material nature? As will be discussed, the understanding of suchlike "currents" is directly comparable to the subtle magnetic currents of the Earth. In the art and science of meditation, collection of the body's life current behind the eyes effects spiritual well being and enlightenment. Similarly the ancient science now referred to as *geomancy* intentionally collected the flowing magnetic currents of the Earth at single places, creating sanctuaries of spiritual resource.

The Great Serpent interpreted as swallowing the solar ellipse may be seen as the mind taking on the immortal source of light and life. This understanding of *soul* or *spirit* is intimately linked to mind's existence, for mind was made for soul to evolve and strengthen itself. Thus the Serpent may be seen as both the *Logos* and the *Mind*, depending on one's point of view.[48] Perhaps the Native Americans of long ago saw it as a powerful ritual sacrifice, with the essence of the sun flowing into the land from the lair of the serpent-dragon. Doubtlessly, the oval is generally cited as an "egg," although it certainly is no kind of egg known to natural science. It is, more accurately 'egg-like,' carrying some meaning associated with the function of an egg-vessel. It should be noted as well that the small triangular feature could easily be interpreted as that which unifies the Serpent figure with the oval feature, being analogous to a hinged and distended jaw. The triangular mound is crucial in the interpretation of several previously cited geometries.

The serpent power is classically associated with Mercury for reasons that should become more apparent. The explanation of the serpent-inclusive Pythagorean Theorem is one example. Many writers have exhaustively researched and presented this knowledge pertaining to Mercury-Thoth, and much of it is most ancient. The "god" governed highways and roads. He was guide to the traveler. He was also a "thief," distributing "wealth" from areas of concentration outward for the benefit of the "needy."

As noted in the Preface, the American Society of Dowsers Great Serpent Mound chapter has performed extensive examination of the earthwork and its vicinity. They have unanimously discovered six energetic lines of subtle magnetism converging in the oval bowl at the head of the earthwork. They are concentric and equidistant lines. It was their finding that helped in the discovery of the hexagon's relation to the Serpent survey. Other such lines of unusual formation and energy have been found on property adjacent to the park facility.

The alteration of the solar energy to a cool utility was a fundamental concern for the ancient engineers of the flowing spirit-force beneath the landscape. As evidenced by the Serpent image displayed in both the 6–8–10 theorem and the hexagon, the geomantic college aligned its subject for maximum exposure to the saturating flux and flow of the magnetic poles. At the same time, the mound figure was conceivably designed to contain and accumulate the subtle energy, being slightly raised and composed of layers of stone and clay. The internal lattice of the hexagon, patterned after the understanding of the spiritual soul itself, allowed for the mixing and integration of all natural energies. Whether it was to be hypothetically transferred to the Great Serpent is a point of philosophy. One thing is clear, however: The picture of the Serpent was framed in classical geometry in part to emphasize harmonious interaction with the magnetic aura of the Earth, as it is in part to display geometrical influence of the sun and the moon.

It has been pointed out that the Serpent is in a striking pose, indicating that our Mercury is active and animated.[49] Native American legends aver that the great serpent rose up from the Underworld to attack the Sun, a myth possibly kept alive through the regular occurrence of eclipse.

This rising up out of the ground is used in Revelation 13, beginning at verse 11, wherein a second beast who has the power of the dragon makes its appearance.

And I beheld another beast coming up out of the earth; and he had two horns like a lamb, and he spake as a dragon.

And he exerciseth all power of the first beast before him, and causeth the earth and them which dwell therein to worship the first beast, whose deadly wound was healed.

The antique symbol for the presence of Mercury is the ank, but with a smallish horn or partial crescent atop its ellipse or circle:

By this example, the Mercury symbol is nothing more than a miniaturized and concise form of the ank. The little crescent is placed as a reminder of the ten and two compass lines as semicircles shown in Figures 53 and 54. The symbol for Mercury was then a second beast, one having all the regal powers associated with the first.

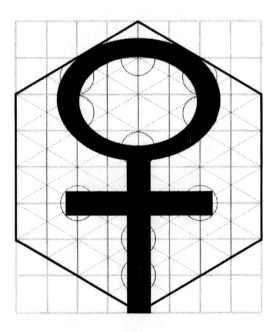

Figure 55. The Mercurial Ank

The Ank was apparently derived from the union between the solar hexagon and the mercurial square of eight.

The figure of the "tree," derived of the square of 8, then proceeded to the dictates of the hexagon, and as will be seen again,[50] its vesica piscis. The power of the sun was thus translated to the coils of the Serpent. The stamp of the mercurial ank beneath or upon the solar hexagon consummated the spiritual power, blended it, and sent it out to the surrounding countryside. According to some, this power once enlivened an interactive network including the entire planet.

As an added note, the supreme symbol for the mercurial ank penetrates the world of matter, focusing on the chemical element bearing its name. Mercury has the atomic number 80, perhaps indicating that the ancients had some insight connecting them to modern physics' approach to matter. Before modern medicine grew wary of the dangers of quicksilver, it was used frequently in combination with other things like herbs and minerals and taken orally. The metal in its pure state easily dissolves gold, silver, lead, copper, and tin at room temperature. Hence the name for the magic square of eight, for its properties liberally encompass the world of numbers as well.

It is logical then that the wisdom of Mercury, whether from a philosophical or strictly material point of view, provided the ancient Mysteries with a wonderful agent of change and transformation.

The Sacred Seven and the Sacred Ten

The ceremonial tree of the kabbalists has been compared by serious students of symbology to the seven sacred centers of the subtle physiology. To make this connection is of some significance, for in this way we see how the "beast" and its "dragon" become a human being (Revelation 13:18). While scripture states that God cre-

ated the human form in his own image, the mystics confirm this in declaring the Universe to be shaped like the human body. The soul entity is also likened to God, the little spirit being a drop in an ocean of loving Spirit.

The seven grand regions of the Universe are in a functional sense contained by the human form. In the strictly physical sense, they are nerve ganglia serving specific regions of the body.

I turned round to see who was speaking to me, and when I turned, I saw seven golden lampstands
And, in the middle of them, one like a Son of man ...
Revelation 1:12, 13

The seven churches of John's preliminary vision are intended to call attention to the mystical body of the son of man. In the Indian tradition, there are seven *patalas*, the heavenly centers which, taken together, form the body of God.

The Greeks, by way of their classical mythographers, further developed and cultured this grand picture of Creation through the living muses, the "amusements" of the "temple." The initiates considered there to be ten.

The muses were responsible for nearly all aspects of artistic and scientific awareness, from astronomy and its astrology (the muses of the two eyes), down to a perfect understanding of history and creative sexuality in marriage, governed by the first and second of these sisters.

Their mother, the tenth in symbolism, was Mnemosyne, the one who remembers all. Hence Mnemosyne is embodied on the tree as the tenth, for in the memory of the soul is the form of the Temple.

All the muses were paired, as if spiritual twins:

Terpsichore and Urania, the eyes;

Euterpe and Kalliope, the ears;

Melpomene and Thalia, the nostrils;

Polyhymnia and Mnemosyne, the mouth and sensorium;

Erato and Kleio, the orifices of life and health (regeneration).

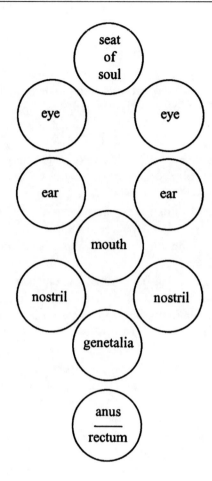

Figure 56. The Tree of Life as the Ten Doors

The Serpent and the Ark

ELECTRICITY IS ONE OF THE GREATEST WONDERS and mysteries of life. Some scientists now believe that through an interaction of elemental molecules with electrical energy, the first life appeared on Earth. From the first solar-receptive cells formed in the primordial stuff of the tidal pools, it is thought that the higher, more familiar life evolved. Philosophical investigation concurs, but in a wisdom not understood as yet by science.

The ark of Moses as recorded in the Old Testament is a box made of *shittim* (acacia), a

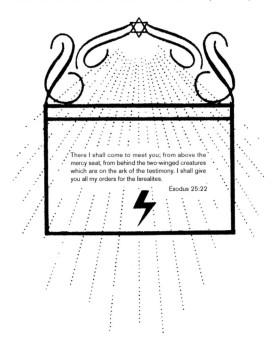

There shall come to meet you; from above the mercy seat, from behind the two-winged creatures which are on the ark of the testimony. I shall give you all my orders for the Isrealites.

Exodus 25:22

Figure 57. The Ark of Moses

resinous wood with special properties. For lack of a better description, one could say that the wood could be made into a wind chime, for it sort of clinks with a musical tone. The native North American wood closest to such quality might be the black heart of an old persimmon. Walnut, maple, cherry and oak are good, but they don't quite have the same resonance. I asked a local carpenter to create a miniature version of the biblical ark, and he had great difficulty in securing the same wood as described in the Bible, settling instead on a variety of acacia, which though quite similar, is native to Hawaii.

In the Bible, the box is made in terms of *cubits,* one cubit usually interpreted as being between 17 and 21 inches,[51] dimensions of 3:5. It was then lined with gold, within and without, and a solid gold "mercy seat" made to fit atop. The sheer weight of this lid ensured a hermetic seal on the inside, possibly necessary for the effect of properly containing the energy produced within. A collegiate institution reportedly put together a similar 1/4-size replica, borrowing the gold from some governmental source to complete the experiment.[52]

Speculation as to the source of the energy produced from the box goes in different directions. Some believe that, at the very least, the ark is a capacitor. But does the box "receive" energy like a radio, store it, and then transmit it, or does it produce energy itself by somehow converting matter into electricity? Is it energy that electrical engineers are familiar with, or is it a more polarized form of energy capable of an entirely different expression in application?

Electricity: History and Mystery

When Ben Franklin performed his famous experiment with the kite and the key, he was of the opinion that electrical force was a fluid or plasma. In traditional natural philosophy, electricity is like a fifth or perhaps even better described as a sixth state of matter. In this it is a sort of liaison between the Universal Ether and the other four conditions of solid, fluid, gaseous, and fiery. The Ether (Aether) is held to be matter in its preconditioned state. It is said that a lightning bolt is solid as it strikes and could be hit with a baseball bat with "stunning" results if one were swinging at precisely the right moment. At the same time, though, the electrons in a bolt of lightning flow like a fluid into or around whatever they make contact with. Similarly, under certain conditions, electricity may appear as wisps of gas, as seen in the Northern Lights or in ghostly forms produced by earthlights.[53] Franklin didn't *discover* electricity, but he did discover that lightning and electrical force were one and the same.

The honor of discovery may go back to the Greeks around the time of Pythagoras. It was recorded that by rubbing the fossil resin of electra or *electron* (amber) with a soft cloth of fur, a static charge was generated that would attract small pieces of dried grass. The Romans found that rubbing lignite produced a similar reaction. This phenomenon along with the lodestone and its magical attraction to the north remained unexplained for many centuries. Then around 1600 along came William Gilbert, physician to Elizabeth I. He was a clever man, and due to his insights the Queen took an interest in his experiments with static charges. In fact, Gilbert created the terms *electric* and *electricity* after the Greek word for amber via the Latin. (Actually, he coined several new terms, still in use today.) He showed that diamonds and wax also produce a static charge. The creation of the *versorium* by Gilbert allowed a pointer to swing to the field of a static charge. So in a way, Gilbert, along with the Queen, got the ball rolling toward more discoveries in the field of controlled electricity.

The Italian scientist Alessandro Volta later demonstrated that when a small amount of moisture is deposited between two different metals, electricity is produced. Volta, after whom the unit of electrical energy (volt) was named, invented the first battery by placing plates of copper and zinc in alignment separated by acid-soaked paper. He showed how electrical energy could flow like a fluid force instead of jumping in sparks. He also demonstrated the easy transference of electricity by wire from place to place.

Later, the Englishman Michael Faraday, generated electricity in a very practical way, showing how a magnet moving inside a coil of copper produces current as long as the magnet is kept moving. It was Faraday who signaled a major step forward, for he made the first generator.

Then came along the American Thomas Edison, who had a real genius for discovering practical applications of electricity in a number of areas. Excepting the radio, it seems Edison put his electrical genius to everything from the light bulb to the phonograph. For a time, Edison attracted the assistance of a young Nikola Tesla. But Tesla was brilliant in his own right, and his is another story. Briefly, Tesla was more intrigued by the hidden or occult properties of magnetism and electricity than was his contemporary, and he ultimately created controversies inherent on the path of the misunderstood.

These are accounts of men attempting to understand something that Nature produces on a grand scale and a regular basis. The computer I'm working with right now utilizes very small amounts of current giving life to silicon chips producing great artificial intelligence. Edison and Tesla would have loved this. But if we can do so much with such small amounts of electricity, what was the ark for? If our ancestors needed the ark in the past, will we need it again in our future? Something about the ark is well concealed. Like the veil over the Serpent Mound, there is probably a very good reason for the golden box being veiled. Like the little computer chip given artificial life, it is feasible that the ancients created special "circuits" that enhanced the life force of local or entire geographic regions. What was the real meaning behind the dragon, its lair, and its power?

Dharma: The Mystery of the Electric Couple

To get answers to questions like these, one should start at the beginning. From the Holy Science of the Indian sage Jnanavatar Yukteswar, we read that there are times on the Earth when electricity and its fine matters are not grasped by the human intellect. Thus humanity goes through various Ages or *Yugas* wherein the knowledge of electricity and magnetism are either on the ascendant or the decline. In other words, during one precessionary cycle (about 25,920 years), we go through four different periods in the development of *dharma* (the "law" governing the mental virtue), each period twice: once ascending and once descending. Either of these periods approximating 12,960 years is termed one-half the *electric couple* that is the period of precession.

According to the Indian Masters, this galaxy we live in is like a snowflake amidst an uncounted swirling of similar stellar formations—

no two alike—all continually revolving about *Vishnunabi* or the Central Sun of the physical cosmos. There are literally *billions* of galaxies, each one larger than we can yet understand, yet just a speck in comparison to the size of the physical cosmos. Our telescopes today are weak in comparison to the capacity of the inner eye of the Saints, and a "central sun" is a common feature of the various (and there are many) cosmic schemes. The suns are like great souls, and their galaxies are their properties and fine matters. Ours is interpreted as blue-white, reflected in the strange bluish color depicted in a young Krishna, an incarnation of Vishnu, the Sustainer.

When our galaxy makes its sweep closest to the Central Sun, the dharma principle (the law governing the mental virtue enabling us to comprehend the nature of Spirit) becomes very strong. Like Faraday's magnetic principle, the flux of the Spiritual Center of the physical universe permeates all matter with its radiation. Thus even as we think and move about, the general populace generates an enlightenment of the Spiritual Reality inherent at the core of Vishnunabi. Right now however, such a Golden Age or *Krita Yuga* is several thousand years in the future for the mass of humanity. As we move away from the grand center, we lose not only our natural spirituality, but our ability to make and keep peace—as we take up and cling to a life of the senses. Hence, politics rule with warfare, and humankind forgets everything it has learned. Coupled with disastrous earth and climatic changes, this state of affairs periodically threatens to annihilate the human race. The dharma is in principle kept intentionally preserved among the Spiritual Adepts and their devoted.

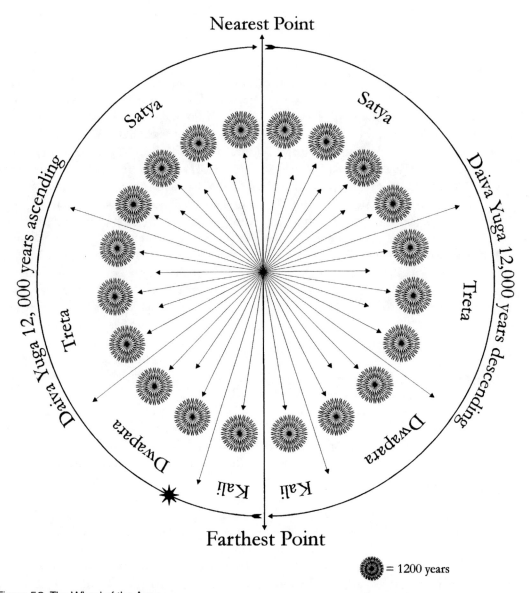

Nearest Point

Satya

Satya

Daiva Yuga 12,000 years ascending

Daiva Yuga 12,000 years descending

Treta

Treta

Dwapara

Dwapara

Kali

Kali

Farthest Point

= 1200 years

Figure 58. The Wheel of the Ages

The circle, divided into twentieths by the flowery aster- isks, describes the development and decline of dharma, the intellectual virtue. The half on the right descends as the Earth moves away from the Central Sun, while the left side indicates the gradual return of the natural genius of humanity. The small star on the lower left indi- cates the present time when we are again familiariz- ing ourselves with the nature and application of elec- trical current. Mankind literally loses its memory during the descending ages, and thus the misunderstanding of how long the Kali Yuga really is. The precessionary cycle is actually a little longer than 12,000 + 12,000 years, but this diagram was simplified for clarity. (Mason- Hamilton, after Yukteswar's explanation)

In brief, the four periods reflect outwardly in the technology of the populace the science of comprehending electricity and magnetism. In the low "Iron" age, humankind possesses only inferential knowledge of magnetic force and electrical energy. This is historically evident in the observation of the lodestone and the result of friction upon amber. In the next ascending period or "Copper" age (in which we currently live), the knowledge of generation and electrical application comes along nicely. In the next cycle—the "Silver"—the understanding of magnetism and electricity are fully explored and developed, with space and time comprehended reasonably in technology. Then in the highest or "Golden" age, the mysteries of soul and Spiritual existence become revealed inwardly. Following this, the cycle repeats itself, only reversed—beginning with the highest age in an addendum to itself. Mankind then gradually forgets, and returns to a state of confusion and lost spirituality.

One notable thing about this cycle is that the length of the precessionary period is virtually identical to the cyclical period of the revolution about the grand center of Vishnunabi. There is evidence that both the tilting of the Earth and the length of her precessionary cycle are intelligently conceived dynamics.

The knowledge of electricity may have existed between three and five thousand years ago—in the last decending Copper Age. In 1938, the basement of the Baghdad Museum yielded what apparently was a battery, possibly used for electroplating, and dating back two millennia, specifically to the Parthian occupation. It was a small pot of about 6 inches in height, made of a bright yellow clay, and fitted with a cylinder of copper about five inches high and an inch and a half wide. It was soldered, and fitted with an iron rod that had apparently been subjected to acid.

An Austrian archaeologist named Wilhelm Konig, whose background in science helped him to immediately recognize the artifact as a battery, made the find. Dr. Konig also found some Sumerian copper vases that were silver plated in a manner that was not unlike the electroplating technique. When tapped, a blue patina flaked off, more characteristic of electrical deposit than gilding. These vases were dated at 4,500 years old. It would appear then that the Persians of the Parthian occupation (248 B.C.E. to C.E. 226) inherited their knowledge of the battery from antique Sumeria, in southern Iraq, where the copper vases were found.

The Current of the Land

A large part of the responsibility of this knowledge of the cycle and its effect on humanity begins with the constructive stewardship of land and sea. Once enlightenment and self-knowledge are lost to the mainstream population, the lands become divided along religious and political lines. With these divisions, the planet as a whole entity with a system of interconnected parts falls into disrepair, and the ability to work with the forces of nature toward the controlling of weather patterns dwindles to the status of forgotten art. The Chinese believed that the *lung mei* or dragon paths extended all over the world. In America, the final vestiges of conscious cooperation seem to have left around 5,000 years ago, with only pockets of the tradition surviving, and then in an utterly degenerated form.[54]

This sacred science is based primarily on the knowledge of terrestrial magnetism as generated with the help of the poles of the planet and the flux of the ensuing field washing constantly over the globe. Today, we are just beginning to theorize the possible reasons for the decline in the intensity and power of the planetary magnetic field, and the protection it extends to the biosphere. We know that without the magnetic field surrounding the planet, there would not be life as we know it. What we do not comprehend is simply that we know very little concerning the true nature of this magnetic energy.

Electricity, akin to magnetism, is a unique state of matter, being an amassing of free electrons capable of movement through any suitable medium. How electrons are generated from matter is a starting point in understanding nuclear physics. The human race has not yet perfected a method to transmit large amounts of electricity over distances without costly loss of the energy. Reports of stray voltage have complicated the issue of safely conducting current over land. Electricity from "leaky" cables will travel through rock and soil by a path of least resistance, tending to accumulate as it finds the high ground. If this happens in a rural setting, the current may travel hundreds of feet to the farmhouse, then continue moving up—perhaps finding a bathtub filled with water! Nature will conduct energy *its* way as soon as man loses control. Thus it is emphasized that with generation comes the responsibility of proper conduction. The ancient science may not have had this kind of problem however, for it was not occupied with conducting electrical current. Rather, it was concerned with the *collection of the magnetic spirit*.

The Science of Natural Magic

To understand the cause of this force, but never to be obsessed and never overcome thereby, is to trample on the serpent's head. In such secrets are contained all mysteries of magnetism, which name can indeed be applied to the whole part of antique Transcendental Power.

Eliphas Levi
19th century Roman Catholic priest

The Earth's magnetic field puts forth a continuous and superabundant supply of flowing current. The prehistoric science evidently knew of a very general technique transforming the magnetic current to an electrically attractive form. Under certain specific conditions, concentrated magnetic flow in the Earth can cause one's arm hairs to bristle—and hence the belief in the subterranean movements of the "dragon" beneath one's feet during an electrical storm—gathering its power to its "lair." Properly directed and, through gathering, made to concentrate, the terrestrial "serpent" may find consummation with the powerful electrical energy emanating from the sky.

In our science's careful observation of its flow above the surface of the planet, the magnetic field has a characteristic "aura." But below, and across the surface, the field changes its concentration and direction in accord with the nature of matter. Heavy weights, such as obelisks and standing stones, may aid in the attraction and alignment of magnetic forces on the surface. But deeper in the Earth, the magnetic field may form rivulets and streams of exceeding strength and penetration.

In spite of all the efforts made in the gentle craft of natural philosophy, it is not acceptable to our modern science that the ancient engineering art consciously practiced the manipulation of magnetic current. However, it was the most sacred art of channeling off streamlets of the terrestrial current from the great topographical sheathing that occupied the attentions of those engineers. Like the careful milking of a cow allowing for plenty in reserve for the calf, the ancient method drew upon a potentially inexhaustible source of energy made available and carried by the driving power behind the magnetic field. This apprehension of the invisible flow through the segregating and corralling of its lines of force brings us into the "occult" or "arcane" understanding of the Serpent Power. Once the magnetic flux is sluiced away from the superabundance of its field, it begins, through concentration, to become something else—something in a stage between magnetic and static electrical energy. But it was how they did it that is of special interest.

Herein is the point of differentiation between the "old science" and the modern. Thus developed, the flux is the primal ethereal-material essence, which, being focused and combined with the sky current, produces the current of life, growth, and healing. Such a reaction is comparable to the alchemical marriage between the elements of mercury and sulfur, the "mercury" principle characterizing the magnetic essence, and the "sulfur" principle characterized as the spark of sky-current. Once taken out of its normal or natural condition and made to coil, collect, and concentrate, the magnetic essence demonstrates the "serpent" principle and, subsequently, the positively charged "dragon's lair."

The ancient science possessed a vested interest in manipulating and culturing the swarming magnetic currents of the natural landscape. The flow was analogous to the supple undulations of the spring serpent, moving, as the sun warmed the land, to the higher rocks, there to join others of its kind. We know as well that before the great cities and mass industrialization prevailed, the planet was completely different in appearance. Before the segmenting and raping of the lands, the gentle, irresistible ether now referred to as serpent or dragon current flowed undisturbed where it wanted to go.

The old diviners were not as concerned with conduction of electrical current as they were with the collection of the magnetic current. They were, aptly enough, thought of as magicians by some accounts. Such a person, having the rights of the land displaying the spiritual concentration, may have been considered as "blessed by the gods" or even a member of some spiritual lineage. On the other hand, having inherited or appropriated the locale by some unscrupulous means, they could, as Megissogwan, foe of Hiawatha, have manipulated the force through a darkened perception of its real purpose, creating disease instead of health. Native American myth and legend, as related by Campbell among others, avers that the magicians knew the subtle arts of both dream projection and shape shifting—practices associated with the manipulation of the divine current. Did the Native American shaman class intentionally claim for their personal property the areas where lightning strikes were most frequent?

Indeed, certain members of our very distant ancestry knew how to recognize the natural rhythm of the ethereal water flooding over the landscape. They knew as well the method to artificially attract, often by straight paths, this "essence" to specific points. It was a world-inclusive system set up long prior to any recorded history. The energy, by its nature neither "good" or "evil," was focused and concentrated without dissipation. This in itself was an important part of the art. After the installation of specialized moats, altars, and shrines at these locations to further the culturing of the energy, these places were, by any evidence, handed down generation after generation. At times they were usurped, being taken as thrones of power. Finally, after the corrupting passage of time, the true nature of the place was no longer understood. Superstition and witchcraft then prevailed, and these places became known for their haunted and spectral environs. Today, even such haunted places are difficult to find, due to a drying up and dissipation of the life current. Only their legends remain.

I feel that ley-man, astronomer-priest, druid, bard, wizard, witch, palmer, and hermit, were all more or less linked by one thread of ancient knowledge and power, however degenerate it became in the end.
Alfred Watkins, *The Old Straight Track*

Inherited and built over by the early Church, some of the old pagan temples in Europe and the Celtic region found themselves inheriting as well a perfect situation over a "blind spring" or crossroads of the magnetic flux. In the ancient Ohio Valley, large tumuli shaped like cones and rising often over 60 feet off the plain were originally believed to have been lookouts. When excavated however, burials of suspected importance were often discovered. Such sacred grounds, like the holy churchyards of the Christians, were not likely intended to be walked upon or similarly violated out of respect for the "resting place of the spirit."

Like a combination of the old pagan temples with their secret caves and churches with their steeples, the conical mounds with inclusive chamber burials may very possibly have functioned as focus centers for the earth current. These tombs would have ensured some respect and sanctity, thereby preserving the sensitive current that is so easily drained off through contact with man or animal. Hence one possible function—though degenerated in itself—of the moats surrounding some of these places. The linear moundworks, at times found by the early explorers in conjunction with such "towers," would have served to both bring and distribute the sacred terrestrial flow, in accord with the level of power built up within the tumulus. Even among the historical nations in America, respect for the sacred burial ground was strictly enforced, and was universally upheld, even in times of tribal warfare. And though it was from a tra-

dition before their memory, it nevertheless was a part of their beliefs, even as the Muslim or Buddhist, by some intuitive sense, would never defile the grave of a departed soul by walking over it.

In Ohio, the large conical mound found in what became downtown Cincinnati contained a log tomb. The burial associated with this mound may have been a great leader, and the mound itself designed for his continuing "influence" in the time following his physical departure. Kept clean and free of any conditioning that would disturb the collected charge before a lightning storm would come, such a special "tower" would have increased the capacity for earth current storage. The engineering would have extended to systematically distribute the "consummated" life-current over measured parcels of land. It is now believed that such mounds may have been recognized as departure points to the "Otherworld." It is interesting to note again that the entire Cincinnati plain in the general vicinity of the tall mound and the Ohio River was literally covered with special geometric and linear earthworks—as though they were "appliances" in some ingenious energy-supply scheme.

That prehistoric people knew of and worked with a separate current already existing in the earth—a current made sensational through the overhead passage of a thunderstorm—is beginning to be better understood. The existence of artificial caves or cairns in Europe and the Celtic region, specially lined with alternating layers of organic and inorganic material, would point to the possible knowledge of magnetic flux capacitors in use by ancient man. The terrestrial current, spirit-like, has a nature able to pass with time through anything. Thus special means were devised to contain the wily "serpent," however temporarily. These tomblike structures, not unlike the pyramids, well served as accumulators of the subtle positive forces of nature. The Great Serpent is itself composed of layers of stone and clay, and rests on high ground overseeing a clean water flow. Its presence not only intimated a place of power, but the symbol of the ancestral guardian of life itself.

Though variations in outer forms and methods are known, all over the world the principle of attracting sky energy to specific earth-current collection points was accomplished. Once the earth-current was attracted where it was engineered to go, those responsible would observe its transformation to its more fiery aspect—from the "subconscious" to the conscious perception. The mysterious combining of the twin forces was used for rites of fertility and yes, "magic."

People of the ancient world believed electricity was a form of heavenly fire (Revelation 13: 13). According to Lawler, the Aborigines of Australia to this day consider that lightning comes directly out of the subconscious mind of Nature. Is this not a reference to the accumulation of the magnetic force of the landscape, turned detectable through concentration and becoming visible through radical attraction to the sky current? The Aborigines are believed to yet associate electrical forces with the spiritual side of life, and tradition indicates that successful attempts were made to conduct, attract, mold, and alter natural electrical-magnetic forces for cultural benefit. As in other places around the ancient world, healing energies, operated by the shaman or priestcraft, are seen to have emanated from centers of power in the earth. Their natural accumulation and outpouring were improved upon through the creation of earth and stoneworks—in some cases finely focusing the life force to display supernatural effects such as the aforementioned earthlights.

Again, in the words of Eliphas Levi:

Magnetism is the wand of miracles, but it is this for initiates only; for rash and uninstructed people, who would sport with it or make it subserve their passions, it is as dangerous as that consuming glory which, according to the allegorical fable, destroyed the too ambitious Semele in the embraces of Jupiter.

In reference to the consummate magnetic essence as "Astral Light," he says:

The Astral Light as a whole, that element of electricity and lightning, can be placed at the disposal of human will.

It is common knowledge among agriculturists that the land becomes very fertile following electrically charged rains. The nitrates of the soil become "activated" with the help of lightning. This is dramatically evident in a control utilizing fresh rainwater-soaked soil in comparison with tap water on plants of the same seed stock. There is, inotherwords, a *third* current, the life-current, brought about through the interaction of the earth and sky currents. It exists latently in both these currents, i.e., magnetic and electrical forces. Yet it is extremely subtle and not as easily stored as either the magnetic or electrical currents.

So it is that as their inherited science matured in insight and technical merit, so did their artistry relax and open into a world of effigies, giants, pathways, and geometrical apportionment of acreage, all expressions in their simple science of controlling Earth energies. To be certain, the Great Serpent Mound is the epitome of an ideal such as the *dragon,* for a straight alignment of over 70 miles suggests it to have been an arbitrator between the two extremes of nature: the light and the darkness, life and death. No doubt many ancient paths once led to or went from the

Great Serpent. Such a divining line or *dragon path* has its lair directly over the point of the golden mean.[55] In terms of Spiritual Science, the Serpent Mound would have been intended to author and distribute the most sacred and subtle life current, and would thereby have been synonymous with the celebrated golden ratio.

Did the prehistoric people of the Ohio region know a method for blending the positive earth and negative sky currents in such a way that a non-injurious current promoting healing and growth was created? It is very difficult for us today—we who have literally disfigured the ancient landscape to an incredible extent—to understand how familiar our ancestors were with the life force flow of the land. If one runs over the garden hose with the lawnmower, it no longer is able to bring water to the extent of the yard. So similarly, when we destroyed the linear earthworks of the Ohio Valley, subsequently bringing in the railroad and the highway system, what chance had we to rediscover the subtle transference of positive current from one place to the next? Indeed, the mysteries of the overland and linear mounds may find the humble beginnings of explanation in this knowledge. Central Ohio's Great Hopewell Road, for example, is over sixty miles in length, and demonstrates the probable use of twin parallel raised earthen embankments, perfectly straight, for the entire distance. But now, with the "circuits" broken and leaking, and with the most fertile points of natural generation forgotten or simply drained dry, we live in a dark world far removed from the natural rhythms and paths known well to the ancient shaman.

In his diary Alfred Watkins quotes Jeremiah 6.16:

Yaweh says this: "Stand at the crossroads and look, ask for the ancient paths: Which was the good way? Take it and you will find rest for yourselves."

The discovery of even a portion of one of these ancient trails can be exhilarating. They are often straight, and, as we have discovered, extend many miles. Like the "pot of gold" at the end of the rainbow, these paths ultimately curtail, and their charge flows into places that served as great accumulators of the subtle energy. Mounds, circular and pyramidal, great circles, squares, rectangles and octagonal structures once surrounded the Great Serpent's lair for many scores of miles in all directions.

Anyone who has felt his or her hair begin to rise during a thunderstorm has experienced the near final stage in the drawing and focusing of earth current to meet the demands of the sky current, equal and opposite. It is an orgasmic flow of energy. As mentioned, the high places of the land, including the ridges and mountain tops, are accumulators and conveyors of the positively charged earth energy. Undoubtedly there were many such places on the ancient Ohio landscape, places where the energy simply tended to move through or accumulate on a regular basis.

With only a few special exceptions, the important mounded structures of the Ohio territory are by water paths. Where water runs above or below ground, the subtle magnetic and electrical forces are imperceptibly stirred up. Gradually they move on by paths of little resistance to natural accumulators. These paths were often engineered, as in the linear mounds of Cincinnati. Additionally, fractures and faults beneath the surface may generate and give rise to streams of gently flowing earth force that finally collect and are attracted to the charge of the sky, creating the *stepladder* phenomenon. This is a spermatic spark that collects and arises straight out of the earth, a small and very brief supply for the heavenly demand. Then comes the sky-to-earth discharge: the awesome thunderbolt.

If we were able to place ourselves into the pre-industrialized world—for example in the prehistoric lands of Europe, Asia, Australia, and the Americas—we would very surely find topography with natural magnetic and electrical flows unmolested. The "serpent" would slither and undulate freely, coiling in its "lairs." Any social group, perhaps having a shaman class and having resided in a given area a generation or more, certainly would have had its curiosity piqued at the occurrence of lightning strikes, at regular intervals, at certain places. Today, where a certain charge accumulates, as in a radio tower or similar tall structure, lightning naturally is attracted. The ancients believed that hills and mountains, caves, and tunneling subterranean water flows were the dwelling places of gods or divinities. It is amusing and amazing to see much of the electrical fury of a spring storm drained off in its passage over a large metropolitan area with its artificial "mountains" of brick and glass. What we have done, and done well, is disenfranchised ourselves from the privilege of comprehending this most exquisite mystery of nature as it once held the ancient nature religion's advocates, in love with the natural landscape, spellbound.

Among the Ojibway (Chippeway), the Mississagua, the Cree, and the Algonkin, the Thunderbird created lightning by flashing its eyes, and thunder through the flapping of its wings. These people believed that the Thunderbird, so engaged, was in the hunt for the Serpent. A lightning discharge from the Thunderbird to the head of the Serpent may lend a clue to the powerful attraction of the old Serpent Faith mentioned by Putnam and others. Pre-Columbian tribes also associated the presence of lightning with the serpent energy, especially as it tore through

trees. In Greek mythology, it was the love of Ouranos (Sky) for Gaia (Earth). Gaia often hid her offspring from the Old Man of the sky, and these offspring represented great potencies contained within the "soul" of Gaia.

Possible locations for sacred architectures arose where this phenomenon of lightning occurred with greater frequency, as the lofty location of the Parthenon in ancient Greece. Advancements over generations in this knowledge may have yielded the understanding of natural batteries for storage of this energy, ideally taking the form of the highest religious or philosophical conceptualizations, such as temples, chapels, and grottos. Both natural and artificial cavities are hallmarks of many ancient sacred sites, and the Great Serpent Mound is no exception, as will be discussed. Further, our subject lies right atop a massive deposit of dolomite, a form of limestone in combination with magnesium. As a natural capacitor, limestone has much to offer—the mountainous Great Pyramid is composed mainly of it.

The Great Anomaly

The following is from an old Pennsylvania county record:

Mrs. Wolf went out early one morning to hunt her cows. She and her dog took position on a large flat rock, where she stood watching and listening for her cows, until the dog moved and whined at her feet, which caused her to look down, when, with extreme horror she beheld a vast number of black snakes, rattlesnakes, copperheads, and almost every other kind of serpent, lying in piles along the edge of the rock, attracted thither, probably, by her and the dog's presence. She took in her situation at a glance, and, in a moment, observing where there was the least number of her besiegers, she sprang over them from the rock, the dog soon following suit, hastened home, and, horror-stricken, related to her husband what had happened, who, with the other men above-mentioned, repaired to that rock and began to kill the snakes, and continued doing so until they were driven away by an unendurable odor. Mrs. Wolf said that none of the serpents offered to harm either herself or the dog until she attempted to escape, which she did unharmed.

It has been the way of western man, as people all over the modern world, to have a dreadful fear of serpents. The snake population has been mercilessly tortured and killed, especially in the spring, as the sleek reptiles approach the warm rocks to sun themselves. This same ignorance of nature extends deeply into the subconscious world of the serpent force, for it too has been "killed" with alarming thoroughness.

Our Great Serpent has its own special "rock" that it has laid upon for countless centuries. The earthwork is at the western edge of a five-mile-wide *cryptoexplosion* feature. While scientists continue to debate the cause of this structure (*crypto* means "hidden" or "concealed"), it is believed that the rock is fractured as much as nearly a mile below the surface. There are a number of faults, cracks, and shifts in the rock. There are sulfur springs and crude petroleum asphalt leaks very near to the Serpent Mound Park. In addition, there are seventeen such cryptoexplosion anomalies spread out over seven adjoining states and into Ontario. Some scientists have theorized that an asteroid broke up into large bits and pelted the earth like a monster hailstorm about two hundred million years ago.

Much research has yet to be accomplished in

Figure 59. Cryptoexplosion Anomalies in the Midwest

attempting to understand the effects of piezoelectric forces in highly faulted areas. Any number of strange, psychic, and physical effects have been experienced and observed in and around the site of Serpent Mound Park. Some people dream vividly of the mound weeks after visiting the site. The various visionary and dream experiences could easily fill a large book. One can only guess at the influence that the cryptoexplosion feature had on the Serpent Mound's builders' site selection. Very possibly the edge of such a feature would demonstrate more dramatically the energy effects of the faulting. The former park manager and his wife spent many years living at the site and experienced definite energies in certain areas. A specific place along the cliff face south of the serpent's helix was one area he preferred to avoid if possible due to the unpleasant feelings he received there.

There are also definite gravity anomalies and strange variations in the magnetic flow right

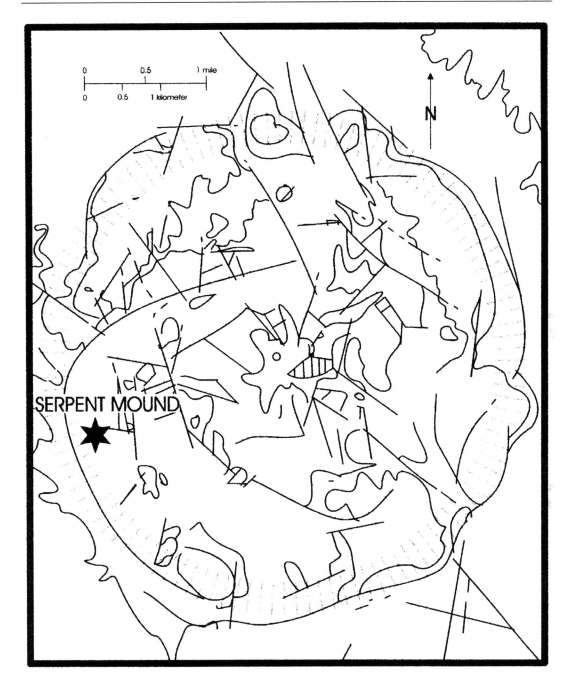

Figure 60. Serpent Mound Cryptoexplosion

The cryptoexplosion feature showing the location of Serpent Mound.

around the park itself. As for the gravity anomalies, one in particular can often be experienced simply by walking the path about the Serpent. A number of people have commented that in the area to the lower right of the head, a sort of lightness can be experienced for an instant.

Archaeological research has shown the probability of the area's attractiveness to the prehistoric shrine's first keepers. There is an open cave facing Brush Creek on the dolomite cliff beneath the effigy. There is also an extraordinarily large bat population. Added to this is the location of the earthwork near the highest topical concentration of uranium ore within a twenty-mile span. Similar findings from around the world regarding the building of sacred sites near radioactive deposits cast even more speculation on the mysteries surrounding the Great Serpent.

Soul and Spirit: A Connection to the Ark

The Great Serpent Mound may well be a tribute to the Universal Energy or *current of life*. Since ancient times, philosophers have spoken of this Universal Flow or Chord as the beginning and end of all creation. It is the source of all electrical and magnetic forces. The human form, like all life animate and inanimate, is attuned to this holy Vibration. Perhaps as a practical reminder, the constant current of Ohio's Brush Creek runs all year round at the base of the Serpent's cliff, and the area gets its fair share of lightning strikes as well. Nature has thus obviously provided the potential for a truly spiritual shrine to flourish. But was the energy available to the ancient engineers of the Great Serpent sufficient for their grandest ideal? What *was* their intent and ultimate purpose?

The Spiritual Science from prehistory knew of the existence of a soul or spiritual entity as necessary for any individual life form. The spirit is like a gyroscope and generator in the body and is the reason for the term "incarnation." The ability for one to remain balanced, physically and mentally, is attributed to the "centrifuge" of the soul. Similarly, the presence of the subtle electro-chemistry in the body, promoting life, growth, and the healing of injury, is directly attributed to the virtually unlimited power the soul is connected with. So the question is raised: is it the *soul* that is being held or regurgitated—taking form as a solar ellipse?

When the soul makes its final exit from the human form, the powerful magnetism is withdrawn, and the body begins a return to the elements of which it is composed. In the case of some of the Saints or Spiritual Masters, cremation is often recommended after passing away, for the very flesh takes on the qualities of the immortal through conscious contact with the deathless Spirit.[56] The masters of yoga speak of breath control and the securing of a rare chemical essence termed *prana,*[57] necessary to prevent decay of the tissues when rising above the senses to higher planes.[58]

Just as the sensorium-oriented soul lends life to the human body, so the hallowing ark was conceivably applied in eras past to promote life and light in certain architectures of the time. Like Moses and others, people found worthy of the trust may have utilized the ark or some similar invention of generation and equilibrium to improve the environment. When the generation of current and its application became so well understood that it was no less than analogous to the relationship between soul and body, then the ark and its use were held as a covenant between humankind and Divine Nature.

Is the Great Serpent Mound the remnant of a once highly active structure designed to distribute copious amounts of life force into the surrounding region? Because of possible con-

Figure 61. The Box, the Tree, and the Sacred Serpent

This unique diagram shows the relationship between the Serpent and the tree contained by the dimensions of the Ark of the Covenant—i.e., 3:5. Using the measure of 1.36 feet (the half megalithic yard), the short axis of the box is 260, an important figure derived of the square of eight (Mercury). Since the measure of 1.36 is believed associated with solar measure, these measures work together to balance Mercury with the sun.

In Revelation 4:6, the four living creatures (the four ideas or parts of the primal Atom) are in the middle, around, in front of, and behind the throne. Similarly, the scroll, as the ark containing the power of God (the Sounding Word), was written on the back and front (i.e., within and without), by the Word. Consequently, all is sealed (to put across the idea of a state or fixed condition of divine knowledge) with the universal symbol now seen as the ank, tree, scepter, man, dragon, etc.

This picture or one similar may have been used by the Mystery College to bring home the understanding of the sacred ark as a vessel of light and power needed to commence a great regeneration.

The Serpent image in this casing meant the binding up of the wily Satan, and a means of conducting the enormous power of nature into a peaceful and cultur-

nections to ancient Egyptian architecture, the use of the serpent design may have been an expression of that school's source of knowledge. In fact, the Great Serpent may have been at the very core of some prehistoric school's most sacred intent. Following a careful study of the geometric expressions already shown to be in conjunction with the Serpent Mound's design, another geometry reveals itself.

Finding the dimensions of the fabled Ark of the Testimony came in the form of an analysis based upon a brief personal visionary experience. Simply stated, it is believed that the dimensions of the ark may have been derived from the creation of an outline around the composite of the *tree* and the *serpent*. If up until this point you've only leafed through this text, you may not understand this part without going back over the last chapter. The fact of the Serpent fitting onto the hexagon, coupled with the square of eight fitting as well (in a customized fashion), lays the groundwork. In other words, these images made *composite* precede the idea of the design of an ark in the dimensions 3:5. The tree of life (ank) dictates the shorter axis, and the Serpent dictates the longer. This is interesting to note as the illustration is viewed.

The hexagon is conceived as a *solar* form, while the square of eight is attributed to Mercury. Thus it is a blending of the sun and Mercury, analogous to the fabled Philosopher's Stone and the Stone's potent power to transfer Spirit into matter, thereby improving matter.

---

ally worthy expression. Contained within the golden box—like a living book of wisdom—the ark may well have literally spoken, instructing the like of Moses. Perhaps in ancient times, it was used by the Egyptian priestcraft, hence an Adam and Eve being influenced by the "serpent." This is a fair warning with regard to the power of the sacred ark, i.e., do not mistake the technology for the Creator, yet do not forsake the technology altogether.

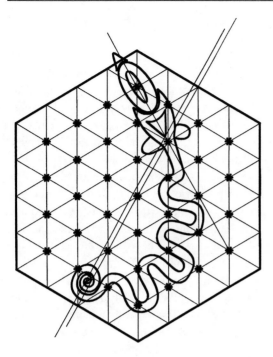

Figure 62. The Great Solar Hexagon Showing True North Alignment

The Great Solar Hexagon showing the paralleling of the true north alignment with the asterisk formations is complemented by the line of the summer solstice setting sun to the southeast.

First came the discovery of the hexagon's serpent image coupling with the tree to determine the dimensions of the box. My findings were published that way in 1993, but after the publication, I noticed that if Romain's North Star line were drawn in, it bisected the box diagonally.

The North Star bisection was a special discovery, for it permanently tipped the scales from the geometries involving the Serpent Mound as being merely interesting coincidence to workable fact. In a way, the understanding of the box made everything very clear. This diagram may well have determined the dimensions of the sacred box.

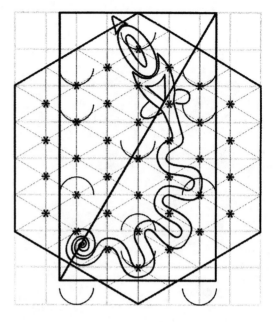

Figure 63. The Furnace of the Wise

The dimensions of the sacred Mosaic ark, believed of possible Egyptian origin due to Moses' background, may be discovered through confining one's lines to the edges of the crescents and the areas immediately to the base of the helix as well as the tip of the Serpent's head extremity. By calculation, the diagonal across the box is approximately 500 feet, and demonstrates the true north-south alignment. This exercise of looking partly to the Serpent figure and partly to the tree figure to create the sacred box serves to bring home yet another seamless joining of principle parts—in this instance creating the furnace of the wise or footstool of the Creator. (Hamilton 1993, after Romain)

Biblical Electrical Knowledge

Figure 63 shows the dimensions of the Mosaic ark, 3:5, virtually framing the ank-dragon symbol and the Serpent. The Tree of Life, believed in one interpretation to depict the ten doors of the human temple, can be seen clearly from within the precinct of the holy ark. The seven seals in this case are the seven sealed levels of knowledge regarding the human form. In this wisdom, the Mystery School was able to encapsulate a great deal of information in a single diagram, even as a book, tome, or scroll. This information, while indeterminably ancient, is evident in Revelation 5:1, again stressing the understanding of a tradition at work.

> *I saw that in the right hand of the One sitting on the throne there was a scroll that was written on the back and front and was sealed with seven seals.*

Biblical academics assert that the first covenant was with the God of Israel, but that the second was with the Son. The ark, a figure of this first trust, gave rise to the analogy of the Son through its internally generated power. Rumi, the great Arbiter of Islam, once made the comparison of the sun to the Son, stating that it is only through the sun's light that the sun may be seen, indicating that through the Spiritual light of the Master of the time, the Master (i.e. the "Son of God") may be known. So it is in Revelation 5:2 that we read:

> *Then I saw a powerful angel who called with a loud voice, "Who is worthy to open the scroll and break its seals?"*

Then in 5:3 comes the enigmatic answer:

> *But there was no one, in heaven or on the earth or under the earth, who was able to open the scroll and read it.*

As tradition holds, the Son, even in human form, is not of heaven or earth, having no temporal reality to call his home, for He is of the Divine Nature surrounding and inundating all. In Revelation 5:5 one of the elders says to John that the Son has overcome, and will open the scroll, i.e., he has risen above, revealing the body with its seven "seals" or levels as the true temple, church, and mosque.

It should be seen how the throne of God (as the hexagon) underlies the ark as a foundation. Mystics aver that the ark is as the footstool or hassock of the Creator. The twenty-four elders and the four beasts surround the throne, giving basis to the ten-crescent form of the universe and subsequently the man-shape. In other words, the throne of the One with its many attributes serves to be sharply focused within the precinct of the ark rectangle, giving rise to the tree of life with its fruits (the nine and one muses, portals, doors, or orifices). In this way, the Son, like God, is self-contained, as the Power of God is contained within the ark in the form of the Serpent (the Word or instrument of the Will) giving birth to the Sun (Son). Out of the holy Logos arrives the soul.

This initiation of the Son is first spoken of in this fifth chapter of the Revelation, more graphically outlined in Revelation chapter 12. The lamb described in 5:6 has seven horns and seven eyes and seems to have been sacrificed. Properly studied or contemplated with time, the mysteries of these exquisite passages are revealed, almost without a doubt unchanged through the duration of their existence. (See "The Xi symbol.")

The Number of the Beast

There is need for shrewdness here: anyone clever may interpret the number of the beast: it is the number of a human being, the number 666.

Revelation 13:18

THERE ARE UNCOUNTED VERSIONS OF THE Revelation's chapter 13, but they all seem to be trying to get the same message across: this figure *six hundred sixty-six* is very controversial. Actually, this number is generally considered to be *evil*. It *brings* evil and it *is* evil. It is a number seen as the harbinger of ill portent, a self-creating auger of bad news, destruction, and chaos.

But in reality, it's just a number. Numbers in themselves have no bad or good qualities; it is what we, as human beings, make them out to be. One is unity. Two is duality. Three is the triune (and God knows how many different triunes there may be). Four—well, that's the number of colors in the human sub-races, the colors of stars, the directions of the compass and the winds, etc. Five—well, now, five is getting too complex and pluralistic to write about in a limited space. Four is more than the limit. Numerology is a science, but it may as well be pseudo-science for lack of expertise in the field. But there is reality in number—wise men and women have always assured us of it.

Six hundred sixty-six is not a primary integer.[59] It isn't the square of any whole number, and it certainly isn't a prime number.[60] 666 is simply this: the sum of the square of six's 36 integers. In ancient times it was a master-figure used in arithmetic, art, and architecture, believed to harbor the special qualities of the sun and the solar influence. There is a Pythagorean connection as well. Why was it used? The answer to this question causes one to examine more thoroughly the use of what are termed *magic squares*.

Being the squares of odd and even whole numbers, magic squares are generally composed so that their body of figures are numerically balanced. For example, each line will add up to the same total as any other line. If done well, even the diagonal lines will add up correctly. As introduced in "The Traditional Tree and the Great Serpent" earlier in this section, a magic square can be a reference-worthy collection of numerical characters. Through connecting their integers in a certain way, graphic representations of that square's master figure are born. From the unconscious realm of the static number eight, one can see how the tree of life and the ank were brought into the world of reason.

In the course of their mastering the creation of these squares, the ancient cosmologists discovered not merely harmonious numerical arrangements, but interesting patterns and unique figures that sometimes repeated themselves in other magic squares, mystically connecting the collection. In this, each magic square was considered a numerical house or domain from where important references to the mysteries of numerical nature might be divined. Obviously, the magic square science may have been an important stage in the development of understanding fractions, decimals, and square roots. But perhaps more important was their probable resource in the derivation of units of measure. If you were working with the circle or hexagon, the measure of the square of six was practical.

So one problem with understanding the use of magic squares in measurement has been the incommensurable relationship of its separate figures with the whole square. For this reason the square's sum was figured first, using that as the master figure. The first century B.C.E. Roman architect Vitruvius assumed wrongly that Greek linear measure held the key to understanding Greek architecture. He subsequently construed the human form as interpretable in the same way. The Greek unit of measure in reality was illusive in architecture, but not so in calculating area. Such an understanding may well have been derived from the science of the magic square.

The magic square of six was called the "Square of the Sun." From within its body of cells, certain other figures could be extracted, all derived from the father figure, 666. These numbers include 37, 74, and 111, their divisions by 2 and multiplication by 2 or other whole numbers.[61] These numbers come directly from the average of the number of cells in the magic square divided into the sum of its cell's numbers: 666 divided by 36. Two average cells are 37. Why then is 666 considered so dark and nefarious? The answer is simply that it was associated with pagan belief systems and a cosmology that was adopted and improved upon by the Pythagorean School—controversial even to this day.

The Square of the Sun is central in the basic premise of the seven (or eight) magic squares standing as the primary integers. The reason for its being central and its being identified as the *solar* square refers back to the Seven Spirits before the throne—as previously noted in "The Spirit of Geometry," the sun was considered a disk in the heavens. By duplicating this circle through the arc of a rope, bar, or string compass, the ancients found that six circles of the same radius perfectly complemented that first circle. Thus, six became identified with the solar rule or philosophy. The number 666 therefore was a very important evolution of this cosmology, and the several steps to its introduction were obvious. The subsequent divisions into this master-figure of the sun coupled with a length of measure created places sacred to solar themes.

6	32	3	34	35	1
7	11	27	28	8	30
19	14	16	15	23	24
18	20	22	21	17	13
25	29	10	9	26	12
36	5	33	4	2	31

Figure 64. Square of the Sun

Besides being used for a system of measure, numbers were also used in writing and speech. For this, a system of symbols with direct numerical correspondence would have to be invented. In fact, it would have to be a fixed collection of symbols so the science could be truly scien*tific*. The Greeks did this about 2,500 years ago, right around the time of Pythagoras. In fact, our first philosopher might be the subject of the opening quote to this section, he whose name embodies the mysterious 666.

Pythagoras, as is well known, was named after the Python. This may have been his own idea, although in the story of his birth, his parents, Mnesarchus and Parthenis, are given credit for the naming after their consulting the Oracle of Delphi. The letters in the name of Pythagoras generally are summed up like this:

Pi = 80, Upsilon = 400, Theta = 9, Alpha = 1, Gamma = 3, Omicron =70, Rho = 100, Alpha = 1, Sigma = 200.

Adding all these together, "Pythagoras" becomes valued at 864. This number has been termed "the Foundation", referring to the first philosopher's work being the basis for much of what has become mathematics, geometry, and natural science.

But this methodology of lending numbers to symbols had certain rules that could be interpreted according to the need. Overall, the science was called *geometria,* a term so similar to *geometry* that it is believed to have derived from the use of the geometric forms of the numerical or magic squares. This coupled with the probable use of the squares to extract numbers for earth measurement (geometry) makes the derivation of the term seem obvious. The numbers 1 and 2, which could not have magic squares, had a broader and more manipulative use in additions. Thus, the rho and sigma symbols, instead of being interpreted at 100 and 200, could become 1 or 2 as the need arose. A further explanation of this system is included in the last section.

By simply altering the value of the final sigma in Πνθαγορας *(Pythagoras)* from 200 to 2, the name of the philosopher changes radically from 864 to 666, the number of the Beast. After all, that's what Python was—the Beast. A more detailed account of this mythological creature is found in the next section under "Apollo and

the Python." Was Pythagoras the name of that "man" or "human being" cited in Revelation 13:18? It should be considered as a possible fact, for scholarship is only now coming to grips with the influence of the Neo-Pythagorean School in that very well-concealed era preceding the Council of Nicea in 325 C.E. At that time, the Revelation was first standardized, having already been in existence some 229 years! How often and to what extent it had been altered we may never know.

In any event, such an example of what was later called "gematria" by the Jewish scholarship (who were also interested in symbol-number correspondence) went wholeheartedly into the Greek version of the Revelation. Subsequently, great repercussions ensued, for so strong was the belief in the kabbalistic word doctrine starting in the time of the early Church that great and serious sport was made in reducing one's political enemies' names to the "evil" number.[62] So in spite of the fact that the 666 had originated as a simple addition of the square of six's 36 figures, the beautiful scriptural art rooted in the original geometria was lost to banal whims of the uninitiated. This is evidenced in the Revelation wherein it is warned that the text should not be tampered with. Of course, the ecclesiastical editors would have nothing to do with keeping the integrity of such a potential instrument of finger-pointing as the Revelation. This is a very sad state of affairs in view of the various sects of biblical literalists so outspoken today, and who consider the Bible "the word of God."

The Great Serpent Mound and the Number of the Beast

The controversial number 666 was intended from the beginning as a master-figure of the Throne of God. Subsequent to this, things related in nature and substance to that throne took on the sacred figure's identification. The Serpent Mound survey and its hexagonal grid epitomize the foot measure of 666. The Serpent + oval feature is suspiciously close to 666 x 2 feet. However, to omit the triangular mound from any other aspects of analysis wouldn't be prudent. This feature may have had a highly specialized function, being used to point out the accuracy of the 6–8–10 geometry, as well as extending the length of the earthwork to meet the requirements for the Thuban Circle. Nevertheless, the doubling of the master-figure of the solar square may have been important in the determination of overall length. Since the Serpent figure is very close to 1,370 feet measured along the center of the mound from tail tip to triangle end, eliminating the 32 feet (approx.) of the triangular mound leaves only about 6 feet in excess of 666 x 2. Of further interest see "The Sigma Symbol."

The Hexagon Proper

Each of the 96 equilateral triangles comprising the hexagon has a square measure of 666 units, five feet each. The triangle side, taken as 81.61 feet and multiplied by 8.161 feet, is 666 feet.

The golden ratio or *phi* also may play a role in the popularity of the number 666. Multiplied by *pi* (3.14) and taking the result to the fourth power, phi-pi produces 666.24, demonstrating a possible mystical relationship between the cir-

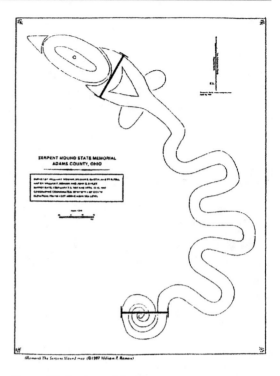

Figure 65. Number of the Beast

The foot measure of the two bracketed lines crossing the head and helix of the effigy is approximately 81.61 feet, a figure derived from both the square of the Sun and the reversal of the golden mean. It also represents Alexander Thom's "megalithic inch." Multiplying the head measure by the tail measure yields approximately 6660 feet. As Oroboros, the worm or dragon was called "tail-biter," a symbol of philosophic regeneration preceding the birth of the angelic phoenix. The sacred hexagon is entirely composed in triangles of this measure of 81.6 feet. The predominance of the decimalized foot characterizes the geometries of the terraform Serpent, creating specific units based upon itself. (Hamilton 1993, after Romain)

cle (pi) and the divine ratio.

This figure of 81.61 is of interest, for it *is* the golden ratio (1.618), only reversed. One multiplied against the other—81.61 x 16.18—offers a figure closely approximating 80 rods or 2 fur-

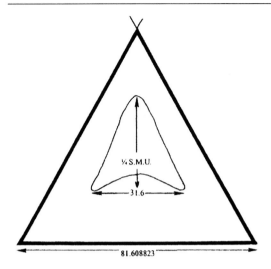

Figure 66. The Serpent Mound Unit and 666

Romain's one-quarter Serpent Mound Unit, interpreted as the square root of 1000 (31.622776), multiplied by the side of any triangle in the solar hexagon (81.6), the product then squared yields 666.

---

longs: the quarter mile. Such bilateral symmetry in arithmetic could have been one approach in the effort to enlarge on something without adding anything foreign, thereby preserving its inherent virtue. The use of the golden mean should never be underestimated, for it is a universal in geometry in spite of its fractional status in numerical expression.

Further, the 1/4 Serpent Mound Unit (see "The Measure of the Stars" next), the precise measure for the triangular mound, when multiplied by 81.61 is, when squared, pleasantly close to 6,660,000. Add slightly to 31.6 so that it becomes more accurately the square root of 1000 (31.62), multiply it by 81.61, and the 666 is, by squaring, produced. More simply expressed, it is:

$$(3.162 \times 8.161)^2 = 666 \text{ (approximately)}$$

The square root of ten will later be linked to the symbol *lambda*, the shape of which is apparently patterned after this feature of the earthwork. As a basic unit of measure for the mound structure as it appears today, it is not unreasonable to suggest that the architect considered ten an all-purpose figure, conceivably understanding an approximation of its square root as well.

The Measure of the Stars

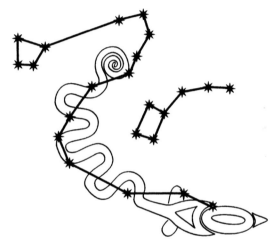

Figure 67. Starry Dragon

In the Italian it is *Dragone, Drache* in the German, and in the French, *Dragon.* The Greeks called it *Drakon* or *Ophis,* the latter term being valued at 780 or 582. The Delphi Circle, shown later, has a diameter of 582 feet, resulting from the multiplication of the golden mean (1.618) by 360. The universal fame of Draco is closely related to its domination of the heavens thousands of years ago, and has, as such, influenced scripture and philosophy more than is generally understood. The very term "philosophy" carries at its heart the roots "ophi" and "soph" related to serpent and wisdom respectively. The Serpent Mound was apparently constructed on the basis of this constellation, albeit with careful thought, enabling the design to take into its folds many other aspects of the arts and sciences.

As this odyssey continued, it became apparent that the "beast" was beginning to rear its serpentine head not only in astronomy and classical geometry, but also in auspiciously conceived measure derived from specific numerology. The number 666 was by any evidence put to use by the earlier Mound Builders long before the New Testament had been written—for the placement of the stars and the depth of topsoil would dictate it. But is what the Serpent *seems* to be saying actually what it *is* saying? If it is the earliest source for a comprehensive understanding of astronomy and geometry, is it also *the* source for an ancient unit of measure?

The answer to this question is yes, and what's more, this mystery unit of measure seems to be relegated to the length (not the standard) of the foot. "Not the standard" means that this unit of the decimalized foot (i.e., a foot of ten parts) is used not in terms of *itself*, but rather in terms of units of measure born out of ratios and, as we shall see, in the distances between the stars themselves as they are expressed on the Earth's surface. At least one of these units is also found in ancient Britain's megalithic sites.

Over the Ocean and Back

The mid-twentieth century saw a retired Scot named Alexander Thom publish a very thorough study on hundreds of stoneworks throughout Britain and Brittany in an earnest effort to uncover the realities underlying Britain's archaeological legacy. Just as Frederick Putnam was a professor at Harvard, later receiving the title "Father of American Archaeology," Thom was a professor at Oxford, later receiving the title "Father of Archaeoastronomy." Like Putnam, Thom was meticulous in his work ethic, his professorship being in engineering. In his surveys of ancient sites, recorded in *Megalithic Sites in Britain* and *Megalithic Lunar Observatories,* Thom made the educated claim of a specific unit of measure, the "Megalithic Yard" (MY), running throughout his surveys as a constant. His statistical analysis showed that this unit in multiples and sub-multiples dominated ancient works in Brittany, Wales, Scotland, and England. Subsequent to Thom's discovery, enthusiastic metrologists suggested that the English foot was allied with Thom's MY as the ratio of the golden mean to the base of the natural logarithm 2.[63]

Oftentimes, the MY was found carried upon Pythagorean-like right triangles that formed the unseen basis for specialized, elliptic-like stone rings.[64] Like the Serpent Mound's astral design fitting flawlessly within the Pythagorean Theorem, these triangles would have preceded the time of Pythagoras by centuries. In addition, like the straight lines discovered in the nineteenth century between sites miles apart in the Ohio Valley, Professor Thom similarly made a discovery of prehistoric sites separated by distance, yet were nearly perfectly aligned. These distances, while requiring some well-thought-out method of arrow-straight surveying, were not, however, related to multiples of his unit.

Although questionable to some, an interesting theory put forth by Thom was his belief that the forgotten engineers of Britain may have created many of their distorted circles in terms of *pi* represented as 3 (instead of 3.14). In this way, the perimeter measures of their oddly construed, circular designs could be pronounced in whole units of their MY and still be based upon the *concept* of the ratio of diameter to circumference. In this theory, the length of 2.5 MY (6.8 feet) was found commonly and was termed, aptly enough, the "Megalithic Rod" (MR). Thom assumed these builders wished to express their geometry in whole numbers while still honoring the secret ratio, and his controversial theory remains widely held as tenable, given the wisdom inherent in the knowledge of how a circle is created.

With Thom's theory as it stands, there is now rather curious evidence that our own Serpent Mound may have been the original source for ancient Britain's solemn devotion to their MY. This theory realizes certain missing aspects for the explanation of the length of the MY, as well as the birth of the decimal foot setting the MY into expression. Whether or not logarithms are taken into account, the Serpent Mound should be looked to by both Thom's advocates and critics. But first, did the designer of our Serpent also have a penchant for pi? Did pi figure into some sacred reasoning underscoring the geometry hosting the serpentine body? If so, was it also a modified form of the irrational figure most familiar as 3.14?

Searching for a Piece of π

As previously noted at the end of the section describing the hexagon, it didn't take long for me to find a place to start. Interestingly enough, any of the seven circles that would have been used to create the 720-MY perimeter hexagon (see Figure 68) would have to be very close to 188.46 feet in diameter. Approaching the problem in support of the ancient stone workers in Thom's theory, the Serpent's builder would have first constructed the mound, secondly created the hexagon on a separate sand table or some similar method of illustration, and *then* created the seven circles. By extrapolating these circles, a unit of measure based upon the ratio of π, could have been isolated.

Just the same, another figure would have to be multiplied by π to attain the required size. The best candidate, logically speaking, would be either 6 or 7, sacred to the circle. But since 7 could be considered the central core of the

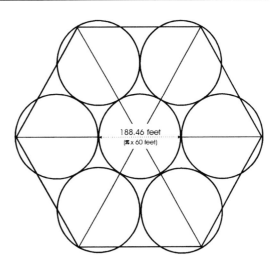

188.46 feet
(π x 60 feet)

flower from which the 6 circles grew petal-like, 6 would be the logical multiple of their pi. Almost unbelievably, the diameter 188.46 feet is π x 60 feet—taking π as an incredibly accurate 3.141, i.e., true pi.

As discussed below in "Divination by Means of Light," after the solar and lunar sightings gave the Serpent its size, the geometry and measure could have been back-figured. Using this method, it was discovered that the unit of the foot could have been found to best embody the ratio of 3.141.

Putting the Foot to the Megalithic Yard— In America

Looking to the Serpent in the hexagon and the Serpent in the 6–8–10 theorem, it was apparent that the size of these geometries was patterned after the size of the Great Serpent—which was perforce patterned after astronomical considerations. The perfect fit of the Serpent Mound survey into these two geometric forms would therefore indicate that the astronomy came first.

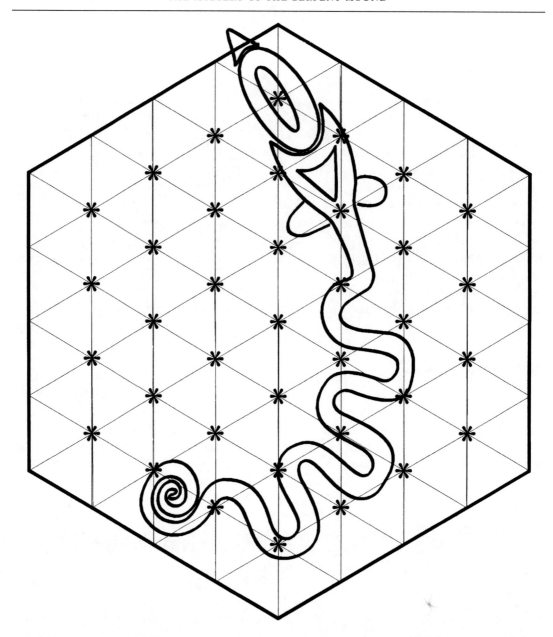

Figure 68. The Primary Hexagon

Primary hexagon with sides of 326.4 feet and a perimeter of 1,958.4 feet: 720 MY.

It would be misleading to suggest that, lacking modern instrumentation, a unit of measure could have been sighted directly from the horizon or the sky. A solid landmark negotiated by the astronomical alignments would have to be in existence first. This would be our Serpent.

There are two forms of the hexagon, each with different perimeter lengths. The first, which dramatically displays the coils uniformly contained, owns sides of 340 feet and a perimeter thereby of 2040 feet. The second, which seems a more creative looping of the coils through the conjunctions of the interior lines, has sides of 326.4 feet and a perimeter of 1958.4 feet. Applying the Megalithic Yard to the first hexagon, each side is precisely 125 MY (50 MR), the perimeter therefore 6 times that or 750 MY (300 MR). The second hexagon, already cited earlier in this section for its triangular parcels having a square-foot measure of 666 units of 5, has sides of 120 MY (48 MR) and perimeter of 720 MY.[65]

The Serpent in the 6–8–10 theorem dictates that the size of the triangle hosting the three squares will have a perimeter of 816 feet, 10 times the length of any triangle side in the second hexagon.[66] The geometrical alignments going into the placement of the 6–8–10 right triangle leave little room for more striking or convincing alternatives,[67] tempting one to draw an important conclusion, for these offer "proofs" of the Serpent-theorem association. This conclusion is simply that the Serpent Mound is either responsible for mediating *a mercurial form of the foot* (see "A Perspective on Miscellaneous Measure" below) or it heralds an uncanny coincidence to something else as yet unknown. Strangely, the Megalithic Yard, so well understood now in Britain, is a stitch in the fabric of the Great Serpent's unseen geometric connections—connections possibly dating from before 2750 B.C.E., the time of the North Star Thuban. The theorem's eight square side measures 272 feet, exactly ten times the Megalithic Yard.

The stars surrounding Thuban (Draconis-α) were so much in prominence then and so clearly recognizable that much attention surely was paid

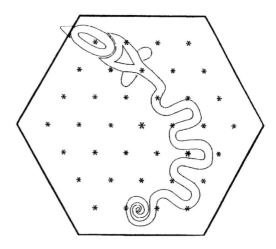

Figure 69. An Alternate Version of the Hexagon

This is an alternate hexagon with sides of 340 feet and a perimeter of 2,040 feet. Note the way the coils fit into the field of asterisks. The distance from one asterisk to another is approximately 85 feet. (Hamilton 1993, after Romain)

to them. As mentioned, the ancients considered the stars to be signatures or houses of the celestial deities. Therefore, it would seem logical to reproduce them on the Earth, for this way one would have sympathy with the heavens.

Who can say how the designer of the heavenly Serpent was able to transfer the positions of the stars with such uncanny accuracy to the Earth? One possible method would have been to carefully create a piece of very thin vellum, or a sheet of some vegetable paper. Then having successfully made it as near to transparent as possible, one could stretch it out between suitable posts, parallel to the desired portion of the night sky. Having accomplished this admittedly rather difficult task, the stars of Draconis could then be sighted and marked with pinpoint accuracy.

A second possible method would be to create a wet glaze of some sort from a vegetable or mineral source. This glaze would be reflective, and the stars could be seen in it as though seen on still water. The key stars could be marked and then the flat mass could be dried, holding the accurate star positions intact, taking into account the reversal of the mirror reflection.

A third method for explaining the accuracy of the Draconis system underscoring the survey map is very simply that a skilled or gifted artist with a very good eye could have transposed the star sequence into any medium desired. Such a skill is a known trait among great artists, and this would place the design of the Great Serpent into the realm of high art.

In any case, the stars seem a worthy place to look for other units of measure, for in putting oneself into the mind of the designer, the following thoughts may occur. First, by accurately representing the desired star grouping on Earth, a sort of *sympathetic resonance* would be acquired. Second, embodying an animal shape over the grouping of stars would not only consolidate them, but would cause their sympathetic energy to be "caught and held" unified in the earthen form. Third, having caught the entities of the star grouping, a detailed analysis of the distance separating them could be made. It should always be kept in mind that these stars were probably held up as heavenly abodes or even living spirits, and thus the distances between them may have had a very special significance. But then this question would have been raised: "What size should the shape be made?" What, if anything, would determine the size of the effigy, and therefore the measurements between the stars underscoring it? Who would have arbitrated and determined such a potentially crucial piece of knowledge?

Divination by Means of Light

If an arrow shot by the strongest man could not reach the stars, then how were the ancient people to tell how far away the lights were, and how far apart from each other? Who would have offered a shaman or priest-scientist help in this regard? Ultimately, there could be but one answer: the sun and moon. For if the Great Serpent's coils, based as they are on the linear pattern of the stars, were any larger, the various horizon events already described might be lost within their folds. Similarly, if the coils were any smaller in width, they would be far less ample to properly contain both solar and lunar sightings while enabling a formidably large effigy. The arbiters would have been no human agency, although only a human agency could set up the arbitration. Someone probably realized that there was a need to apply a very thorough rationale, for a unit of measure worthy of being applied by *men* might be at stake.

Once the geo-astronomy was completed, then the size of the Great Serpent could be determined, conceding that the astronomy may have logically been undertaken at the proposed site for accuracy.[68] Thus, the situation of the Serpent Mound may have been determined even before its size. Then at last a system of *most sacred measure,* conceived through observation and devotion to natural principles, could be born.

Ohio Valley Metrology and the Serpent Mound

Whether or not it is possible to measure with any accuracy the earthworks of the Ohio Valley is fraught with disagreement and confusion. The terribly degraded condition of most of the geometric earth renderings has made their mea-

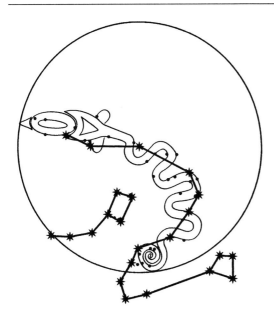

Figure 70. The Circle of Thuban

The Circle of Thuban has a diameter of approximately 680 feet or 100 Megalithic Rods. Could this have been an ancient standard or source of measure?

surement subject to interpretation. Most of this present work is defined by measure characterizing geometric forms projected over the Serpent Mound's image. Thus it is a different approach than that taken by many others who have gone directly to the earthworks in the attempt to decipher a logical and possibly broadly based unit. It is the opinion of this investigator that the use of superimposed geometric form is ideal is the case of decoding the intent of the Great Serpent. Conversely, measure directly applied in the field may be the best method for finding related units among the earthworks surrounding our centrally located subject.

Looking to the Great Serpent's Circle of Thuban, it should be noted that the diameter is very close to 680 feet, if not conceived to be exactly that. The possible difference is just the

same as the difference between the circle of the serpentine vesica piscis and the side of the base of the Great Pyramid: 1.8 feet.[69] In the case of the vesica, it is less 1.8 feet, and in the case of the Circle of Thuban, it is greater by 1.8 feet. If there is a connection—whether mystical or not—would be lovely to see proven.

The figure of 680 was apparently conceived through the contrived addition of the small triangular mound to the front end of the earthwork, completing the full balance of the circle. Whether it was intended to be *precisely* 680 may ultimately be a point of philosophy. Nevertheless, 680 feet divided by the Megalithic Yard is exactly 100 Megalithic Rods. I have serious doubts that this is a mere coincidence.

Now if the Great Serpent's size and locale were determined to some extent through the circumstance of natural astronomy, wouldn't this circle, owning a radius of 340 feet,[70] have been a tempting source to commence with some authoritative standard of measure? After all, it contains the whole body of the Serpent while at once clearly pointing out the central position of the once-celebrated North Star, Draconis-alpha. There is no adulterating circumstance here, for it is a universally acceptable, simple circle. It is a stark and plain representation of the facts. Admittedly, this picture could have been made before the Great Serpent was created as an earth sculpture, but afterwards specific measure could be taken and a standard definitively arrived at.

But does the Serpent Mound *itself,* disposed of any geometrical complements, display important measurement? For the answer to this question, we again look to the analysis of William F. Romain's work on Serpent Mound.[71]

Romain discovered two key units of measure. The first he named the *Serpent Mound Unit* (SMU), 126.4 feet, by which he precisely demonstrates his theory of how the effigy was constructed. The second he named the *Secondary Serpent Unit* (SSU), 149.5 feet, which strength- ens his theories of proportion, especially in the coils.[72]

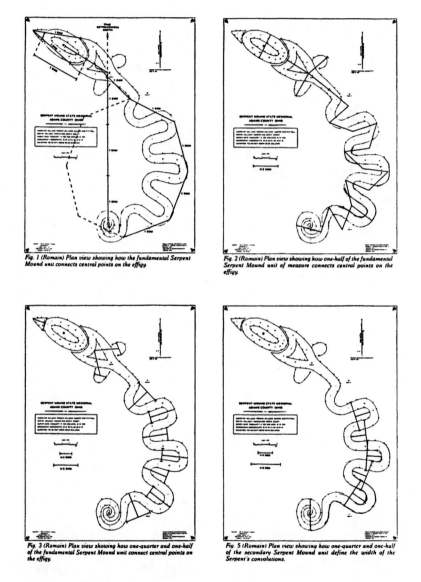

Fig. 1 (Romain) Plan view showing how the fundamental Serpent Mound unit connects central points on the effigy.

Fig. 2 (Romain) Plan view showing how one-half of the fundamental Serpent Mound unit of measure connects central points on the effigy.

Fig. 3 (Romain) Plan view showing how one-quarter and one-half of the fundamental Serpent Mound unit connect central points on the effigy.

Fig. 5 (Romain) Plan view showing how one-quarter and one-half of the secondary Serpent Mound unit define the width of the Serpent's convolutions.

Figure 71. Romain's Serpent Mound Units

Romain's units include upper left: The fundamental Serpent Mound Unit; upper right: half the fundamental unit; lower left: one-quarter and one-half the fundamental unit; and lower right: the one-quarter and one-half Secondary Serpent Mound Unit.

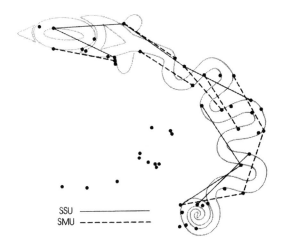

SSU ——————
SMU ---------

Figure 72. Romain's Units in the Star Pattern of Serpent Mound

(Hamilton 1998, after Romain 1988; graphic by Mason 1999)

On a hunch, I took the Serpent Mound Map and carefully plotted the stars of the Draconis asterism in an overlay. I then made two templates, one for the SMU and one for the SSU, as illustrated.

Marshall's Rule

James A. Marshall is known as a surveyor of Native American prehistoric sites. Mr. Marshall is a civil engineer, and not unlike Professor Thom before him, he early on displayed a passion to unlock the secrets of the ancient engineers. He has, by his own admission, spent much of his adult life carefully researching, surveying, and mapping hundreds of antique sites in the U.S. Yet he does not consider his work finished.

Marshall has intimated that the Hopewell geometric earthworks (which have their richest concentration in Ross County, Ohio) differ from the Pythagorean ideal *only by degree*. Like Thom, Marshall claims to have discovered a number of

rare and interesting right triangles, on an extensive scale, throughout the Hopewell earthworks.[73] Although he personally found no evidence for the obvious figure of the Pythagorean Theorem, a number of his proposed Hopewell 90° triangles carry whole numbers on at least two of their sides. In an effort to keep his work free of personal bias, Marshall is plain in his language, keeping his illustrations simple and to the point.

Archaeoastronomers who claim to have discovered a prehistoric unit of measure have to demonstrate that their unit was utilized in the steps of the design and layout process.

Marshall has criticized the number and variety of measurements discovered by the archaeoastronomers, including both the Hardmans and Romain at the Serpent Mound. However, the Great Serpent is so exquisitely crafted and laid out that it would be a disservice to dismiss any unit as irrelevant to the designer's intent without a complete investigation. Marshall places emphasis on the fact that neither the Hardmans nor Romain utilized a central point from which might be extrapolated a logical unit. However, the Great Serpent is an animal-like effigy, and the rule of decipherment would logically be different from that of the more geometric earthworks, with which Marshall is more familiar. This is especially true in light of the fact that the Great Serpent is based upon an extensive star pattern—unlike the Hopewell earthworks as analyzed by Marshall and others.[74] Thus if a central point is required, we may look to the star Thuban beneath the first coil from the head, for it is central to either extreme of the giant's length.

Marshall's Hopewell work began in the 1960s. It was inspired at the outset by the work of René Millon among the prehistoric Mexican temples

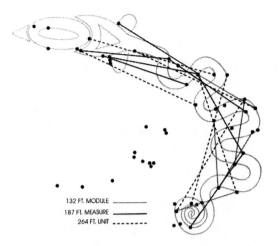

Figure 73. Marshall's Units in the Star Pattern of the Serpent Mound

(Hamilton 1998, after Romain; graphic by Pat Mason, 1999)

at Teotihuacan. Marshall has demonstrated the discovery of the 187-foot, the 264-foot,[75] and related foot measures among the eastern North American earthworks in several publications. In addition, he has shown a possible Native American facility with Pythagorean-like mathematics, an attempt to both enlighten and reform a long-established school of thought regarding these ancient people.

Both Romain and Marshall's units have a strong common denominator, in spite of the fact that they were discovered through different methodologies stemming possibly from separate philosophies. By the observations following, these men have mutually strengthened each other's theories and broadened the work commenced in 1934 by Alexander Thom.

A Perspective on Miscellaneous Measure

The science of *archaeometrology* has long entertained the whimsical thought of there having been a classic unit of measure created by some forgotten bureau of weights and measures in the distant past. Should this unit be rediscovered, then a great light might be shed upon the creative engineering of the past. It is now feasible that the discovery of the Megalithic Yard is an important cornerstone in the unfolding of the rediscovery of this phantom unit should it really exist.

The figure of the Megalithic Yard modified to half reflects the sum of the square of 4, the numbers 1 through 16 added together, 136. Because the figure of 1.36 feet works over and over with the geometric forms intimate to the Great Serpent, it would seem reasonable to assume that on this side of the Atlantic, the 1.36-foot measure was also popular. This figure of 1.36 feet, when it is itself divided in half, comes to .68 feet—approximately 1/1000 of the diameter of the Circle of Thuban.

The figure of 187 feet, possibly discovered by Marshall in North America and also by René Millon amidst the Mexican stoneworks, when quadrupled and divided by this 1/2 MY is exactly 550.[76] Similarly, Romain's Secondary Serpent Unit (149.5 feet), divided by the cardinal 55 (1 through 10 added), lends a figure a mere 2/1000 foot off the MY. As can be seen by the accompanying star maps with lines connecting the Draconis members (Figures 72 and 73), both these figures may have been divined strictly from celestial resources and reasoning, casting new light on the theoretical conception of the MY.

To make the theory a little more interesting, two other published investigators of Ohio Valley sacred sites, Ray Hively and Robert Horn, proposed yet another well-researched unit, 321.3 meters—a meter being 3.2808 feet. Translating this, their unit comes to precisely 1054.121 feet. Divided by Thom's Megalithic Rod (6.8 feet) this is 155.0, and by the 1/2 MY, 175.0.

Marshall, in *Ohio Archaeologist* (Spring 1995), revealed yet another example, in feet, that could be construed as a possible use of the Megalithic Yard in North America. The precise length of the circle-octagon work found at High Bank, including the short connector between the two main geometries, is 2,149.1 feet. Divided by the interesting figure 790, the Megalithic Yard is revealed.[77]

It should be noted that these examples are not conclusive and do not offer indisputable proof of the use of Thom's findings here in America. On the contrary, it would seem more likely that our universally applicable Serpent, as a template, possibly served as the inspiration for a world-inclusive system of measure, owning a number of relative units. **This system may only have claimed** *the length of the foot* **as its most important measure, and the other units cited here were merely expressions or "spin-offs" of this mercurial unit.** Originally, the foot may have been decimalized, although it is more familiar to the modern world divided into 12 parts. The foot is rarely, if ever, used alone judging from the ancient examples, but rather was the standard or underlying unit from which many other expressions came. They arrived from ratios, magic squares, and multiples of units all based upon this secret length. In some instances, seemingly unrelated units appear based upon units originating from the foot unit length.

Further, and by way of astronomy and geometry surrounding the Great Serpent, an apparent mastery of an advanced flowering of a system we relate to as Pythagorean, using this unit of the 10-

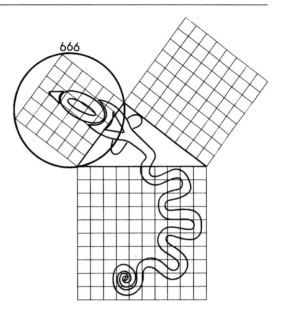

Figure 74. How the Foot Relates to the Megalithic Yard

The Pythagorean Theorem demonstrates how the foot circumference of the circle around the six square in the upper left of the equation is 666 units of 1.36 feet, half the Megalithic Yard.

part foot, displays itself. It reveals a system of number and geometry that not only predates Pythagoras, but also has either dictated or strongly influenced prehistoric megalithic measure as well. Pythagoras himself was a mid-first ante-millennium traveler, collector, and philosopher. It now is becoming more apparent that this man successfully consolidated or divined a tremendous parcel of the ancient wisdom, an effort worthy of a great scholar and teacher. A likeness of our Great Serpent, whether taken from an example nearer his home or intuited by him from the resources of his genius, may well have been possessed by him, even as a "teaching tool." Herein is a great part of the intrinsic mystery of the Serpent Mound, for its design is approximately 2,000 years older than the Greek sage.

The Mystery of Measure

The importance of measure is no better empha-sized than in the records of the Bible, which holds numbers, geometry, and measure as vital to the enriched and comprehensive interpreta-tion of scripture. The beginning of Revelation 11 states:

> *Then I was given a long cane like a mea-suring rod, and I was told, 'Get up and mea-sure God's sanctuary ...'*

There are two *witnesses* sent to prophesy in this chapter, analogous to number and geome-try. Their commonality, prophesying, is therefore no more than measure. To the College of the Mysteries, measure determined the science of celestial harmonics in architecture, and this was conceived through number and geometric pro-portion. The powers of these witnesses are in this greater than any human agency, and yet these two people are described as simple—wear-ing only sackcloth (burlap). Then in 11:7 we read:

> *When they have completed their witness-ing, the beast that comes out of the Abyss is going to make war on them and overcome them and kill them.*

The phenomenal doing-away with the two witnesses by the beast only points out that once number and geometry have done their work, the result can overshadow its origins. It is to say that the initiate should not lose sight of the impor-tance of number and geometry going into the creation of such a great symbol as the Serpent, for in forgetting the source of such an awesome architecture, it might easily overwhelm the imag-ination.

The Sages guarded the sacred science of num-ber and geometry, for properly comprehended it could be a positive aid in understanding the nature of the Divine. This is evident in the last portion of chapter 11 beginning at verse 11 wherein God reanimates the two witnesses after their death in front of the worldly people, the uninitiated. The two are subsequently taken back up to heaven in a cloud, i.e., forever beyond apprehension of the worldly view. Thus lacking the knowledge of how to use number and geom-etry correctly, the people experience the loss of a considerable amount of their architecture (one-tenth of the city) when it is summarily destroyed by earthquake, along with a symbolic number of people. The rest of the people are filled with fear, and this is the result of the loss of knowl-edge illuminating the mind (and thereby free-ing it from unknown or imagined dangers).

A very thorough knowledge of number, geometry, and measure apparently was the essence of the outer portion of the Mysteries. Similarly, knowledge of the human form was regarded as the essence of architecture. Some scholars, understanding the Greek influence on the New Testament, have considered that the scripture may have originally been intended for study by those accepted to the Mystery College of the era. The Greeks were known for their pop-ular mystery societies. Perhaps a modern mea-sure of receptivity to the apocalyptic writing is lost due to an almost complete lack of traditional astronomical, numerical, and geometric knowl-edge possessed by the average lay person.

It bears repeating that a visitor to the Serpent Mound will quickly notice that it was not con-structed on a flat plain, but rolls on a promon-tory similar to a peninsula which itself appears to have been custom-made for the earthwork. Following the adept use of number and measure to fashion the various geometries as cited under-scoring the serpent form, it would seem as though the Serpent was deliberately isolated in some remote place inhospitable for discerning its geometric matrices. This in effect draws the attention to Revelation 12:9:

The great dragon, the primeval serpent, known as the devil or Satan, who had led all the world astray, was hurled down to the earth and his angels were hurled down with him.

The *angels* (Greek: "messengers") could be construed as the stars, the lunar and solar alignments, as well as the geometries giving meaning to the serpent form (and vice-versa). It was partly in this way that the Old World serpent became Satan to the common understanding, i.e., through a loss of knowledge concerning its creation and its affiliations.[78] Chief among its true meanings was, of course, the *Logos* itself, the Word. The student of the Mysteries had no misconceptions here and likely was forbidden to isolate the image of the beast, as it would eventually be misunderstood by itself. This of course draws atten-

tion to the famous lines from Revelation 13:14 which say:

... it was able to lead astray the people of the world and persuade them to put up a statue in honour of the beast ...

Again, "people of the world" is a reference to the uninitiated, they who are of the world (i.e., of the outer senses). It is conceivable that in the very early pre-Christian era, some of the knowledge of the Mystery College was intentionally or unintentionally disseminated among those unworthy of the trust. The image of the serpent may have been isolated like the *crux gammata* later appropriated by the Nazis as the swastika, or the *crux ansata* (the ank) used by occultists for reasons other than its original intent. The once-numerous serpent effigies throughout the world have been nearly obliterated from the face of the planet. That the Great Serpent has survived seems a miracle.

The Serpent and the Mysteries

I VIVIDLY RECALL FROM CHILDHOOD A FOSSIL-hunting field trip with my aunt, whose hobby was geology. We were looking for trilobites, an extinct sea creature that lived before the age of dinosaurs. While my cousins and myself were wandering up and down the streambed, turning over rocks and making much noise, my aunt calmly cordoned off a small patch of stones with her eyes. It didn't take her long to come up with a good specimen.

It is similarly through a calm and deliberate study of the enigmatic Serpent of Adams County—a dinosaur of sorts—that the arcane code is penetrated, and the Serpent again speaks the secrets of Mother Earth. Serpent Mound is only now being liberated from the shadows of preconceived notions and theories linked strictly to gross physical evidence.

The Great Serpent, a crown jewel among the world's prehistoric architectures, may easily be construed as philosophic *rebus,* giving birth to an icon of the *Word* or Logos. Designed to embody the concept of such a metaphysical singularity, the simple construction of the earthwork belies its sophistication among the more highly touted architectures of ancient stoneworks. It cannot be emphasized enough that this is a work in earth *fortified* by stone. Moreover, it has proven to stand the test of time, remaining well preserved even as its peers around the world have fallen victim to weather and vandalism.

Assuming the fact of this longevity, the stage

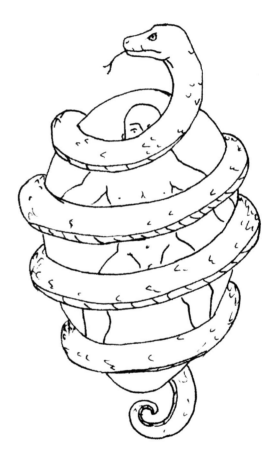

Figure 75. Man in his Embryonic Stage Awaits Maturation within the Great Egg

The Serpent represents the Mysteries of the Logos or Word, the evolutionary power holding and controlling all things in the Universe.

is set for intuiting a higher purpose for the structure, the artistic mandate of achieving celestial harmony fulfilled, before tackling the more esoteric aspects of what is termed in philosophy "the great work." Some of these aspects have been discussed in previous sections, but the question remains: what is it that prompted these people so long ago to create such an intellectually and spiritually encompassing sculpture? Moreover, what is the mystery of the Great Serpent itself, and why are we only now seeking to understand it with greater enthusiasm and clarity?

To this day, archaeoastronomy has not been able to figure out how the ancient architects of Stonehenge discovered its amazing locus whereupon an incredible number of heavenly paths apparently converge in a certain way. The Serpent Mound also may keep among its secrets a specific placement on the ancient landscape, though not necessarily for astronomical considerations. When all is told, the astronomy lending character to this venerated site may merely serve as an aesthetically pleasing dust ruffle over an extensive and well-conceived bed of knowledge. In theory, it will show the little giant as the focal point of a subterranean scheme grown out of the labors of a remotely ancient race having the responsibility to catalog and preserve the technological and religious wealth of a once glorious surface civilization.[79]

Apollo and the Python

When the young god Apollo took on the primeval serpent Python, it is said that a number of arrows of light were pumped into the beast from different directions. The creature was the only survivor of a distant age now forgotten, and all others who knew of this age were long gone. Similarly, the Serpent Mound may be the sole surviving entity of a period so remote it is shrouded in mystery. Yet by illuminating the earthwork with the straight attentions of a surveyor's transit, and rediscovering the light shafts of its astronomically pregnant form, our Serpent may reveal the same remarkable oracle of Gaia long ago "slain" by Apollo.

Indeed, it may be best to establish the importance of the serpent image as an indicator of ancient wisdom. For this we may look to Greek mythology. By definition, the term *mythos* means "word" as contained in a story. It is believed that the fact of the classical myths surviving intact as long as they have in Western culture is due, not in part, to their historical value marking the age of poets, playwrights, and mythographers. To philosophers, the myths represent sources of hidden truth and are to be treasured as such. An excellent example of this is the story of Apollo and the Python. It is one of the great classics in mythology, although its true content has not been known for quite some time.

In accordance with one of the oldest recorded Pythias[80] of the Delphinian Oracle, the first to have benign prophetic power was Gaia herself. She in turn gave the appointment of her oracular duties to an Oread (Mountain Nymph) named Daphnis. Later, Themis, a water divinity of the highest rank, took over the properties of the Oracle's locale, subsequently passing them on to the Titaness Phoebe. Phoebe ("Enlightened") in turn awarded the Oracle to her grandson Apollo for his birthday, for the place was very much to his liking, save for one obstacle.

Apollo had gotten it into his mind at a very young age to create an oracle. He had been searching for a place with moving water for some time. It is said that finally he petitioned his grandmother, Phoebe, to acquire a certain place having a waterfall, necessary for his work. A formidable dragon dominated the area—a serpent named Python. So before the area could be cleared for the young Lord's project, the guardian Serpent had to be sized up, figured out, and ultimately vanquished to a non-injurious status. For this it had to be "slain."

It was believed that the Great Serpent had always lived in the "womb" of Gaia and was in fact the mother goddess' original mouthpiece before any formal oracle had been considered. The Python had survived the great flood or cataclysm from the previous age and was thus the sole transmitter of knowledge to the kings of the world. Python, however, was not accommodating to the majority of visitors seeking advice and wisdom. It has been said that only a man may teach another man, and thus possibly Apollo considered that the responsibility of oracular response should take a form other than the monster. The Oracles of Gaia, Daphnis, Themis, and Phoebe were short-lived, perhaps due to their other responsibilities. But in truth, the aboriginal oracle was still the primeval Python, and no woman—even a divine one—had successfully supplanted it. However, the Oracle was rightfully destined to be under the auspicious pronouncements of the feminine voice, and Apollo must have had this communicated to him by his grandmother, even as a condition on her gift. Apollo's work then was to preserve and transfer the Python's Power while removing its problematic presence.

Apollo was not a god or divinity invented to portray the sun as it burns in the sky, for Helios more aptly represents that. Apollo represented the *Solar Mysteries*, the mysteries associating the soul and its relationship with the Creator. Gaia represented the spiritual entity (the shape of the Atom) as the mother-soul. The Python was the latent *Principle of Sound* hidden deep in the folds of her being.[81] Hence the Python as *Word-giver* of Gaia.

In accord with the traditional myth, after the

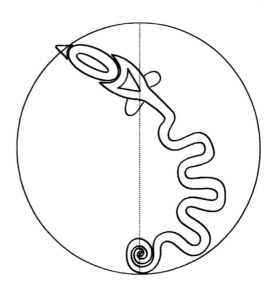

Figure 76. The Delphi Circle

The Delphi Circle has a diameter of approximately 582.5 feet, being the result of multiplying 1.618 (phi) by 360. Of old, the serpent was called Οφις *(Ophis)* by Eratosthenes (276–195 B.C.E.) and Hipparchos (190–125 B.C.E.), both considered to be initiate astronomers. Ophis by Pythagorean numerical reduction is 582, being the result of adding 70 + 500 + 10 + 2. The name of Pythagoras is similarly reduced, when the final sigma (as a word ending) is valued at 2 rather than the usual 200. The circle is used to form the basis for certain symbols by way of the phi ratio in the Arbelos. The circle is also called the Lasso of Apollo, with which the young god successfully corralled and subjugated the Python.

death of the beast, Apollo let the body rot in the sunlight for a while. He then removed the skin, and carefully slicing the body into a *number of parts*, threw it down the abyss from whence the serpent came. Over this entry to the underworld he erected his famous golden tripod,[82] covering it with the skin of the creature like a drum. Within the tripod, he placed the sacred bones of the Python.[83]

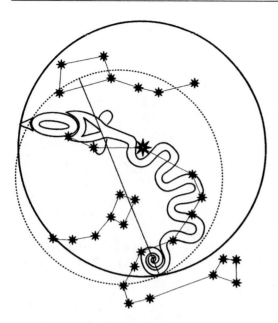

Figure 77. The Circle of Thuban and the Delphi Circle

The Delphi Circle (diameter 582 feet) in comparison with the Thuban Circle (diameter 680 feet).

This serpent, if anything on the order of the serpent featured in the Orphic system, was a grand and universal diviner, a fact underscored in the aspect of Serpent Mound's collaborative effort in the sciences and arts. Its body, comprised of light, lent it the authority of the Logos, the tongue of Truth. As stated, after the great flood Python dominated and was the sole oracle available to men. As the Earth repopulated, it came to be the work of Apollo to transfer this power from its elitist aspect to a worldly oriented service. The rotting of the flesh symbolizes the transfer of this rather esoteric expression to a more humanity-focused one.

The subsequent stretching of the skin over the tripod symbolized the universally binding *Sound Principle,* and the bones within lent real weight and substance to the seat, making it able to take on the demands of the world. The bones were the *parts* the skin held together as a single entity. These metaphorical parts, as illustrated in the last section of this work, represent the basis for the symbols of a complete word-structuring collection, an alphabet.

Once this Great Serpent (the Universal Word) was slain and sliced, it fell literally into many distinct "vowels" and "consonants." Through the interment of the bones beneath the Oracular Seat, the Pythia was able to utter the prophetic truths once reserved only for those bold enough to petition the living Python itself. The slowly decaying flesh of the Great Serpent was said to have put off a sweet and spirited smoke from deep in the abyss beneath the tripod. This in turn inspired and exhilarated the lady to correctly translate the divine Word into intelligible sentences. Thus began the age of prophetic truths spoken by the Delphinian Oracle, offering a valuable insight to the probability of a Sound Current-based system of divination dating from prehistory. The creation of the Oracle of Delphi is, according to one way of considering it, the greatest of myths, for it truly embodies the meaning of the term *mythos.*

As the leading character in this story, the man we call Apollo organized the founding of an institution here purported to be older than its accepted historical reference. This "god" may have been an actual person, an enlightened initiate of a former Golden Age, who, with the help of friends and family, was empowered to start a Mystery College. From this school, the principles of sound philosophy through language would be passed on to those who were considered worthy of it. Later exponents of this college would include Pythagoras of Crotona and Apollonius of Tyana, both revered sages of their respective eras and, by any evidence, both wordsmiths of the highest order. Both are believed by initiate philosophers to have directly carried on the intent of Apollo, and both, predictably, had their achievements downplayed, and their characters maligned, especially by the early Church.

The Oracular Voice dominated civilized culture for centuries. All throughout the ancient world, the Delphinian Temple was the final word of advice for many. From that seat, that tripod, flowed the linking wisdom conceived to aid in the intentional uniting of humankind with its own divine nature through a simple service performed, the service of the spoken word. The Pythagorean commission surely was in part executed to regain to some degree the original intent of Apollo. This was to reveal, through astronomy, geometry, and arithmetic, the origins of the written and spoken word. By this plan, and in developing a few excellent students and disciples, the Master might see clear to reveal to them the true Word—the internally comprehended Sound Principle and Music of the Spheres.

The Python of Pythagoras

Few people know that the proto-philosopher, Pythagoras, is believed so named for the reason that his parents, Mnesarchus and Parthenis (later Pythasis) were deeply impressed by the words of the Delphinian Oracle. It was prophesied to them that they would have a son who would surpass all other men in beauty and wisdom. He would be a great benefactor of the human race, and his service would be recognized for generations and generations.

The story of the virgin birth (Parthenis is an epithet of Athena, after whom the Parthenon received its name, meaning "virgin") was a part of Pythagoras' legend. As in the story of Jesus, Pythagoras was held to be a messianic incarnation, a teacher of the esoteric *word* and things

related in number and form. There are similarities in the two men's lives. They were born in the same area of ancient Syria. In both cases the parents were informed by means of prophecy of the birth. The mother of both had a visionary experience preceding the birth of the child. Both children were brought into the world when their parents were away from home, Mnesarchus on business and Joseph for census.

In the Pythagorean Theorem section, the question of the source of Pythagoras' information was raised, and the answer is simply that it was *eclectic*. No matter what a man's background in former lives, he must perforce take a "refresher course," even in subjects of previous mastery. The coming of the Messiah always signals change in some form to the populace, but it is rarely predictable what form the change will take. The messianic charge takes on different responsibilities in accord with the needs of civilization, and while he may be a religious reformer in one case, he may be a philosopher in another.

It is recorded that during his travels, Pythagoras assimilated the teachings of the Jewish Rabbis concerning the mystical doctrine of Israel. It is well known among initiate scholarship that hundreds of years later the Essenes were organized to gather and study the works of Pythagoras. So it stands to reason that the Jewish mystics considered Pythagoras a link to their heritage. The impact the Essenes had on the later Gnostic School and consequently the later Church[84] is well understood. Pythagoras was very conveniently suited as a philosophic "hunter and gatherer," for it is written that he applied for and received initiation into the Egyptian, Chaldean, and Babylonian Mystery Colleges, doubtlessly receiving quite a load of astronomy and mathematics from these sources. But this was only the beginning for the man later to be recognized as the *first philosopher*. He traveled from country to country, ultimately locating the best and wisest teachers. He assimilated the Eleusinian Mysteries,[85] the Mysteries of Isis at Thebes,[86] and even the Phoenician Mysteries concerning Adonis.[87] Finally, he passed through Persia on his way to India. In India he received the highest and finest initiation the world could offer at the feet of the Brahman Masters.[88] Herein was the secret of his spirituality.

We don't know the reasoning behind Pythagoras' arrangement of his encyclopedic learning to form his own school, but we do know that he accomplished it in a way that would remain insightful over time. While Pythagoras' penetration into the Mysteries served well enough to inspire even Plato, it is his incorporation of Spiritual Science that has caused modern materialistic science to ridicule his work. It should be stated that when the dimension of the Transcendental is added to anyone's teachings, he or she is to an extent automatically eliminated from credibility by the modern sensibility. It is inconceivable to the materialist that a peer can somehow sense the Unseen when others of reasonable education, wealth, fame, or power cannot. Thus has the name of Pythagoras, like Apollonius, been subjected to all sorts of harsh criticism, their words taken out of context and harped upon as fallacy, etc. So today, strangely enough, the thinking of Aristotle is often given precedence over that of Pythagoras.

So thorough was Pythagoras, along with his later counterpart Apollonius of Tyana, that we today find it nearly impossible to attribute to the man so much ability. Numbers, geometry, music, and astronomy were only the vehicles he used to put across the higher teachings. So when we review the works of Michelangelo, the discoveries of Kepler, or the inventions of Edison, we find their genius easier to accept, for these later exponents of art and science were more or less specializing in their particular endeavors.

Serpent Mound as Python

Given the solid evidence of the collaboration between the design of the Serpent Mound and the famous 3–4–5 theorem, there is good reason to suspect that the theorem, like the Serpent, preceded the Philosopher. We know this because of the several apparently intentional conjunctions of straight lines within the serpent-theorem combination,[89] and because of the new dating of the Serpent Mound placing its design more than two thousand years before the birth of the Sage. In this, we also may deduce that Pythagoras had a true mission, the kind of work given to those who labor tirelessly, even from former lives, to preserve the knowledge. From this we may also figure that in his travels and analysis of information, Pythagoras in some way *came to possess* the image or likeness of what we think of as Serpent Mound. Subsequently, he used it as a teaching tool.

The Python, as "fixed" by Apollo, may have been the *Rebus of the Masters* from prehistory, a solitary symbol containing in itself all speech, writing, and knowledge pertaining to the literal art of keeping the Mysteries. A single, grand, unifying icon of all learning and erudition was, by the exercise of this work, the Great Python. The existence of such an icon would be a very important institution in itself and would have been protected scrupulously.

The preliminary purpose of this work is first to demonstrate the Serpent as a coded harbinger of the chief natural sciences known to the ancient Mystery Tradition. Secondly, and as the result of this first purpose, this work aims to show Serpent Mound as the source for the arcane and original alphabet as invented by the Greeks from

Phoenician and Semitic sources. Pythagoras and his community of natural scientists would have created the alphabet as the final and concluding entry in the Python's *book of knowledge.* On the other hand, it could have been *revived* and properly reconstructed by Pythagoras and his Pythagoreans. Very little is known in this respect, save the obvious Near Eastern influence on the symbols. We do know, however, that the alphabet of the Greeks appeared around the time of Pythagoras, and that places where he lived and worked became strongholds of alphabetical dispensation. As noted in the final section of this book, the Samians were dictating their versions of the eta and omega to the Athenians considerably less than one hundred years after the death of the Sage of Samos.

In the myth of the slaying of the Python, the arrows from Apollo's bow may refer to the various alignments with the shafts of sun and moonlight converging on the Serpent's coils. In this we might speculate that his sister Artemis, goddess of the Moon, assisted him in the "kill." Similarly, the cutting up of the body may have been the segmentation produced in part through the geometrical and astronomical analysis of the Serpent. If these things are indeed the case, then the real mystery of the Serpent Mound is not only who designed and constructed it, but also *for what purpose?* The understanding of a Pythagorean connection is a linchpin in any proper future comprehension of this mystery.

The Revelation

The mysteries of the Revelation, like that of the Python, are intimately joined together in the overall mystery tradition. The Great Serpent would appear to be at the very beginning of this tradition, commencing about 5,000 years ago.

The Revelation to John is a religious text, full of strange and wonderful imagery, the last book in the Christian Bible. It is the rather mystical testimony of a man familiarly known as Saint John the Divine,[90] a personality taken to have been a member of the early Christian community. Although few modern scholars claim to know well the procedures of the early Church councils, by later standards it was blasphemous to bestow any saintly title upon anyone other than the Apostles[91] without a long period of information gathering, analysis, and waiting. Some believe therefore that John must have been the Apostle John or another named "John of Patmos."

The epilogue of the Revelation plainly speaks in the first person ("I, Jesus"), which has been assumed to be a vicarious penning due in part to the invoking of Jesus at the end. In addition, there is a clear warning *not to tamper* with the wording of the book, doubtlessly set forth due to the extreme care taken in its numerical structuring and poetic format. Nevertheless, many scholars believe that at the least the book has been combined with other manuscripts. This is probably a gross understatement. The later editors of the manuscript were as far beneath the original author as a pig to a professor.

The name or title "Saint John the Divine" appears to have been sanctioned later by a Church that valued the Revelation as a sort of tool or mace with which Rome would serve as intermediary regarding all future prophecy.[92] Using it to its advantage, the Church could continue to invoke doom and delight, reward and punishment on its potentates, congregations, or enemies. The utility of the scripture is quite evident even today. Threats of doomsday and hell are ceaselessly rained upon the unwitting faithful, the priests and preachers gaining modicums of power through naive and cleverly orchestrated misinterpretation based upon the distorted scripture. It might come as a surprise to uncounted people that "Jesus" may indeed have penned the work originally, and that his real name, like his true mission, has been virtually obliterated from the historical record.[93]

While there is strong evidence in support of the above statement, the intent of this chapter is mainly to point out the true meaning of some of the Revelation's enigmatic imagery. The Old Serpent referred to in the Revelation so well describes our own effigy that the influence of the Pythagorean School on the Revelation is unquestionable.

It should be kept in mind that the Revelation text has been altered and interpolated to a degree that has removed it from the realm of its original and sublime credibility. However, there are apparent whole portions which, while having their connections to the body somewhat mutilated, nevertheless substantiate the fact that the writer was thoroughly familiar with the Pythagorean or Neo-Pythagorean College. Since the sole exponent and chief defender (apologist) of this College was Apollonius of Tyana,[94] we may look deeply into the imagery provided by the Serpent icon as an aid in deciphering some of the Revelation's confounding puzzles.

It should also be borne in mind that this is the same time period (96 C.E.) that the Jewish mystics and scholarly rabbis developed the basic forms and formularies comprising what is currently called kabbala (cabala, kabala; in Hebrew: qabbala, tradition or something received, passed down). This tradition may have been of Egyptian origin. Indeed, the modern tree of the sephiroth is no less than the image of the traditional Egyptian ank, though surely this visual focus of the kabbalistic science has not been attributed to the ank any more than the Church attributes the cross to it. According to the best records, the kabbala became orthodox some time in the sev-

enth century C.E., and was subsequently developed by the rabbinical structure all the way through the mediaeval and renaissance periods to the eighteenth century. Interestingly, it strongly influenced Christian thought at its peak in the twelfth and thirteenth centuries.

The kabbala by way of the familiar Jewish tradition is a rather strict system of religiously oriented science in what is termed "magical" form. Its intent is to increase the receptivity of the soul-oriented mind toward spiritual realization and a firm knowledge of the Godhead with its angelic hierarchy. In the fundamentalist sense, it is a mystical technique of number and geometry by which scripture may be both written and interpreted. In an advanced understanding, it becomes a literal touchstone for the wise. The initiates of this College once claimed the ability to comprehend the sacred mysteries through *penetration*. Among the fruits of their labor in this garden was the gift of accurate self-analysis, and with this came the equally accurate foretelling of future and past events. In reality, the origin of this school of thought was not the exclusive property of any religion, but was a universally acceptable system and methodology applicable in many areas of philosophic endeavor.

The figure of St. John purportedly wrote in a period that is, to understate it, controversial to unbiased scholars. The messiah had made his appearance. There were political and social reforms being made. Battles and triumphs of the pen and spoken word were common. There is scant documentation of the Apostolic and pre-Church centuries save through the New Testament itself. This is profoundly complicated by disagreement in current scholarship over the words believed actually spoken by the messiah. The exquisite attention paid to number and format in the Revelation as well as certain fragments of the Gospels indicates the full bloom of the flower of the kabbala being been very much present. But since the New Testament was written in the Greek, what have the Jewish scribes to do with these accounts?

About two centuries before the beginning of the Common Era and extending to two centuries after, the Essenes were in full command of the scholarly pursuit of the lost teachings of the first philosopher, Pythagoras. Apollonius of Tyana, like the "intrepid joiner" Pythagoras before him, is believed to have sought and received various initiations. That he sought out this desert sect, assimilating the knowledge it had to offer, is a foregone assumption, for it was Apollonius of Tyana who was destined to create the Neo-Pythagorean School. The fact of Apollonius appearing right in the middle of that sect's heyday is a mystery unto itself, and one ignored by mainstream scholarship down through the centuries. Part of the reason has been the systematic elimination of Apollonius' record, even as Pythagoras' record was intentionally destroyed or corrupted. It has often been said that when one dares to speak the truth, he makes more enemies than friends.

Probably finding its way into Neo-Pythagorean culture from the painstaking researches of the Essene Brotherhood, then aptly transcribed through the instrumentality of the Greek Apollonius,[95] the *tradition* makes itself clearly known in the Revelation writings. The later Nicene editors, knowing little and understanding less of the intent of the wonderful Mystery text, saw its believed message as too difficult to be applied, in a practical sense, for both themselves and the masses of the faithful.[96] Probably formatting the work as a future prophecy to suit their own version of destiny, certain parts were deliberately worked over or shuffled until their sacred meanings could no longer be directly divined and the numerology made very difficult to reconstruct.

The following illustrations are displayed with the purpose of demonstrating that Revelation's serpent—"the old devil"—is one and the same with our own Serpent Mound. Further, this "image of the beast" was likely to have been well known to the high initiates from the outset of dynastic Egypt, if not earlier. The tradition of this wonderful template, without which there would be *no empirical evidence* for the life and work of Pythagoras' secret teachings, was apparently brought to the North American continent so long ago that Native Americans, in their tradition of oral history, hardly recall the people associated with the designers of the Great Serpent Mound. Who constructed it and what took place there are mysteries that may or may not be solved.

Other research has been completed regarding the myths and traditions of a number of nations and tribes surrounding the area of what is today Adams County, Ohio. In short, a Great Serpent lived and moved about in this area, a serpent that had an eye emphasizing a rather formidable light source. One of the names for it comes from the Cherokee. They called it "Uktena," and it was a monster.

Was the great Serpent Mound created by a mysterious race, the end of whose lineage was the beginning of the Adena People? It is a little-known fact, and one rarely pursued by archaeologists, that the very early pre-Adena folk had members who were of very tall stature. But long before the Cherokee, the Native American legends speak of a people of gigantic stature, who, in the words of Heckewelder were "capable of great exertions and doing wonders." Could such an ancient race have been instrumental in creating the Great Serpent Mound?

While we do not know the answers to this question, one thing is quite certain, the image of the Great Serpent of Adams County is fraught with extraordinary coincidence and precision in a comparison with the poetic dictates of the Revelation to John, itself a direct recipient of a spiritual-philosophic tradition stemming from an unknown past. And while this scripture is suspect for interpolation and reorganization, this same image of a serpent is, through association, connected with the Pythagorean School, which subsequently became the Neo Pythagorean College, affecting the New Testament through the Essene and Gnostic Colleges. Yet before these mysteries were associated with Pythagoras, they were apparently part of a deeply developed religio-scientific culture, the roots of which seeming to draw nourishment from a remotely antique philosophy based upon the firsthand knowledge of one God.

The Woman in Revelation

The vision of the woman and the dragon by John the Revelator offers further and deeper evidence of the science and art of the Mystery College. It assigns yet more information to the symbolism already described with a view toward introducing the necessity of the Son being born through the womb. In this process of birth, the Son takes on human form, manifesting the appearance of God on the Earth.

> *Now a great sign appeared in heaven: a woman, robed with the sun, standing on the moon, and on her head a crown of twelve stars. She was pregnant, and in labour, crying aloud in the pangs of childbirth.*
> Revelation 12:1, 2

The heavenly woman, robed in the sun and standing on the moon, is depicted as the vesica (representing the womb of the Mysteries) set into the solar hexagon. Her standing on the six lunar alignments lends substance to the theory

Figure 78. The Celestial Woman

Revelation 12 speaks about twelve stars crowning the head of the celestial woman. Carefully interpreted, these "stars" are first her crown, then the fruit of her pregnancy. Subsequent to these symbols a "huge red dragon" appears, dominating the imagery. Her crown of twelve stars likely indicates the complete knowledge of geometry possessed by the Mystery College. The throne was central to nearly everything in this school of thought and thus the more the hexagon was utilized, the more central the knowledge of the Godhead is indicated. This geometric knowledge coupled with astronomical knowledge served as a powerful force in educating those who were receptive.

of the Serpent's astronomical status having been known, in some way, to the Mystery College.

The woman's pregnancy is revealed graphically by the Serpent's oval feature as it resembles an umbilicus within the womb, well contained. The celestial Serpent is, subsequently, a veritable cord tying together Heaven and Earth. The body

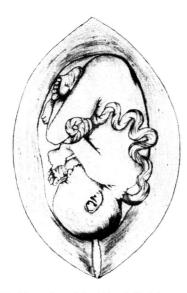

Figure 79. Mysteries of the Womb-Delphos.

Here the serpent takes on the aspect of umbilical cord and the internal navel of the Mother is the umbilicus, The Serpent Mound may be interpreted in this way as well, for the serpent in this aspect is the cord tying together Heaven and Earth, God and Man. Here the Serpent takes on the aspect of Logos, nurturing the fetus of the Child Humanity. Hence we may understand the sacred Omphalos of the Delphinian Oracle. (Kathy Valentour, 1995)

of the child this cord nourishes is the ten-crescent body previously described as the nine-and-one orifices, the tree of life. The Serpent, as an umbilical cord, bridges the difference between the divine world of archetypal images and the concrete world of earthly measure, called geometry (*ge* or *geo* —"earth" + *metria*, "measure").

The Revelation continues with the creation of what might seem a paradox, in reality showing the versatility and diversity of its symbols.

> *Then a second sign appeared in the sky: there was a huge red dragon with seven heads and ten horns, and each of the seven heads crowned with a coronet.*
>
> Revelation 12:3

Saturn	♄	1
Jupiter	♃	2
Mars	♂	3
Sun	○	4
Venus	♀	5
Mercury	☿	6
Moon	☾	7
Wounded Head		8

Figure 80. The Seven Heads of the Beast

The seven "heads" of the beast are shown under their occult titles as seven figurative planetary designations. Spiritual Science used these in order to conceal their simple numerical counterparts. The ten heads were originally twelve, but one head was "wounded." The woman standing on the moon could be interpreted as either the astrological moon below (as the number seven) or the astronomical alignments of the coils. It is astonishing today to hear the priests and preachers in their attempts to stir up their masses and flocks in the effort to externalize the meaning of this scripture into political and geographical name saying, ignorant of the possible astronomical and geometrical mysteries enjoined by the early college.

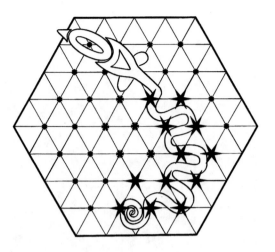

Figure 81. The Tail of the Dragon
The "tail" of the dragon is sweeping one-third of the stars from the sky. While very possibly a reference to Draconis at its height in the sky about 4800 years ago, the wisdom of the geometry is more practical, for it is timeless and not subject to precession. One-third of the asterisks within the sacred hexagonal figure are near the long tail of the Serpent.

The second sign is seen in exactly the same space as the first, great sign. Then continuing, we read of the tail of this dragon:

Its tail swept a third of the stars from the sky and hurled them to the ground ...

The meaning of this first portion of 12:4 is illustrated by the picture of the Serpent upon the hexagonal grid as well as in the sky. The 36 + 1 asterisks geometrically represent the stars of the heavenly throne. One-third of these, 12, are shown as those points closest to the serpentine body. Thus the "tail" of the dragon is the Serpent. Approximately one third of the number of stars in the old constellation Draco, although variously interpreted, fall on the tail of

the beast (our Serpent Mound). Perhaps the geometry of the hexagon standardized this possible this possible double meaning, one astronomical, and the other geometrical. The second part of 12:4 then states:

... and the dragon stopped in front of the woman as she was at the point of giving birth, so that it could eat the child as soon as it was born.

These lines are interpreted to mean that the tree of life or human form should never be taken lightly or mismanaged by the traditionalist or initiate. The science of this tree should be considered as sacred as one's own self, for that is what the symbol represents. The tree, growing right in the middle of the throne or garden of God, is potentially a wily, uncontrollable "red" (fiery) dragon if not managed and groomed properly. If this dragon is permitted to go wild, he overwhelms the mystery of the womb, i.e.. he will figuratively obscure ("eat") the child, replacing the tree of life with his own image and intent.

In just these few lines of a single chapter of the Revelation can be seen a critical amount of information stored in a small area. Revelation 12:5 through 7 has our heroine give birth to a son, who is subsequently taken "straight up to God" and the throne. Then she escapes to the desert, where God has prepared a place for her to stay for three and one-half years.

Here, beginning at Revelation 12:7, the multiple-meaning symbolism commences again, returning to the solar hexagon or throne of God. As the dragon already enjoys the like of the throne, the son born to the celestial woman must confront it, for he has been taken there:

And now a war broke out in heaven, when Michael with his angels attacked the dragon. The dragon fought back with his angels, but

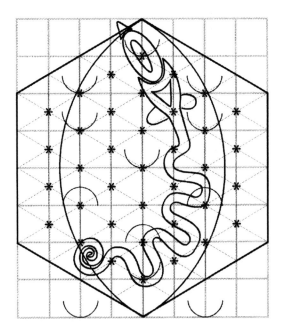

Figure 82. The Dragon Waiting before the Womb

The vesica piscis, isolated from its circles, demonstrates how the tree of life or man-body (represented as the ten doors or nine and one muses) finds fruition in the "womb." Here the serpent is the umbilical cord, but very soon thereafter is recognized as the dragon "waiting before the womb." The multiple symbolism of the Great Serpent and its related geometries is appreciated through careful study and dedication to the ways of philosophy

they were defeated and driven out of heaven. The great dragon, the primeval serpent, known as the devil or Satan, who had led all the world astray, was hurled down to the earth and his angels were hurled down with him.

The primeval serpent has been driven with his angels out of heaven. The *angels* are likely no less than the geometric matrices surrounding the serpent, i.e., his *messengers.*

The remainder of chapter 12 appears to deal with the practical reality of the dragon *power* as it may have been perceived by the Mystery College. For the astute scholar or investigator, there is considerable couching in the language of alchemical metaphor.

The celestial woman, who is made to have both divine and human attributes, is apparently the vessel of the Solar Mysteries, figuratively and actually. She is so intimately linked with the messianic appearance that even her life becomes a potential sacrifice.

The Name of Jesus

Ιησους is said to have been the Ogdoad of the Christian Gnostic tradition. It was a word or name created to have the exact value of 888, the resurrected or perfected 666 (the Son transformed from the Sun). By way of symbol-number correspondence, the name appears like this:

iota	=	10
eta	=	8
sigma	=	200
omicron	=	70
upsilon	=	400
sigma	=	200
Jesus	=	888

It is by means of the 24 perimeter points of the solar hexagon (indicating the various limbs of the creation) multiplied by the 37 interior points (representing the weaving together of the four *ideas*) that the number 888 (and therefore Man) is achieved. The glory (light) of the throne, no longer dependent upon the image of the Great Serpent (Logos), takes the form of the Son, Word-made-flesh.

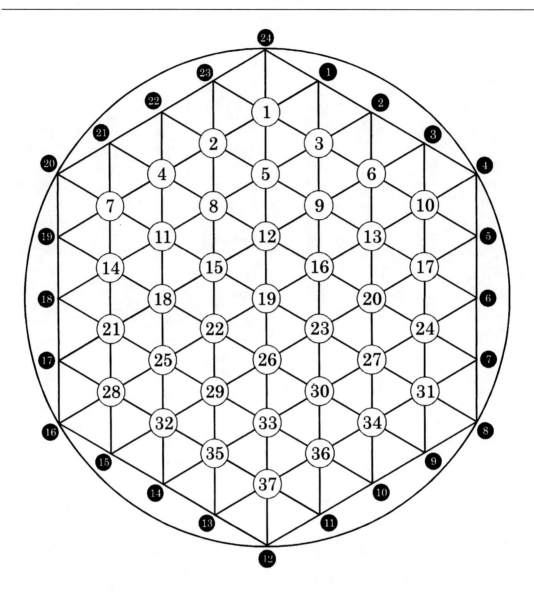

Figure 83. Numbering the Hexagon
24 x 37 = 888

The advanced students of the tradition held the throne of God as the departure point between pure Spirit and the material creation. It is the Seed Mind, containing the principles that ultimately extend to create the material universe and the shape of the human body. The Great Serpent is the Creator's Instrument (Tool) or Signature (Logos) resting upon this faceted

Figure 84. Dawning of the Great Serpent
As the light of the spiritual sun dawns within the Great Serpent, the creature gradually evolves into a humanity-oriented existence. With the admission of the Solar Principle, the body of the Logos commences a process of ultimate change, transforming into the Son.

jewel, and the Spirit (as the Sun or Son) voluntarily sacrifices to reconcile or evolve this Tool through light. Like a fish or whale swallowing the bait, the creature's jaws literally entertain the Sun-spirit. That the soul of a man may only relate to the soul of another man for spiritual enlightenment is an axiom of Spiritual Science, one qualified in this example of *Word-becoming-flesh.* Thus the Michael engaged in "battle" with the celestial serpent.

Masters of Spiritual Science concur that the human form is indeed a wonderful casing by which the powers and perceptions of the inner spirit are literally multiplied. To receive the human form is considered the greatest good fortune, for the Spirituality is developed with it, a privilege even the angels are said to desire.

The Term Christos

The term Χριστος (Greek, "anointed") is not very well understood in modern parlance, although Christian eschatology considers the anointing of the messiah to be academic in its study. Eschatology is mainly concerned with death and matters leading to or stemming from it. Since the Mystery College did not see death as theology views it, the original meaning of the term *Christos* has been misplaced for the general laity.

The wisdom associated with the anointing of the elect of God may have been preserved by the Merkaba mystics from an earlier tradition, although this may be relatively unimportant in light of the Gnostic spelling. "Merkaba" indicates literally "a part of the Tradition."

chi	=	600
rho	=	100
iota	=	10
sigma	=	200
tau	=	300
omicron	=	70
sigma	=	200

Christos:	1480

The conceptualizing of the Grace of God involved the knowledge of the flowing Spirit. As the audible Word or Voice of the Divine, the Spirit could be intermingled with matter, forming the very flesh of the chosen one. Once the Son became established, the factor of the cell of the flesh was used with the factor of the warming, quickening Spirit. Like Hermes, the blood carried the essentials of life to become the flesh. In this, the cell of the square of the Sun was multiplied by the Mercury factor, 8:

$$18.5 \times 8 = 148$$

Although the following is speculative, the atomic number of quicksilver, 80, could conceivably have been applied in this math by the Mystery College. Thus 18.5 x 80 = 1480. However, the knowledge of atomic numbers may just as easily not have played a role here, and the mercurial eight was simply expanded in terms of ten to become the dominant factor in the term's conception.

Interestingly, when the square of eight (64) is utilized to multiply the internal number of the

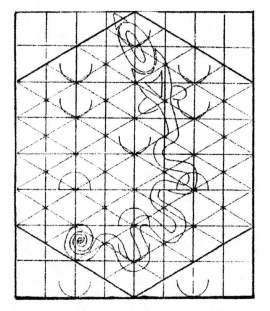

Son (the 37 eyes of the throne), the result is the total number of Jesus Christ:

The Resplendent Sun or Son: The Spirit of 1776

The conceiving of the sacred number 888 may be compared to creation of the ironclad magnet. Surrounded by a casing of specially prepared steel, the currents of the magnet's field of force are concentrated, increasing its power. By enlivening the geometric form of the throne or primal Atom, the spirit's powers are concentrated.

Called an aura, halo, aureole, gloriole, or nimbus, this energetic field of sublime light is often represented about the heads of saints, martyrs, and true philosophers or mystics. It typifies the health and well-being of the soul, being the result of proper care and nourishment. Mystics refer to this as partaking of the bread and water of life, received through spiritual practices.

The vital aura of the soul, numerically based in the number 888, is therefore extended ceremonially to twice its size, philosophically a redoubling of the resources of the spiritual soul. The seed of the soul, being only the size of one atom, in this learns to extend itself beyond the boundaries of the throne. Therefore the gloriole of the Spiritual sun or Son is enumerated as 1776.

The Cardinal Number 1776

The Ogdoad or 888 numerically represents the throne of God and the body of the Son. This cardinal philosophic number doubled to the number of the Son (1776) divided by the number of great union, 96, is 18.5, the cell of the square of the Sun. In this way, 1776 and the operation of the Solar Rule are intimately related.

The cardinal 1776, as the number of the Great Work (the grand union), is called the eagle of eagles or the phoenix in the terminology of the Adepts. As the number of union, 96 is analogously the addition of sulfur (atomic number 16)

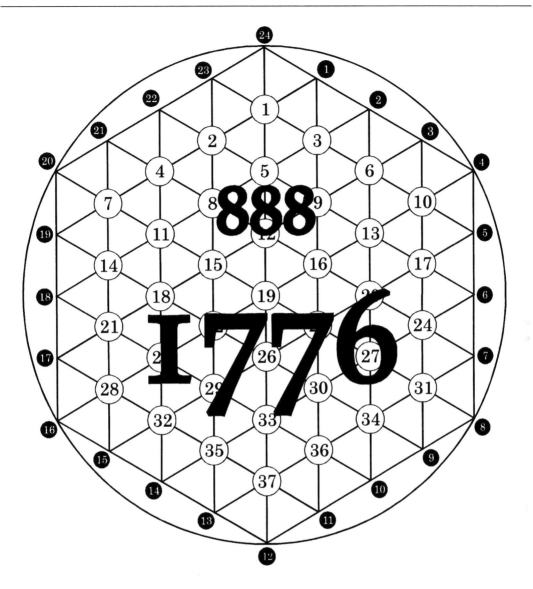

Figure 85. 888 and the Spiritual Son

and mercury (atomic number 80). The 96 equilateral triangles of the hexagon represent this union.

The multiplication or exaltation of the Stone (the throne of God) is accomplished through the addition of 816 (the number of solar amplification) and 960, signifying the completion of the magnum opus (the Great Work), 1776.

Thus the Philosopher's Stone, the throne of God, the Sun or Son, Jesus, the Atom, Adam, etc., are all essentially derived from this numerical wisdom.

Interestingly, when the numbers 1776 and 888

1776

Figure 86. 1776

$$1776 + 888 = 2664$$
$$2664 \div 4 = 666$$

The Measure of 1776

The foot measure of any of the hexagon's triangle sides is 81.6. Subsequently, the number of these triangles is 96. These two figures, 81.6 and 96, added together make 177.6.

The Throne as the hexagon, owning a measure of 326.4 feet on each of its six sides (4 x 81.6) thereby owns a long diagonal measure (see Figure 68) of 565.4 feet. This figure multiplied by π (3.1415) relates the foot circumference of the circled hexagon as approximately 1776 feet.

are drawn together and quartered, the number 666 results:

The Phoenix Mystery

Spiritual Chemistry

IT WAS IN THE EARLY 1970S THAT I STARTED MY study of alchemy. It is a serious hobby and highly recommended for anyone with an interest in the Mysteries. Alchemy is in fact Spiritual Chemistry, and anyone who would use the term

Figure 87. The Devouring of the Sun

A very important analogy of spiritual chemistry, the taking of the sun by the lion or dragon meant the integration of the coagulating and order-bringing principle of immortality. The old Masters used such metaphor when explaining the sacred sciences and arts to their elect. This picture was published in 1550 C.E. in *Rosarium Philosophorum.*

"alchemy" in a derogatory fashion undoubtedly would similarly abuse the title "philosopher," though perhaps unwittingly. There is essentially no difference between an accomplished alchemist and a true philosopher, for the former gives rise to the latter. Philosophy is not earned in the degree mills of modern universities — rather it is discovered through earnest love and dedication to the ways of Nature, regardless of the trial. Universities will offer it for a price, but it cannot be bought or taught. Rather, it is *caught.*

It is said that he who does not know the *mercury* of the philosophers is not fit to be called a philosopher. The *mercury* is that which reduces all things in order to make them receptive to the divine nature, literally resurrecting them to a higher form. The Great Serpent with its plethora of harmonic associations has come to be a symbol of that Universal and all-purpose substance, for it nobly refines certain truths. Such knowledge is the doorway opening to the transcendental mysteries of life. Philosophers, perceiving inwardly the light and guided by the inner Sound Principle, will often share their insights with others. Some philosophers always remain behind the scenes, however. Such a gentleman or lady is rarely (if ever) self-serving, but sacrifices so that others may come to know the work. Philosophy is a gift given to those who wish to search for and discover the secrets of nature from a more advantageous point of view. Most men choose the worldly path, and in this decision they are seeking less to know their true selves as to understand and master the reality of their outward situation.[97]

There are some obvious alchemical interpretations of the serpent and the ellipse, perhaps the most prominent being the idea of the creature as a mercurial deity, swallowing up the sulfur, a solar manifestation. Sulfur and mercury combined produce cinnabar, a legendary mineral compound known for its black-gray powder or red crystals. The interpretation of compounding cinnabar is no better portrayed for hands-on alchemical analysis than in the Pythagorean Theorem combination.

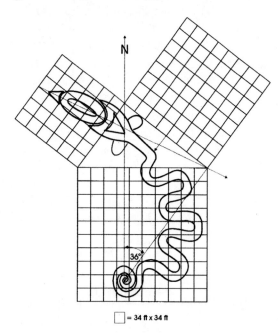

= 34 ft x 34 ft

In the theorem, the upper left square's smaller squares added together with the upper right squares equals the number of squares in the base square. In this example, the square of 6 (known as the square of the Sun) has 36 squares. Adding these to the 64 smaller squares in the square of 8 (the square of Mercury) equals the number of squares in the square of 10 below, known as the square of the Earth. Thus sulfur added to mercury makes cinnabar. In ancient Egypt, one root term believed responsible for *alchemy* meant "black earth," the crude stage of mercury combining with sulfur.

The naming of these squares as the Sun, Mercury, and the Earth stems from a long time ago and was based on the attributes of their whole numbers (6, 8, and 10). By some special coincidence which seems to relate the elements of sulfur and mercury to these squares' names, the formula for producing cinnabar is presented in a mathematical and geometrical form, complemented by the image of the beast swallowing or giving forth something. This "swallowing" and "regurgitating" is represented in the famous term *solve et coagula,* meaning dissolve and then recoagulate. Cinnabar of the divine variety[98] has been referred to as *Adamic Earth*: that from which man was fashioned, a pure material. In this interpretation, what the serpent is doing with the ellipse becomes rather esoteric. For this reason, the effigy may also be seen as regurgitating something termed both the Orphic Egg and the Egg of Brahma. Both these signify the matrix enclosing the emerging creation, Man.

The Sages tell us that man is the externalized soul, which was itself born out of the Word of the Creator.[99] From this comes a second interpretation from Spiritual Chemistry. The Serpent on the hexagon reveals an interesting meandering of the tail that carefully attempts to circumvent the various asterisk conjunctions within the geometry. The description of the throne, as explained in "The Hexagon," is an effort to express the understanding of the human form as patterned after the attributes of the soul. Man is a *living soul,* but the soul made entirely extroverted and materialized.[100] In this way, the body, unlike the soul, may grow from a seed.

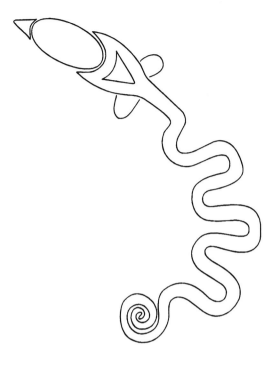

Figure 88. The Serpent and the Egg

The Serpent and its elliptical feature are sometimes considered to be the union between sperm and egg.

be the most obvious and sweeping alchemical symbolism. It is multi-leveled in its interpretation. As stated in that section, the twin circles arising from the throne are likened to the dual pre-creation principles of Omniscient Feeling coupled with Omnipotent Force producing Vibration, the Great Word or Logos.

Perhaps the most intriguing aspect of the vesica piscis' alchemical interpretation is that it renders an abundance of measurement relating to key philosophic principles. Considering the age of the design of Serpent Mound (approximately 5,000 years), it is very interesting to note that the circumference of either of the twin circles is 2368 feet, the total numerical value of the name *Jesus Christ* as transcribed from the original Greek. Since the man Jesus was believed to represent the Word or Logos made flesh, it is fitting that the numbers of his name would be given in the vesica piscis geometry. More to the point, this would offer further proof of the Tradition having preceded by millennia the life of the man referred to as Jesus Christ.

The Great Serpent is therefore at times likened to a spermatic entity entering into a union or conjunction with an egg, perhaps the ultimate alchemy. However, as the hexagon is seen as the "blueprint" for the proto-soul,[101] the serpent thereupon is seen as the Power laced throughout—the Logos having as its work the labor of creating the soul of Man. In this, the union of sperm and egg may be analogous to the creation of the spiritual entity. Hence body and soul engaged in an undeniably close relationship.

The Alchemy of the Vesica

The conjoining of the twin circles as depicted in the section entitled "The Vesica Piscis" may well

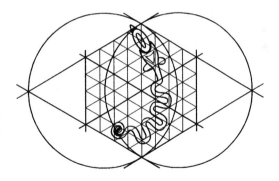

Figure 89. The Mystical Number of Jesus Christ

The figure 2,368, the numerical value of Jesus Christ, is found equal to the foot circumference of either circle of the vesica piscis.

The Great Alchemical Furnace

This numerical figure of 2368 shows up again in the composite picture of the ark containing the tree of life and the serpent. Recalling that the Tree stands for the man-body with its ten doors, one internalized, the understanding of the great alchemical fusion takes place. The square of eight gives birth to this Kabbalistic Tree through its 64 interior squares. The hexagon or throne owns 37 points within, symbolic of the "weave" of the Atom. The alchemical union of these two figures serves to emphasize the principle of multiplication—in this case, the twin internal numerical Figures 64 and 37 multiplied produce 2368. In this, the numerical value of Christ-Jesus was very much a part of a tradition earlier than the present Christian era.

In Figure 90, the great ellipse (the "oval feature") coincides perfectly with the highest *sephiroth* or Muse, like a fruit on the tree of knowledge. It appears as though the Great Serpent (as the Logos) is sampling this "fruit" as if to suggest that in the Logos is contained all knowledge.

In this interpretation, the serpent is gathering strength and growing in wisdom prior to its maturation. Yet the containment of these things within the ark adds a dimension of Godly alchemy to the picture—the wisdom of the great furnace that fuses Spirit, soul, mind, and body together as one thing under God.

The Serpent and the Cross:
The Mystery of Distillation

Students of symbolism are familiar with the enigmatic presence of a serpent apparently crucified on a cross or tau symbol. This has never been intended as a mockery of the Christian crucifix, but rather explains the staying power of the cross in the mystical tradition.

The cross, like the serpent, has been used extensively in pre-Christian and non-Christian imagery. Native American symbolism in fact incorporates many versions of the cross signifying many different things. The ank in the form of the caduceus or the Lamp of Hermes is applied in myth to escort the recently deceased to the next world, a *crossing over,* so to speak.

Nicholas Flammel, a late fourteenth-to early fifteenth-century alchemist celebrated in France, depicted crucified serpents in describing a part of the chemical process. As the mobile and wily mercury, the cross was the fixation of that illusive element thought impossible to fix. In this, Flammel and others made the daring analogy of the alchemical process to the life of Christ. But this was nothing new, for the Chinese and Arab philosophical schools had long included the Universal in their practice. The fixation of mercury was analogous to the controlling of sense and mind to the end of achieving higher Spiritual receptivity. Such receptivity was characterized by success in both laboratories: the one using the hands, and the one searching for visual and auditory revelation from within.

So it is that advanced mystics, disengaging the attention from worldly things, learn to lift their focus above the level of the senses, absorbing and withdrawing into the light within the forehead. This distillation of the vital force through redirection of the attention causes the spirit to rise above the phenomenal serpent cunningly concealed in the mind and its related matters. This aptly reflects the words of the Apostle Paul, the poet Khayyam and others when they speak of "taking up your cross," "flinging off the winter garment of repentance," or "dying" (to the worldly life) on a daily basis.

The serpent was therefore compared to the physical state of being, but at other times the image was evolved into a subtler concept. The

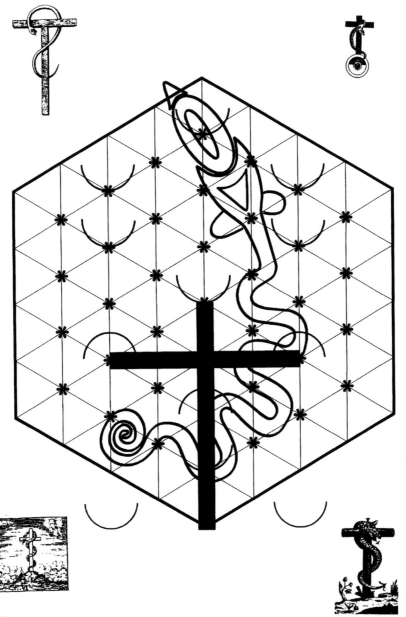

Figure 90. 777

By way of tradition, the sigma-tau combination, normally valued at 200 (sigma) plus 300 (tau) or 500, at times could be valued at 6, a substitution for the enigmatic *digamma* now missing from the alphabet. Michell notes that the term *stauros*, meaning "a cross," could be val- ued at either 777 or 1,271 by this interchangeable system. As 777 represents a stage between 666 (the beast) and 888 (the messiah), it could be inferred that the cross represents a heavenly transition.

serpent taking wings to fly is an outstanding analogy of the spiritual transformational process in the human being but was more suitably adapted to the image of a winged person or phoenix. With this in mind, the early chemists touted the practical importance of flight where their subject (the soul) was concerned. In the words of one commentator on Valentine's *Triumphal Chariot of Antimony*: "Let Mercury instruct it in the art of flying." This states the need for the philosophic subject to become airborne so that the separation from its gross body can be whole and complete. The need for flight is a spiritual verity, and so practical that its principle may be applied down to the most mundane levels of experience. The Saints from the several important world religions stress the necessity for rising above the narrow limits of mind and the senses. For if the vibrant soul remains fast where it is placed right until the time of natural death, that is the nature of the bird who cannot see beyond the nest or the serpent crawling on its belly.

The ABC of Spirituality begins above body consciousness.

Sant Kirpal Singh

To John the Revelator, the "voice like a trumpet" said to him plainly, "Come up here ..." (Revelation 4:1). In this alone, it is clear that the flight or lifting image has long been effective in expressing the miracle of recall to a spiritual reality. According to the Mystic Adepts, getting back to the origin of Spiritual existence is the depth of desire burning in the subconscious soul.

The principle of distillation is one of the crucial aspects of advanced alchemical knowledge. My Master used to demonstrate the advantages of *rising above body consciousness*. After giving a talk or discourse, he would often withdraw and perform the feat right in front of us. It was like the room was taken under the magnetic spell of a great spiritual gyroscope. We enjoyed a sort of charged atmosphere and a peace that cannot be described in words. Our karmas would literally be blown away or drawn into his presence when this happened, making it much easier to see and understand how the Messiahs and Masters and Avatars help their chosen initiates to progress more quickly.

This feat of rising above also allows the Mastersoul to become re-saturated in the essence of the *Water of Life* existing above the physical world and the level of the senses. Like a parent bird, he flies up and away from the nest, returning with foodstuff for the hungry souls. Often the Master is likened to the provider of Amrit or Ambrosia, which, following his return to the physical form, is passed directly to the disciple through the eyes.

Alchemy is not a subject to be taken up by the worldly-wise, for the lure of gold-making easily dissuades the seeker from the true path. Initiation by a competent Master is above all a prerequisite, for without the proper discipline and the working out of certain karmas, the responsibilities accompanying the knowledge of the Philosopher's Stone are quite overwhelming.

The Worm and the Dragon

Western archaeologists in Mongolia earlier in the twentieth century suggested that the Chinese belief in dragons might be due to the plentiful number of fossil remains of the giant lizards found throughout the region. As it turns out, this was speculative, and at best only partially correct. The wisdom of the dragon to the ancient Chinese was more realistically linked to the discovery of a flow of what is termed *qi* or *chi*[102] through the landscape, and dinosaur remains would not be a requisite in the discovery of such a magnetic current. This energy, already described in "The Serpent and the Ark," took an unusually well-ordered form in some places across the Chinese landscape.[103] Yet even with this rather erudite knowledge regarding the true meaning of *dragon,* there is considerably more to learn.

Mythologies and legends of old are peppered with references to the worm or serpent. Though often another name for a young dragon, the worm or serpent tends to actuate the mythological premise that spiritual forces take up the role of living creatures. The serpent-dragon myth occurs throughout virtually all our major ancient cultures and is in fact one of the important common themes pervading the most antique subjects of ascetic mysticism, philosophy, and spiritual chemistry.

The dragon as worm (eel) associates itself with water, but also harbors fire of the occult nature, i.e., electricity. The Celtic dragon metamorphosed into a reptilian giant with the wings of a great bat. It could belch fire, presumably from flammable gases produced in its digestion of everything. Like the winds and clouds, the dragon rode with supremacy through the atmosphere, having its stronghold in the belly of mountains and its lairs in the secret places of the earth. Ultimately the dragon is identified with the ethereal condition, in essence lending it the credentials of regal majesty with supernatural wherewithal. Such dragons as produced by the Chinese were suspect as creatures of *art.* Legends from all over suggest that certain dragons were living things created through an extensive knowledge of an array of divine crafts forbidden to the commoner. The mighty and dreadful dragon of old was no less than the reputation and wand of great magicians well versed in the lore and rituals of sorcery—according to their critics.

In Britain and France, legends of dragon slayers remain a part of popular folklore. This is very probably due to the systematic removal of the

Figure 91. Symbol of the Fish

In Japan, the crane and koi (colored carp) are national symbols. Like the Japanese flag featuring the rising sun on a white background, both these creatures have the red *Hi* mark on their heads. The koi having this red seal on top of the head coupled with a pure white body are called Tancho, same as the word for crane. The belief in spiritual transformation seems to permeate all established world cultures, and as the serpentine worm that transforms to the phoenix, so the Tancho koi complements the Tancho crane. It is of interest to note the similarity between the Great Serpent's head projections and the pectoral fins of the koi. As a dragon, the worm is often associated with water.

Mystical Christian tradition considers Jesus as the Fish. Just as Ιησους (Jesus) has a symbolic numerical value of 888, so the term for fish as Ιχθος (Ichthos), has a value of 888 + 1, i.e., the Son and the One seated on the throne.

signs and trappings of the old Serpent faith from the sacred places. Oftentimes churches and cathedrals were constructed right atop the old centers in order to retain familiar settings for the people. Christmas and Easter were similarly coordinated to hold true with long-established rites. Thus it is that St. Patrick's legend assures us that the serpents were driven from Ireland even though there is no evidence for any snakes in the region at the time. It is believed that the old Druidic College may have degenerated toward the beginning of the Common Era, and that its priestcraft had become prone to human sacrifice.

Whether this notion is true or not, the hasty trail to wealth and power taken by the unenlightened magicians was always a shadowy interpretation of the much-desired path illumined by the Sages. The enlightened philosopher conceived the lowly worm as forerunner of the regal phoenix. Unfortunately for the uninitiated, would-be master of the divine process, any attempt to create the phoenix's worm in the laboratory ended as abruptly as the magician's philosophical integrity. In the testimony of the adepts, the airs used to abound with the poisonous fumes (dragons) of the dark magicians, and this was the expression of an inept foray into the matters of spiritual substance.

While it would be relatively unimportant to argue the possibility of actual fire-breathing, land-sweeping dragons now or in the remote past, it is not unrealistic to support the presence of allegorical truths associating such accounts with philosophical investigation. Much of the awesome power and character attributed to dragons has doubtlessly been contributed through the old chemists' diaries, couched as their writings were in language comprehensible only to those initiated into their particular school.

In perhaps the earliest known manuscript

Figure 92. A Prehistoric Native American Flying Dragon (Moundville, Alabama)

dealing with the subject of chemistry, the *Golden Treatise* of Hermes the Egyptian describes the three states of matter in these cautionary terms:

> *But a dragon inhabits all these and are his habitation; and the blackness is in them, and by it he ascends into the air.*

The dragon image abounds in both Eastern and Western philosophy, medicine, and religious mysticism. The Native American nations held both fear and reverence for the serpent form. In Longfellow's *Hiawatha,* gathered from oral tradition, there are passages citing the bravery of the hero in vanquishing the malevolent magician Megissogwan, the Pearl Feather. This man has twin serpents called the Kenabeek who play in the "black-pitch water."

On the other hand, the Japanese and Chinese used the dragon to promote the many aspects of natural healing and longevity. Dragons as primeval fish or big cats could be ridden by the genies (divines) that had successfully mastered some aspect of the great mystery of life. Alchemically, the dragon in some form was a necessity in the high art of swordmaking. Certain compounds or agents were specified in the terms of the dragon. Dragon teeth, blood, and scales were used; dragon grease was applied for the dissolving of silver. Metallurgical art and science were most concerned with the evolution or transformation of the primitive to the highly refined and perfect. In this, direct parallels to the spiritual content of life were popularly drawn.

The early chemists, the alchemists, may have originally created the image of the phoenix as it is popular today. On the other hand, it may simply have been rediscovered. The Philosopher's Stone, which is analogous to the Primal Atom or throne of God, has been referred to as the phoenix requiring nine eagles to complete its transformational flight. While the Greek and Arabian phoenix was an exalted denizen of an angelic climate, the earlier records of Egypt depict the phoenix as a winged man.

The colonial American Congress selected the eagle over the phoenix as the national emblem.

In a colored sketch submitted as a design for the Great Seal by William Barton in 1782, an actual phoenix appears sitting in a nest of flames. This itself demonstrates a tendency toward the use of this emblematic bird.

—Manly Hall

From the *Tales of 1001 Arabian Nights* comes the Roc, evocative of an aspect of the phoenix ideal. The Russian Firebird and the Native American Thunderbird bear some of the divine qualities of the phoenix. The Europeans, like the Greeks, considered the swan as a phoenix, and Hans Christian Andersen uses this theme in his story *Ugly Duckling.* The peacock with its multicolored fantail has been compared to the various stages of the phoenix's maturation. Even the pelican with its ability to carry weight to heights has been used symbolically to describe some quality of the great one's cycle.

The etymological basis for the term *phoenix* is found in the Greek, compounded from two seemingly opposite roots. This again is an anal-

Figure 93. The Great Seal

ogy to the Primal Atom or perfect material, created as the result of two seemingly opposite attributes. The root for light is *pho-,* while the name for night (the darkness) is *nix.* Nix was the goddess of the night, representing in the mythological scheme of the Greeks the *little power of darkening,* as in conjunction with Erebos her mate, who was the source of darkness (the Ignorance: Sanskrit—*Avidya*). Like the compounded Sanskrit term *guru,* taken from roots meaning light and darkness, the term *phoenix* (Greek. *phoinix*) was created to mean literally the "dispeller of darkness." The phoenix, like the soul, was associated by the ancients with the sun.

The phoenix is an important mythic symbol pervading the ancient world. While legends make the phoenix a venerable harbinger of divine light and wisdom of a divine nature, the bird is held to return to the world at specific intervals to be reborn and ascend again to heaven.

At the death of the aged bird, the ashes of the phoenix's bier nurture a small worm. This tiny, glowing creature contains in itself all the mystery and majesty of the phoenix. The worm, serpent, dragon, and phoenix all appear to be linked as successive stages of an ideal belief that the ordinary man and woman may transcend the lower worlds of matter, overcoming all to reign supreme in the principle of the Divine. In this, the phoenix gives way to another, higher form, that of the human being. All the time-honored world religions as well as the great schools of philosophy regard this ideal as the very core of their systems.

While the serpent and the dragon appear to be nearly the same thing, the second seems to be a development of the first in the understanding of acquired or accumulated *knowledge*. The English and European fairytale dragon is notoriously a collector of rare and wonderful items of wealth, power, and beauty, and lovely princesses seem to head the list of most precious collectibles, for such is the height of treasure-gathering in philosophic metaphor. In this, the phoenix represents all-knowledge and an erudition that transcends all, alleviating the gravity of worldly matters through light.

The phoenix, to paraphrase Pythagoras, is no less than truth clothed in living light, for the only thing higher than truth is actually living it outright. From earliest times, it has been the greatest aspiration of the world race to perfect the mind and body with a view toward releasing the soul into the highest mystery, that of the Word, the Thunder of the Throne becoming the Divine Light. The human body, whether male or female, has always been the true church, mosque, and temple of the living Spirit, and this before race, religion or social status.

Just as the serpent of full trappings, Quetzal-coatl, became a man to illuminate the needy and receptive of the ancient Aztec people, raising their culture to unknown heights, so it is that the

Figure 94. A Heraldry Phoenix
(Courtesy of Andrew Bomkamp)

Word *becomes a human being*. People learn from the example of others, not from inanimate objects or incorporeal spirits, real or imagined.

The Word of God became a man that you also may learn from a man how a man becomes (as) God.

—Clement of Alexandria

While there is little reference to the diet of the phoenix, philosophers will aver that it *acquires* the atmosphere of its environment, and that this process is far too subtle to be perceived by the human eye. It is also said that the phoenix constructs its nest of the resinous acacia. Is this not a reference to the sacred ark from which the hallowed *divine fire* burns, resurrecting the creature of matter to one of pure spirit?

The Great Magnetic Line

Britain's Alfred Watkins is said to have seen "in a flash" a pattern beneath England's countryside that hadn't been seen for thousands of years. Perhaps the two most spectacular ley lines[104] discovered in America are the *Great Magnetic Line* and its counterpart, the *Western Meridian*. The two have encouraged much speculation as to their coincidental true north alignments. The Western Meridian seems to link Phoenix, Arizona, to Helena, Montana, with Salt Lake City between, but this alignment (though indicative of true north and quite acceptable by some ley researchers) is not as interesting as the Great Magnetic Line.

Stretching from Florida's Tallahassee to the general vicinity of Sault Ste. Marie, this line is over 1,000 miles in length and passes through Atlanta, Lexington, Cincinnati, and Lansing. It has been dubbed the Great Magnetic Line because of its apparent true alignment from north to south.

Human beings are irresistibly moved as the result of past actions. The Masters of Spiritual Science teach emphatically that every individual, and humanity en masse, has a well-defined destiny in accord with what has been accomplished, good or bad. This great wisdom of cause and effect seemed the most logical as I pondered and pored over the map of the United States one morning, attempting to theorize an acceptable course of events that may have brought about the mysterious alignment of the cities. My mind would not entertain the idea of pure happenstance. Although Cincinnati had been a major center of ritual, was that also true for prehistoric Lansing, Atlanta, and Tallahassee's areas? Did a race of prehistory once have a single nation

The Great Magnetic Line

The Great Western Meridian

Figure 95. The Great Magnetic Line and the Great Western Meridian

extending from the Great Lakes to the Gulf of Mexico, the White Man simply building upon a miraculously straight line originally surveyed by an unknown, technically adept people?

Phoenix Resting

It was then, after putting attention into these surface city centers, that the vision began. It didn't just jump out in fullness leaving me breathless, but came in small flashes. First Michigan became animated, and the Great Lakes highlighted what seemed to be the head of a great eagle. As I continued to focus on the cities, the wings appeared to unfold, stretching eastward to blanket New England, and westward to cover Minnesota into the Dakotas. Then the entire Upper Peninsula of Michigan glowed like a crown plume.

It was as though I looked upon a most enlightened "overview" of half the United States and parts of Canada, a perception that made obvious certain features of the landscape that are easily passed over in the usual viewing. It was a multidimensional vision, gradually including aspects of a strangely well-ordered subterranean scheme. This underworld, as a foundation, gave substantiality to the surface manifestation of the great winged effigy. The vision was at once thrilling and frightening.

As a deeper focus slowly came, I looked past numerous underground aquifers, rivers, and waterways, and began to see countless miles of interconnected tunnels in an expansive pattern. Here, before my inner gaze, was a subsurface network of precisely created passageways linking together a great series of massive repositories. They were composed of small and large sepulcher-like rooms, too many to number. Some of these repositories had developed a connection with natural cave systems over the millennia, and this confounded my ability to discern them separately. Some of the chambers were large in height and breadth and, like the smaller rooms, accommodated objects and treasures of inexpressible value. From the impressions conveyed, the materials and things that were stored were of scientific, artistic, and religious significance. The design of many of these repositories was like a wagon wheel—though often there was no outer rim, just the extended "spokes." There were tunnels connecting the wheels. The effect was like a huge, underground clockworks, the repositories being its jeweled gears.

It was otherworldly as well, for while I was absorbed in this vision, an ominous accumulation the likeness of *mist* circulated like armies of guardian apparitions, filling the ancient halls. Words fail to describe the effect, but I knew that a great blockage and veiling was temporarily lifting, as if the hand of Moses had parted the sea of the subconscious world. It appeared that the entire landscape, above and below, had at its base an unbounded region of sacred burial, haunted by legions of ghostly spirits. Hidden in the necropolis' mystical fog was a legacy of transcendental wealth and resource, all suspended in activity, yet sustained by some force of life. There were pillared, mausoleum-like tombs of forgotten titans and gods from the earliest ages of the world, seemingly undisturbed, and carved right out of the Earth's deep rock layers. This aspect of the vision was foreboding and of an antiquity far beyond what I could hope to comprehend. It was a grand catacomb confederation of cryptic and monumental expression. It was clean and well-ordered, maintained by some overseeing authority responsible for the whole order of things. The experience of this vast underground sanctuary was intriguing and heavily laden with mysteries layered upon mysteries.

Access to this shadowy region was protected in its broad circumstance through a well-coordinated, supernatural, artificial "intelligence" using illusion and diversion to maintain its mind-boggling secret. There was interesting water management taking the form of movement and collection, waterfalls and pools, ponds and small, reservoir-like lakes throughout the expansive chambers, breaking the stillness of the sanctuary. The water was very pure: its pristine character created beauty spots and lovely sounds that successfully transformed the monotony of the gloom. There was a detectable light source there made known by the water's presence, but for the most part it was inactive due to its system's age or because it was powered down to a minimal expression for conservation. It seemed to come right out of the rock.

Conversely, there were ingenious booby traps and formidable "creatures," perhaps automatons, resembling goblin-reptiles, crawling, standing, and walking erect, wandering the halls and extremities of the netherworld in the more "sensitive" areas of each region and large repository. They made terrifying sounds intended to frighten away intruders. Failing this, they acted as watchdogs, protecting, with deadly force, the areas that *could not be violated* due to the importance of that being stored there. Most of these places were vaults, hermetically sealed, and locked.

The surface world of the United States, both in nature and its manmade aspect, seemed to be "modeled" after what was underground. The situation in the subterranean world to some degree dictated the way things were on the surface. I noticed that one of the largest repository systems to my view was located beneath the Smokies, but that other areas, such as Michigan and the Great Lakes, had more components contributing to the "big picture" over a larger region. Although I couldn't count them, I was given to know there were approximately 162 main multi-leveled repositories, going across and down the eastern U.S. and Canada, and numerous others between them. Nearly all these others were smaller and of the same era, created, as I was

given to understand, in a cooperative effort through private agencies, including families. Others were of a far older age. It was the longevity of these that in part inspired the creation of the relatively newer vaults. The network comprising the Phoenix effigy was part of a greater project begun some time prior to the finale of the last Ice Age. It was a part of a conservation and preservation project enacted by a world government of the time. It was my understanding that there were approximately 700 of these government-sponsored repositories worldwide. What was on the surface was removed and taken below. This work went on for a considerable number of centuries, a little at a time, until the last vestige of the world that knew the Phoenix no longer was visible.

The Great Magnetic Line clearly irrigated the entire representation of the Phoenix with life energy. The thought occurred that the Phoenix, rooted so far beneath the landscape, was virtually too difficult to see by any natural means save through the kind of experience I was being given. Yet there is a mysterious continuity to the legendary homelands of certain Native American nations, such as the Allegheny, the Adena, and the Hopewell, that is strategic to the surface likeness of this angelic representation of the Phoenix. In this I knew intuitively that the native people must have known something of this underground world, for the natural signs were perhaps more easily recognized before the White Man's hasty re-shaping of the landscape. Nevertheless, the surface changes made over the last two centuries were unwittingly influenced by the subtle forces beneath the landscape, the influence of what I term *the Phoenix resting.*

The power maintaining the shaping and energy of the whole *Tartaros*-like phenomenon originated from deep in the Earth herself. The impression was that it similarly serviced the entire globe—that there were representations or "seals," i.e., great works of extremely ancient scientific and artistic endeavor, all over the world similarly rendered inactive, taken below, stored efficiently, and protected for some future age. I was made to understand that the Phoenix, because of its symbolic nature, was to be the first to become re-activated to the surface worldview. Moreover, who would doubt the prophecy of the Phoenix rising?

A careful study of Native American religion, mythology, and current philosophy reveals an almost universal belief in one Great Spirit, often a Creator-spirit, and specific sacred sites, many of which have been lost. Once, before the White Man came, these sites featured natural beauty spots often coupled with energetic and spiritual forces, and the dead were honored through having their final resting places there. But even as we have forgotten what we are in spirit because of the demands of the materially perceived world, have we not lost also our connection to the last remaining gathering places of the ancient Earth-oriented spirit? I believe there is a direct correlation between lost spirituality and lost par-

adise. Like the knowledge of the soul, these sites are so important that they must be preserved. Fortunately, concerned groups are exercising political and educational channels with steady success.

As a direct result of this visionary experience, I strongly feel that the Serpent Mound is among the most important of sacred sites, for in my vision the Ohio and Miami Valleys were literally the *heartland* of a grand eagle—the "nest" of the proverbial Phoenix. As the vision of the Great Thunderbird[105] gradually receded, all its energies seemed to find their focus in southern *Ohio,* the Native American term for "beautiful river," named by the ancient Mengwe People (later Iroquois) according to the legends.[106] Suddenly, the reason for the greatest concentration of the Hopewell prehistoric earthwork design being located in Ohio was intuitively understood. Then, as I looked on, the whole energy of the vision fell wholly into the Great Serpent, central among all those ancient earthen treasures. I realized that the Serpent Mound *was intended to be perceived* as the glowing remnant of the Phoenix.

In Search of the Alphabet of the Gods

The Power of the Word

(Author's Introduction)

When the first edition of this book was released in 1993, it was important to me to deliver the understanding of Serpent Mound's connection to the Pythagorean College. In that way, the understanding of the source of the first alphabet would be an easier connection to make. What seemed difficult to express is that this serpent effigy is an empirical embodiment of not only the source of the first formal word of man, but that of *Logos* from the time before its conversion to the spoken word. The main stumbling block has been historical evidence for the Pythagorean School being fully responsible for the first alphabet. In fact, the whole notion seemed outrageous and incredulous, but for the uncanny correlation between the numbers, the geometry, the astronomy, and the coiling Serpent's body.

Each geometric form reviewed in this work, as well as the body of geo-astronomy, has gone into this final presentation. There is nothing extra, and all has been presented for the reason underscoring this concluding section, i.e., to prove the Great Serpent's use in the creation of the original alphabet of the Greeks. Even the tree of life, derived from the square of eight and validated by the hexagon, is a part of the alphabetical science, for the majuscule *psi* depends wholly upon it. And while the serpent is mainly responsible for the various minuscule forms, the positioning of the geometries is standardized to view these symbols correctly. This is another reason why this book is best read from cover to cover.

The origins of all modern alphabets are not hard to trace by scholarship, for they were formed long after the scripts, picture forms, and hieroglyphic forms stemming from different ancient cultures—most all of which were situated in the Mediterranean basin. The first numerically fixed alphabetical collection is essentially held to be a Greek invention (hence the term *alpha-bet* from the letters alpha and beta), based upon a Canaanite (Phoenician) form of North Semitic script. The Greeks themselves had been writing for centuries prior to that time, and this is evidenced in the second millennium B.C.E. syllabary[107] found in places such as Crete and Mycenae. This first fixed, numerically oriented system appeared around the time of the middle of the first millennium, B.C.E., and the questions raised by scholarship are concerned with what connection the earlier Greek writing had with the invention of this alphabet. The last portion, especially including the symbols for phi, chi, and psi, are not traceable to any Phoenician or Semitic source, lending insight into the creative workings of the Greek genius.

The "collection of letters" was designed to tell the story of the transformation of a spiritual quest, and to do it in a unique and practical way. The brilliance of the Pythagorean School, so typical of the Greek genius in those exciting and extraordinary days of the first millennium B.C.E., somehow knew of the Great Serpent as the centerpiece of an ancient scheme of science, art, and religious experience. **In fact, the various symbols**

of this Greek alphabet, properly interpreted, modified, and placed, will form a picture of what we are familiar with as the Great Serpent Mound, probably known to the Greeks as *Python.* As an enduring mythological symbol, our Great Serpent was intended as the starting point of a future work for the human race in the slow reclaiming of our spiritual legacy and its gradual return to the fountainhead of truly cosmopolitan existence.

By some irresistible effect of karmic law (the law of cause and effect, action and reaction), this spiritual legacy was segmented long ago, transformed into so many individual symbols, developed on this separate basis in different climes and times, and then reassembled, stronger than ever. It was like a great water source, first evaporating, then raining many drops, and then recollecting purer and more robust than before. This is the way of a certain aspect of karmic law—especially when the subject, in this case the Great Serpent, is intelligently conceived in the first place.

Thus, to restate, the Great Serpent's design is seen foremost as the Logos, Word, Aum, Sabda, Mazda, and a thousand other titles, each attempting to indicate what is essentially not enunciated. It is the Primeval One, the holy instrument of the Invisible Creator and was intended to be witnessed—not worshipped—as such.

I

There are few things that can stimulate the imagination like a good mystery. While we reach out and explore the solar system with a view to the future, there remain many questions unanswered concerning our past. In our enthusiasm to explore the external world and gather the riches of nature, we have nearly forgotten the vast reaches of the inner cosmos. In this, we have lost sight of both our heritage and inheritance of

mysticism and philosophy in their most pure and essential forms.

Though we have made strides on the road toward improving our historical plight of warfare upon one another, we are reminded each day that much needs to be accomplished before a lasting peace *with harmony* may be established worldwide. Then there are the problems of controlling disease, feeding the hungry, and of course preventing a great environmental Armageddon.

Historically, the wisest of our world leaders have been those men and women who held a balanced education as the best means for preparing an individual for what the world may have in store. Due to a misplacement of this superior philosophy, the world exemplar called Western Civilization has produced a mighty business empire complemented by an astounding array of professional sports. While impressive and appealing to the external sense, this "empire" leaves us weak and vulnerable in the areas of internal development such as basic and advanced literacy, explaining why we have fewer poets laureate in a century than Olympic gold medallists every four years. So in attempting to prepare our children for what the *world* may have in store, we forget about what the *Spirit* may have waiting. Though as a populace we have almost forgotten, the study of language and its essence as expressed in poetry serves to culture the most delicate and subtle tissues of the mind which connect to the spiritual entity called *soul*. Without this process of consciously connecting ourselves to the divine nature or source *within*, the human spirit falls beneath the feet of external interests, blanketed into unconsciousness by the machinations of the mind. The soul literally becomes a prisoner. It is by means of a fully conscious spirit that the world dominated by mental impressions, pursuits, and pleasures may begin to reorganize itself to an integrated state, with all goals in direct harmony with the magnanimous ideals of Godly wisdom.

In the high tradition of the East, where all religions had their start, the *Word* is presented as having two distinct aspects: the inner and the outer. The internal Word is not very well known in the West. It is seen as the Unifying Principle in the Spiritual Science, that which (in Western terminology) would link physics to metaphysics. While Western science has very astutely discerned four forces at work in the known universe (the *weak* and the *strong* [which bind molecules and atomic nuclei, respectively], *electromagnetic* force and the force of *gravity*), the Spiritual Science apparently mastered the Atom long ago, qualifying it beneath the holy Sound Principle.

The difficulty with turning one's attention within to catch the philosophical Word or Music of the Spheres was well understood by the Masters, even those of ancient times. Their solution did not begin with physics anymore than the contents of a good book may be wholly discerned by studying its cover. Numbers, geometry, music, and the spoken word served to culture the initiate's mental make-up. Once these disciplines were satisfied, the neophyte was given the keys to the ascetic science, learning to clear and control the mind with a view toward a perfect submission and attunement to the Word—the Logos or Voice of the Divine. This Word or Sound Principle owns a supreme authority in all human affairs, and in fact has the distinguished honor of being at the core of each and every major world religion—for each has a different name or names referring to It. The Hindu religion calls it *Bani* or *Nad;* the Buddhist *Transcendental Sound;* the Jain *Maha Mantra;* the Zoroastrian *Sraosha;* Islam *Kalma;* the Sikh *Naam;* and the Jewish tradition *Word.* It has often been emphasized that the Sound Principle is the one unifying factor of all things, serving to open the door to all higher spiritual experience.

II

It was the creation and discerning application of a very carefully conceived system of writing that definitively marked the difference between not only what we term historic and prehistoric, but the differentiation of intellect into the material and the spiritual. Committing the word to written symbols opens new portals of communication, allowing ideas, as events, to be accurately recorded. Since everything from dinosaurs to the pre-dynastic Egyptian Nile culture occurred prior to any evidence of intelligible, organized record-keeping in the Western view, all has been labeled *pre*historic. North American *pre*history is considered to run right to the time of the first literate Caucasian explorers. *History,* from the early Spanish, French, English, German, and Dutch point of view, communicates understanding, culture, and even wisdom through the accumulation of proper records over time. The much earlier Greeks considered history to be one of the cardinal cultural virtues, attributing it to one of the loveliest of the divinities, the muse Kleio.

With the advent of writing under the inspiration of the wise and beautiful muse, language flourished, and poetry was developed. Similarly, the later Jewish rabbinical culture, taking God as its inspiration, conceived an alphabetical system which, like the Greeks before them, assigned numerical value to each symbol. In this, they were able to assign certain value to key words, phrases, and sentences in their mystical tongue corresponding to classical axioms of arithmetic, geometry, and measure. The initiate scholarship of the Greeks and Jews added a new dimension to the written and spoken word, qualifying it with the divine archetypes of their spiritual cosmology.

An exquisite science requiring deep thought and inner revelation accompanied the composition of scripture and philosophic treatises. This science was conceived to the end of harmonizing the thoughts and utterances of the literate with the spiritual aspect of the human being. Although it is not apparent to some linguists, the scribing of numerical symbology occurred in the highest cultures simultaneously with that of alphabet. Numbers and letters were one and the same. To the Wise, the two were intimately a part of each other just as the elements of the periodic table are automatically associated with their numbers by a good scientist. Merely because we presently do not form our words and phrases through the harmonic blend of poetic tone in combination with number does not make the much-neglected science a fatuous pursuit fit only for eccentric scholars. Certainly the composition of scripture has proven the value of the art, and this in spite of reorganization and its evil companion *interpolation,* committed by collectors and inheritors of earlier texts and fragments.

Unfortunately, there are a few in the ranks of modern scholarship who would agree upon the term "pseudo science" to describe the Jewish *gematria* (from the Greek gaiametria, *geometria:* symbol-number correspondence having its basis in classical geometry). However, prior to the ludicrous overemphasis placed upon the Revelation's *666,* a number having its origin in the magic-square aspect of the sacred science, the symbol-number pairing of Greeks and Jews was not generally perceived by scholarly critics as bordering on the ridiculous. In fact, a most serious college of philosophical science had established a logical order to the perfection of language, making it possible to express and successfully convey the highest concepts of truth through speech.

In the Western way of considering things, a science is based upon data gathered through investigation and experimentation, its repute and verity depending upon its proof being observable in successfully repeating the experiment in the appropriate laboratory. In a very similar sense, the gaiametric science was discovered and developed through the pure logic of elemental form, not contrived, fabricated, and manufactured by an elite group of linguistic wizards. In the same way that Western civilization has mistaken poetry for dollar signs and field-goals, so we have become unaware of the sublime science linking the material world to the realm of spirituality. There indeed is a science to the Word, both within and without, but it has become as inaccessible as a rose in the dead of winter to one who does not believe in florists.

The real crux of any argument is not whether there is some practical science in the gaiametric art, but do the words and phrases conceived actually possess some inherent potency which affects the listener in the desired way?

The answer to this question was well understood to the advocates of the science-art but relies upon the philosophical background of the interpreter. **Alpha**, for example, the first symbol, is also the primary vowel. **Beta** is the mean of the mutes. **Gamma** is the basic velar. **Delta**, the fourth symbol, is the classic dental. Following in a prescribed and deliberate fashion, the alphabet was conceived by means of subtleties in rule and enunciation coupled with numerical value that might cause modern linguists to fail in comprehension were *they* given the task of creating a system linking the tongue of men with that of angels.

The view that some Egyptian hieroglyphics influenced the Semitic symbols opens the door to the notion of the ancient Sky Serpent having been the source of most all cultural inspiration. After all, it was at the very center of the heavenly dome at that time—at the very dawn of history as we understand it. By logic, the natural law of cause-and-effect would dictate the gradual re-assembly of a system of excellence as inevitable as last summer's seeds germinating in fertile ground after the cold months. Pythagoras may very well have inherited not only the image of the Great Serpent, but also the understanding of the use of its various parts for the recreational work of both astronomy and geometry. The society of the Pythagoreans likely went through much thought, and trial and error. Each of the seven sacred coils would have a number, and each would subsequently become a numeric-letter symbol. Further, certain parts of the head or neck would be used to indicate the area from which man would utter a certain sound—nasal, dental, guttural, etc. Thus while an objective viewpoint would not accept the Great Serpent as a monument created to bridge the difference between the celestial *Word* and the terrestrial spoken word, a subjective analysis might provide substance for a sound counter-argument. The solar Phoebos-Apollo slew the starry Serpent (even as the dawn dispels the night) so that its heavenly Logos would be made available to men.

To reiterate, it is the contention of this last part of the book that the alphabet we familiarly refer to as *Greek* has at its roots the direct influence of the Serpent as template. This is in light of the earthwork's associated geometric, astronomic, and mathematical interests. But as I hope I have intimated, the structure serves to embody and present information yet more profound: an embodiment of the spoken and written word in the form of a remarkable cyclopean creature linking the human race to the esoteric Sound Principle, the *Word of God*.

III

As discovered earlier, the designer of the Great Serpent utilized the conjunction of the twin circles, Force and Feeling, to serve as matrix for the creature, which in turn represents the Principle of Vibration, the Word of Spirit. At the same time, the vesica signifies *delphos,* the womb of Gaia, i.e., the place of conception and life for the oracular mysteries. In this sense, the Serpent also is the umbilical cord, and the *omphalos* (the navel of the world mother) is the umbilicus (the hollow oval feature). In this analogy, the Serpent is the symbol serving as intermediary between heaven and earth, mother and child, and finally the celestial Logos translating to the terrestrial word.

In order to present this abstract Sound Principle—audible as an actual musical sound to the inner ear of the initiate into the Mysteries—the creator of the Serpent image carefully included the creature in not only the area common to the two circles, but in four additional classic backgrounds. One of these, the *Delphi Circle,* was subdivided to form the sacred *Arbelos.* These include the Pythagorean Theorem, the Sacred Cut, the Solar Hexagon, and the Delphinian Circle. These five primary illustrations are analogous to the lofty concept of the *five electricties* or *Pancha Tattwa (Panch Sabda),* manifesting their lowest aspect as the currents serving the five senses. The Revelation to John refers to them as four-and-one angels, as recounted below.

Over the centuries, certain parts of the Tradition have been developed separately from the body of the Spiritual Science, and they have become integral aspects of organized social religious ritual. The mystical practice of remembrance (sweet remembrance) is considered to be the saying of the Rosary by the Christian, or the recitation of prayer with fingers running over beads by the Muslim, serving the purpose of preparing the votary for deep reverie or meditation. It is also the practice of *mantra,* familiar in India as repetition of the charged names of God *(Simran).* As a mental exercise, the words or phrases are uttered with the "tongue of thought" only. This charges the mental state of the initiate with subtle electricity so the mind does not wander or interfere in periods of deep devotion and concentration. The practice requires sufficient time for the attention to fully concentrate at the seat of the soul, the sensorium. Once it is fixed there at the place behind and between the two eyes, the worshipper may have firsthand experience of the Divine, often taking the radiant form of the Son, subsequently leading to higher stages of Spirituality.

In the spirit of sacred analogy, these five illustrations represent a summary knowledge regarding the essential expressions of the Holy Sound Principle in the Creation. While the Serpent image seems to the new student an unlikely (or even improper) vehicle to carry these signs, it is in fact the form selected after considerable thought and labor. It is the medium of philosophical worth used to bridge the intellectual gap of understanding between the spiritual realm of unalloyed vibration and the material world utilizing matter in various forms to produce sound. One could hypothesize that when the constellation Draco occupied the highest area in the heavenly dome, this wisdom was possibly at the core of a singular world religion.

It is the loss of the sacred symbolism of the Serpent image in Western culture that has made this understanding seem so abstract or "foreign." This coupled with a lack of guidance on the mystical, inner path of Spiritual Science has put Western scholarship at odds with enlightened Eastern thought. Virtually all masters of the various spiritual sciences, including the yogas, have taken embodiment in the Mediterranean area and the Indian subcontinent, including Tibet, for as my own Master has stated, the people of those cultures require it. However, definite strides have been made in this century to remedy the sad isolation of Western culture from its Eastern counterparts, a first and much-needed step in bringing more and more enlightened souls to the West and even Western embodiment.

The human form, said by the Great Saints and Sages to have been made in the image of both Creator and Creation, subsequently has certain vocal capacities that collectively put forth the components of the Universal Logos in the form of song and speech. While there is a distinct difference between internal and external hearing regarding the spirituality of the soul— the spoken word was intended from the beginning to interpret (as in translation) the inner Word.

Even if the human race owned but a single, unifying language, that language would be incapable of imparting any more than the wisdom of the Spiritual life and the instructions for walking the ethical, moral and practical Spiritual Path—that of discipleship. It is the Word of *God,* say the Masters of Spiritual Science, that imparts the soul to the body, nurtures it therein, finally aiding in its departure at the time of physical death. It is this Word that effects a literal *rapture* of the individual soul in its spiritual journey upward and is ultimately the most sacred revelation. In the Western Christian culture, the Word of God is almost exclusively printed out, a most limiting measure on the Infinite!

The *Word* is carried as the conscious essence of the Son in his descent from the region of Pure Spirit for the purpose of spiritualizing the Atom, *Chitta.* In this, the Son and the One God (seated on the throne) are as one. To simplify, any of the protonic atoms within the vast Universe are not unlike the *essential* soul (the Heart) of a human creature, the difference being the *inhabiting* of the atom by the Spiritual Essence, quickening it, transforming it to the Atom (the Heart).

The reader should know that there are three distinct aspects of the Word. One of these is the vocal, while the other two govern natural and Spiritual law. One of these later aspects is first described as one of the *four ideas,* mentioned in "The Serpent as Universal Template," under the heading of "The Hexagon." This aspect of the Word is bound up in the material universe, sustaining the countless atoms. In this, the Word may be considered as the *strong force* of physics, with the *weak force* being its complementary polarity, sustaining the matrices of the molecules. These weak and strong (duality) aspects of the Word or Vibratory Principle preclude the material atoms from becoming the abode of the Son. Thus the other noted aspect of the Word governs the supernal worlds, as is the true Logos: the omnipotent power of unalloyed Spirit. In this, it sustains the Atom (Causal Man) with its four ideas. This Grand Word is, in reality, the scriptural *First* and *Last.*

The College of the Mysteries knew the difficulty of imparting this knowledge of the two Words (not to mention the spoken word), and thus they called the lesser *Omicron* and the greater *Omega. Mikro-* means "small," and with the suffix *–on.* Omega means "greater O," (Om) the Word of unalloyed Spirit. Once the Atom has been conceived, an influx of Spirit improves, unfolds, and enlivens its potential, like fresh warm water awakening a tight seed. The Omega Word, transforming the atom to the Atom, describes the descent of the Son into the atomic matrix.

God shaped man from the soil of the ground and blew the breath of life into his nostrils, and man became a living being.
Genesis 2:7

The Word of God is the Holy Breath. The great Adepts of Spiritual Science describe the *Power of the Word* as That which reverberates in the Universal Creation amidst all the atoms and their molecules. Its influence also extends beyond the Creation of Illusion (based as it is upon the four ideas) into the Spiritual Planes, which Christ spoke of as heaven or the Father. Surely Christ was not alone in this pronouncement.

IV

When a strong electrical charge is inadvertently contacted, a person or animal becomes temporarily suspended in general activity, or rather, magnetized and made to conform to the passage of the current. The elusive concept of the Will of God has been likened to electrical force, and in the classical myths, thunderbolts become a metaphor of Zeus' will. Similarly, the use of intensive, prescribed prayer or sweet repetition of sacred names, phrases, etc., tends to gradually suspend, quiet, and ultimately subdue the thinking and wandering mind with a view toward reacquiring full possession of one's soul. The mind was specifically placed in tandem with the conscious entity or soul in the creation of the human body in order to perfectly handicap the spiritual entity, which, under less confining circumstances, would rise and easily reintegrate back into the Spirit or Oversoul.

Thus the human form is said to be the highest gift awarded by God, for with it, all negativity may be confronted and overcome. Hence the words spoken by Christ and others concerning Satan are put in perspective, i.e., gain control over yourself.

So it is the initiate or disciple of the Master is given the names or phrases or prayers to keep sacred and use constantly in remembrance of the Spirit. The five currents, invoked through such devoted practice, charge the mind with calm and stillness, rendering it devoid of mischief while proceeding to bestow greater light and spiritual awareness to the awakening soul, the conscious entity. The Revelation to John describes these currents as four-and-one angels who, holding the four winds of Earth, maintain control over this external creation with its three dimensions of height, width, and depth, i.e., the ordinary atom:

Next I saw four angels standing at the four corners of the Earth, holding back the four winds of the world to keep them from blowing over the land or the sea or any tree.[108]

Then I saw another angel rising where the sun rises, carrying the seal of the living God; he called in a powerful voice to the four angels whose duty was to devastate land and sea,

Wait before you do any damage on land or at sea or to any trees, until we have put the seal on the foreheads of the servants of our God ...

Revelation 7:1–3

The initiates, inferred to be the servants of God, are asked to fix their attention at the seat of the soul, the sensorium, located between and behind the two eyes. The attention, say the Saints, is the foremost expression of the soul. Where one's attention goes and concentrates, whether upon an external object or on the internal principle of the Sound Current, the individual becomes what he or she meditates upon. We go where our attention goes; we become what our attention rests, fixes, and meditates upon.

The "four angels" refer to the root understanding of the four ideas as they are transformed to the four currents after their establishing the ordinary atom. The fifth angel, wisely introduced in a separate paragraph, commands the other four. To repeat, these first four are no less than the inseparable constitution of the illusory atom called *Avidya* (the Ignorance) due to its quality of repulsion—the condition of the illusory world, Maya.

The fifth angel is therefore the Power of Omega, the greatness of the Word, the Grand Word. Literally dictating to the other four angels not to bring chaos into play (the active power of the mind), this angel becomes the commanding fifth of the five electricities, subsequently fully characterizing the seed mind *(Chitta),* maintaining control over it. This seed mind is the Heart and is often considered the *psyche* or soul as it is in its most pure form existing as a denizen of the material regions. The initiate then learns to hold a rein over the seed mind through constant remembrance of God in direct conjunction with the audible Sound Current emanating from above in the Spiritual Region. The Omega Word is the true source of life and power, by grace tapped into for irrigation of the entire mental faculty to permanently calm and subdue the mind.

The Word alone may be contemplated for longer and longer periods. Through this, the initiate and devotee is made eligible for higher insights and perception beyond the blanketing, limiting nature of the Ignorance, the ordinary atom, in the enlivening of the *self* or Atom-extra-ordinary.

The Son of God[109] carries the Feeling and Force of the fifth angel[110] and is commissioned to competently instruct the other souls,[111] who are called *jiva,*[112] into the correct method of securing a place above the Creation of Darkness, *Maya,*[113] the abode of Satan.

This describes the power of what has come to be called *Christos* or Christ, properly introducing the student to the formal study of the Mysteries and the direct connection of the anointed Messiah[114] on the Earth.

V

It has been said that the wholesale obliteration of the Alexandrian Library, a center of philosophical study located in Egypt, was among the greatest of political blunders in the known history of the world. Even today there are attempts made to literally burn books that appear to detract from a given faction's beliefs. Such radical groups think that they have patently isolated the very essence of their philosophical system and, with a clear view of the future, safely destroy all that is impertinent. Such a fool's mission is comparable to doing away with the rooster and hen once an egg has been fertilized and laid. Now what have we lost in the frenzy of the early Christian zealots?

The roots of *sound* philosophy, be it religiously oriented or directed to the enhancement of science and its art, are like the roots of a mature tree. Even if the tree does not please the eye, detracting from the practical beauty of its fruit, to destroy the tree will mean having no fruit until another tree matures. The very wise have always encouraged us not to break ties with our past.

In the account of Nicodemus before the powerful Pharisees (John 7:51), Nicodemus says that the Law entitles anyone to a hearing and the proper procedure to discover what he is really doing, not prejudicial treatment. It is out of such human prejudice that both history and mythology have been passed down to us altered, enhanced, detracted from, and interpolated in accord with the prerogative of the ones entrusted with the task. In ancient Egypt, for example, when one king or pharaoh would succeed another with whom he did not agree politically, all evidence of that previous leader would be systematically erased from the stone and papyrus of the land. Ikhnaton the reformer was overruled in this manner. A more sweeping example would be the orthodox histories of our main world religions: their exponents would have the faithful believe that the accounts of their founders and messiahs to be truth unblemished, the factor of need has altered such historical accounts to the status of exquisite myth and allegory. Perhaps it required Buddha considerably longer than seven years to achieve illumination. It may have been that the events of Krishna's life were more internally than externally oriented. It may well have been that Mohammed, having knowledge of the true Word, was reluctant to ever do anything in violence. Was there a *crucified* Jesus or is it a story that is used to emotionally pressure us into acceptance of something that would, by nature, take considerably longer than a single lifetime to properly comprehend?

In the same understanding, the classical myths were not conceived in their present charming form but were probably derived largely from ancient legends—events of remote eras carrying with them axiomatic truths of philosophic import. Intended for preservation in some literally suitable vehicle, the classical myths of Greece and Rome reveal the subtle hand of philosophically astute mythographers.

Probably the foremost example of the knowledge possessed by these adepts of myth (without understating the value of Hesiod's *Theogeny*) is the story of the finding of the first Oracle of Apollo. The acquisition of the sacred site from divine sources (family), the slaying of the giant serpent, and the subsequent dismemberment and depositing[115] of the corpse down a certain shaft in the earth all combine as key elements of events describing the gift of the interpretive

Word to mortalkind. The slow, sweet-smelling smoke that was the essence of the Python intoxicated the Pythia on her golden tripod, enhancing her abilities to deliver insightful oracles. All considered, the mythology contains the crucial ingredients in a perfectly linear series of moments enabling the translation of the Word into words.

Analogous to the Son descended from the heavenly abode or Prometheus giving fire to humankind, Phoebos-Apollo descended from the heights of Olympus in order to bestow the True Word upon humanity. While the mythologem of Apollo and Python was better suited to a distant age, there are a number of parallels to the story of Christ and other Spiritual Masters or great prophets contained. Apollo, not unlike Pythagoras and others who would follow, was primarily concerned with establishing the Word in the form of speaking and writing, ultimately to initiate people into the mysteries of the unspoken and unwritten Tongue, the Word of God.

VI

It has been widely assumed that the Semitic culture contributed much of the material adopted by the Greeks in their scribing. However, bearing in mind that the Greeks *invented the alphabet,* it may be prudent to suggest that their facility with Semitic symbolism surpassed that of the Semitic culture itself.[116]

Fortunately, archaeology and scholarship have exercised remarkable open-mindedness in the centuries-long effort to discover the origins of alphabetical systems. Even when researchers aver that *aleph* (ox), *beth* (house), *gimel* (camel), and *daleth* (door) gave rise to the Greek *alpha, beta, gamma,* and *delta,* a curious reverence or belief that the Greek system embodies a sublime originality is intuitively understood. The Semitic meanings do not apply to the Greek let-

ters. So when the scripture says, "I am the Alpha," it surely was never meant to construe God as an *ox* (Semitic: *eleph*). Thus the Greeks seemed to have worked up something that was full of promise to a perfect status, like refining gasoline from crude oil: both burn, and although crude is natural, its refinement is an exponential improvement. This is why it is said the Greeks invented the alphabet, for their system embodied the letters as a single entity, as though they had rediscovered the lost secret of how the jumbled symbols inherited from the Semitic scribes were arranged.

Likely undertaken by the Pythagoreans, the refinement of the Word from Semitic and eclectic design enabled the Greeks to *reconstruct* the true system of alphabetic communication, a literal resource of writing and speaking that unexpectedly may have been kept preserved in its original form on the North American continent. To bring home the theory that the Greeks knew more about the origins of Semitic symbolism than the Jewish scribes, a discussion of the alpha symbol's spelling and *numerical value* is of interest (see "The Alpha Symbol"). Explaining the transference of the Spiritual Sound Principle into the material world, alpha, the first letter of the system, is unique geometrically. Instead of animals and objects being represented by the symbols (letters), the gifted Pythagorean Greeks likely explained the symbols through the body of the Serpent and the geometries associated with it. With kindergarten flashcards we see an *a*pple, a *b*ear, a *c*at, and a *d*og to help in memorizing. The Pythagoreans, while dismissed as fanatics even today by some, were not of a preschool disposition. The Semitic system was at best an insight to higher understanding for them.

Further, the spellings of certain key symbols, viz. *beta* through *iota,* are assumed altered by later schools of inheritance with the result that the numerical values do not reduce to those ascribed to the symbol's number. Alpha, valued at 1, reduces correctly, as demonstrated below. It does not require much explanation to show *how* the letter spellings were changed; the *why,* however, is likely wrapped up in either the secrecy of the alphabetical science or the political implications surrounding the life and death of Pythagoras. In every case (as shown), the spelling of these primary symbols was intended to reduce perfectly, lending excellent evidence for not only the enlightened thought going into the system, but the Great Serpent serving as the host-subject for the alphabet. It should always be remembered that this metaphorical Serpent was evidently a successful effort to derive the mundane word from the Logos or Divine Word. The initiates alone were privy to this sacred Word, heard within, and passed on from a Master of the Science.

Working hand-in-glove with archaeologists, language experts have set up and broken down any number of theories with a view toward establishing a definite reasoning behind the uniform alphabet introduced by the Greeks at about the middle of the first millennium B.C.E. What Spiritual Science finds objectionable is the almost strictly external approach used today to gather information to form conclusions on this subject. The esoteric philosophical studies should not be considered taboo, as though they could affect one with a credibility-disabling infectious disease. Herein is the difference between the academic and philosophic approach to archaeology. The academic training was always intended as a discipline to reach the greater and broader wisdom that sound natural philosophy has to offer. But now academia has become a fixed and permanent "school" unto itself, and only those who are serendipitously favored to reach beyond academia's self-set limits will be able to "enlighten" the receptive populace.

VII

Who constructed the Great Serpent Mound? Was it the Allegheny, the Adena, the Hopewell, the Mississippian "Fort Ancient" culture, or was it another culture entirely? It is like no other earthwork in existence, and surely it would have been considered a sacred sign and relic to any Native American culture happening to inherit it. Even the White Man, bent on uncovering or destroying anything in his path of greed (which he termed *progress),* could not consent to the obliteration of such a unique treasure. For in truth, the Great Serpent Mound is the great and mysterious **Thesaurus** (implying *theo-*"god" plus *sauro-* "lizard," i.e., the Great Serpent). Literally translated as "treasure house," *thesaurus* is a literary reminder of the wealth inherently a part of the dragon's lair.

Although someone may come up with a better theory of how well the Greek symbols adapt to the astronomically oriented coils, geometries, and measures of our ancient dragon who touches the solar umbilicus, one thing is quite clear: The so-called "Adena" and subsequent cultures were drawn, perhaps through an irresistible effect of their own distant past, to the site of what was intended as a *grand marker* and omniscient *signature,* having no likeness anywhere in the prehistoric world.

Even as the White Man found his way to the future metropolitan centers of the Magnetic Line without knowing their straight north alignment, so the Serpent Mound area may have drawn and inspired these ancient native people—even as the beginning of wisdom and the rekindling of faith.

ΑΑα	Ββϐ	Γγ	Δδ	Εϵ	Ζϛ	Ηη	Θθ
1	2	3	4	5	7	8	9
Ιι	ΚΚϰ	Λλ	Μμ	Νν	Ξξ	Οο	Ππ
10	20	30	40	50	60	70	80
Ρϱ	Σσς	Ττ	Υυ	Φϕϖ	Χχ	Ψψ	Ωω
100	200	300	400	500	600	700	800

I am the Alpha and Omega, says the Lord God, who is, who was, and who is to come, the Almighty.

Revelation 1:8

Do not be afraid, it is I, the First and the Last; I am the Living One …

Revelation 1:17

Those who prove victorious I will feed from the tree of life set in God's paradise

Revelation 2:7

To the One seated on the throne and to the Lamb, be all praise, honour, glory and power, for ever and ever.

Revelation 5:13

There is no practical reason to fear this Serpent. Join please with the greatest of dragon-slayers from before the dawn of history and dismember on the cutting table of acute intellectual discernment the mysterious fruit-eating serpent of *Yahweh.* Penetrate to the very core of this

Figure 96. The Greek Alphabet

The 24 letters of the classical Greek alphabet influenced Western writing more than is generally understood. Under each is its numerical value by which the writings of the New Testament are discerned by esoteric scholars. Three symbols are not included in this grouping, falling out of use some time ago, supposedly for practical or sacred considerations. They are *digamma,* valued at six, *episemon bau,* valued at 90, and *sanpi,* valued at 900. There may be other symbols which were once used for purposes no longer comprehended, symbols which may one day be reintroduced with a view toward ever improving the human ability to communicate even the most spiritually sophisticated concepts of religion, science, art, and philosophy.

The majority of the symbols are derived from the Athenian and Samian renditions, with samplings of other scripts included as the need arose to produce a complete picture.

mystery and learn the disciplines of the Spiritual College, the secrets of the wordsmiths, and the wisdom of the prophets of all faiths. For the Great Serpent is none other than the Word of the one God of the ancients.

The Symbolism of the Serpent: Alpha through Omega

The Alpha Symbol

A S THE FIRST SYMBOL OF THE *alpha*BET, ALPHA HAS long stood for the first, the primary, and even the best. Perhaps the most frequently used vowel sound, the short *a* is an important means of expression. Actually, the other short vowels, e, i, o, and u, are the fundamental *ah* sound with variations of jaw, throat, and tongue added. To open everything and simply voice a sound reveals alpha. This apparently is what alpha is intended to mean—the primary sound vibration.

The alpha symbol may have originally been considered as the small triangular feature at the head end of the Serpent, representing the in-flowing gate of energetic forces enlivening the creature. This idea probably will stand the test of time. It is at the beginning of the creature, and so logically it was chosen to represent the primal vowel. Similarly, the tail of the creature, opening or uncoiling, may have been the original inspiration underscoring the majuscule omega symbol, opened at its base (see "The Omega Symbol").

However, since both the delta and lambda majuscule forms also find an affinity with the area of the small triangular mound (both representing important dentals), and because the tail is used to represent the minuscule rho, both the alpha and omega majuscules may have been given special consideration. The alpha is at times represented as narrower than the lambda. Thus

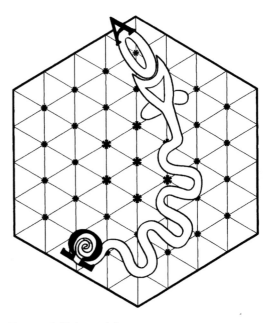

Figure 97. Alpha and Omega

The hallowed Alpha and Omega, the First and the Last, are associated with the beginning and end of the Great Serpent.

an encompassing and vital geometry was likely selected, to be used only once to bring home its importance: the vesica piscis. Since the alpha is the First Principle of Vibration that the Serpent in essence represents, it is one of the symbols that does not directly employ any part of the sacred creature to express itself. Because the vesica promotes the entire Serpent, it was a logical choice.

— 153 —

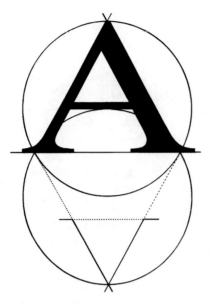

Figure 98. Alpha

The spelling of the term "alpha" uses lambda and phi to explain its unique function. *Ah* enters into *1* as a liquid medium, not unlike the way life is transferred by means of seminal fluid, preserved and developed in the amniotic fluid. Lambda then translates this vibration into *phi,* key to the progression of growth in the material world. This is subsequently transformed into alpha again at the end of the term. Thus the Primal Utterance is brought from the uncreated state through the gate of the material world, externalizing the Spiritual Power.

Αλφα   **Figure 99. Constructing the Miniscule Alpha**

α   The minuscule alpha is phonetically rep-
        resented as a minuscule omicron with a
Ο + ι   minuscule iota crowding on the right. The
        difference is almost unnoticeable save for
studying it, and clearly shows the delicate effort put into this system. When enunciating a long *o* into a long *i,* a short *a* is heard as the two vowels blend. This is perhaps the best vowel combination which this occurs so demonstrably.

Alpha equals 1 (a) + 30 (1) + 500 (ph) + 1 (a), therefore equaling 532. Subsequently, 532 is 5 + 3 + 2 or 10; and consequently 1.

The Beta Symbol

Comprising the last syllable of the term alpha-*bet,* beta arrives with inferred power or strength. Being non-aspirated, and instead one of the muted consonants, beta prepares the way for any vowel's effective voicing if it goes before, silencing the vowel if it appears after.

As shown in Figure 100, the Serpent is turned over on itself using the hexagonal matrix. Ceremonially doubling the subject, we see that the second coil from the head of both forms the twin characteristic loops of the letter, while the vertical line of the hexagon serves as the backbone for the symbol. The use of the twin Serpent form is not to imply that there are now two Serpents, but only to convey the idea of beta representing the number two.

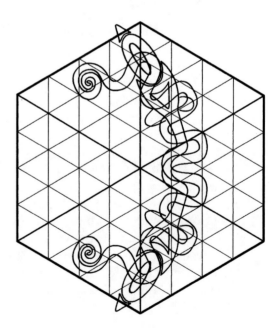

Figure 100. Beta's Twin Serpents

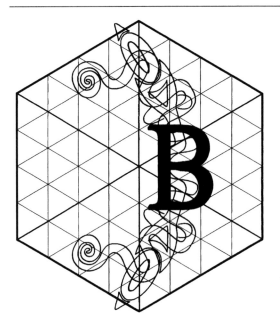

Figure 101. Majuscule Beta

Beta is then the first of three symbols that utilizes a double Serpent. The second is kappa, valued at 20, and the third is sigma, valued at 200. Philosophically, the reasoning for this progression becomes obvious to the initiate, relating the gradual, complete separation of the three constituents. The philosophic *triune* is a common underlying factor in most religious schemes. The Pythagoreans said that two gave rise to three, and this understanding has been captured in Figures 103 and 104 which reveal the two minuscule forms of the letter most popularly considered. Both emphasize the second coil from the bottom while putting some thought into the third. Figure 104 adds the tail, holding respect for the majuscule, and in fact being the same size. Figure 103 demonstrates how the modern English *b* developed from a gradual exclusion of the top loop.

As will be shown, all the letters representing

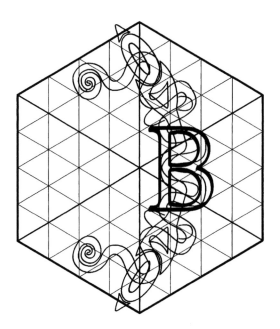

Figure 102. Majuscule Beta Shown in Transparency

Figure 103. Minuscule Beta

Figure 104. The Forerunner of the Minuscule English *B*

The Gamma Symbol

Gamma is third in the order of the Greek system and, interestingly, was originally considered as a c, having evolved, according to scholars, from the Etruscan. The Etruscan culture originated in very ancient times in the western part of what is now Italy.

Long ago favoring the left side and being somewhat reluctant to form a perpendicular main stem, the modern gamma provides a hint regarding its original exposure. The Etruscan counterpart is thought to have simply changed over time to the familiar gamma through the convenient selection of scribes. Aligned to the north-south axis of the Serpent, and favoring the creature's tendency to the left, the seemingly backward Etruscan version may be viewed in Figure 105.

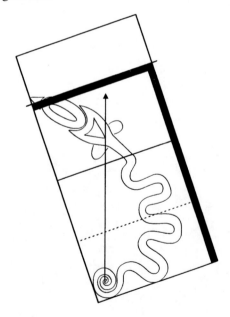

Figure 105. Majuscule Gamma is Defined by the Sacred Cut

the numerical value of 2 have two forms of minuscule. Since the beta is the first of the three owning this artistic ambiguity, it describes the beginning stage of the three-part separation yielding salt, sulfur, and the mercurial element. The philosophical schools believed that all matter was of a dual or twofold nature, while one of those parts, the spiritual, had twin components—the metaphorical sulfur and mercury. Thus the Great Serpent divides into twin aspects, ultimately to rejoin back upon the *salt* or hard geometry.

Beta is currently spelled out *beta-eta-tau-alpha*. Were this to be reduced to discern its basic value, the number 311 results, subsequently reducing further to 5. This points out a first example of the possible tampering with the original system. The Pythagoreans would likely have spelled the term beta-*epsilon*-tau-alpha, reducing to 11 and finally to 2.

The Etruscan scholars are said to have not particularly differentiated between the *c* and *g* sounds, as the later Greeks certainly did. It thus requires little insight to see how the *g* may have supplanted the *k* sound (c).

The word *comma,* derived from the Greek *komma* (from *kop-,* meaning to strike or create a chop), very neatly describes the creation of the sacred cut, depicted in the section under the same title. The compass stroke marks the parallel long axes of the double square in order to draw the line defining the golden section. The arc may be reduced to a simple comma to do this:

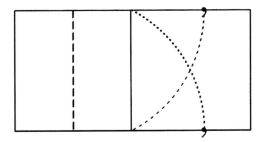

Figure 106. The Comma and the Sacred Cut

If the Greeks considered that they formally isolated the *g* sound, then they likely evaluated it as evolving from the hard c (k). Noting that the kappa symbol is also formed from the geometry of the sacred cut, the symbols would sum kappa (20), alpha (1), double mu (80), and alpha (1), equaling 102, subsequently reducing to 3.

Figure 107 shows the majuscule and minuscule as they are better known. The majuscule, defining the golden mean, gives special notice to the minuscule, contained in the perfect golden box. Note the tendency of the lesser gamma's left fork to curl in the direction of the Serpent. The minuscule gamma is placed in the velar-producing area at the back of the throat.

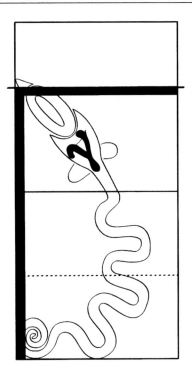

Figure 107. Majuscule and Miniscule Gamma

The Delta Symbol

As the fourth symbol of the Greek alphabet, akin to the Semitic *daleth,* delta's triangle has come to be widely accepted as a sign for the letter *d* in English. It is not difficult to see how the minuscule Greek form gave rise to the minuscule English.

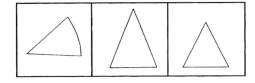

Figure 108. Daleth and Delta

The North Semitic and two Greek forms shown left to right, representing the early daleth and delta.

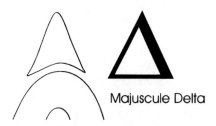

Majuscule Delta

Figure 109. Majuscule Delta

Figure 110. Minuscule Delta

Figure 109 shows the probable origination of the majuscule form at the head end of the Serpent. As rivers are considered serpentine, or in some ancient cultures actual serpents, the fact of the delta symbol being taken from the mouth-end of the Serpent structure is not difficult to envision.

As delta represents the classic formation of a dental (in which the teeth are used to form the consonant), the idea arises that the triangular mound feature represents a great horn, tooth, or tusk-like fang. The stylized capital delta, owning a straight line as its base, would have distinguished it from the majuscule lambda, which, also a dental, is patterned after the same feature of the Serpent.

The familiar character of the minuscule delta with its little curl atop is actually an inclusive form of the fourth coil with a fine thread of the fifth extending like a gossamer on the right edge of the fifth coil. The fourth winding from the tail of the Serpent is also used in the construction of the minuscule mu and upsilon symbols, valued at 40 and 400, respectively. This partially explains why an oval form was selected for the little delta with its lifting thread, helping to clearly distinguish the three fourth-coil characters.

It is of interest to note that together the terms *daleth* and *delta* employ most of the dental articulations. The term "dental" itself includes the missing *n*. The numeric value of delta is 4 + 5 + 30 + 300 + 1, summing to 340, subsequently reducing to 7. Were the Pythagorean methodology as meticulous as has been averred, it is likely that they retained the North Semitic *th* in place of the harder *tau*, enunciating the tau-alpha as a theta-alpha at the end. Since theta is at times pronounced as a softened *t* with a little breath behind it, so the change could have taken place, merely replacing one dental with another. In this, the literal value of the term changes from 340 to 49, reducing to 13 and finally to 4 due to the theta over the tau.

Because the delta is a dental, the minuscule form may have used the oval in sympathy with the theta oval three symbols ahead.

The Epsilon Symbol

Epsilon is valued at 5 in the Pythagorean system, and is apparently a reference to the fifth coil of the Serpent counting from either direction. *"Psilon"* is an interesting term and may be understood as indicative of bareness, smoothness, and baldness, characterizing the seven coils of the Serpent. Thus it is *e*-psilon, the character marking the fifth coil. It should be considered that with the advent of the creation of the alphabetical collection, any number of expressions owning references to the serpent might have been developed. Further, it is a logical theory that with an excellent knowledge of the mother form, the various symbols of the Greek alphabet, fitted together, would recreate Pythagoras' Python.

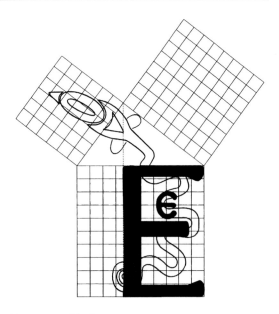

Figure 111. Epsilon

Like phi and chi, psi was once expressed in a double consonant form, in this case pi-sigma. One reason for its condensation to a single symbol is conceivably found in the spelling of epsilon. The prefix *epi-* coincidentally has five uses, viz. on, upon, at, by, and near, and infers resting or situation. Were the spelling of the term evaluated as pi-iota-sigma, i.e., ep (i) silon, dropping the iota due to its inference through the pi, the term would reduce to 455—being sure to include the inferred iota in the summation: $4 + 4 + 5 = 14; 1 + 4 = 5$.

The minuscule epsilon rests on, upon, or at the fifth coil of the Serpent counting up from the tail, and the central branch of the majuscule is resting at, by, or near the fifth coil counting down from the head. In this arrangement it can be seen how psilon could remind one of the coils of the creature. This possibly helps to explain why psi represents the number seven. Epsilon's usual spelling sums to 865, virtually the same value as the usual summation of the name Pythagoras. In this may be discerned the reason for the use of the Pythagorean Theorem in describing the epsilons (see "Pythagoras and the Sigma" in the sigma section). Paradoxically, the name also reduces to the figure 666. (See "The Number of the Beast.")

Not coincidentally, the spelling of eta, which is the long *e* alternative to the shorter *e* of epsilon, also creates an "alchemy" or perfect joining of sounds, absent to the eye but inferred to the ear and proven in the numerical reduction. The two *e*'s, as the other four vowels, represented the bright spirits of speech, as without vowels, we would all be mumbling. Recalling that there are twenty-four parts to the soul of man (the twenty-four elders), these five were thus the five elements or conditions of matter in that Spiritual Science—fiery, gaseous, solid, liquid, and ethereal—for all matter was sustained by the Universal Logos or Voice of God.

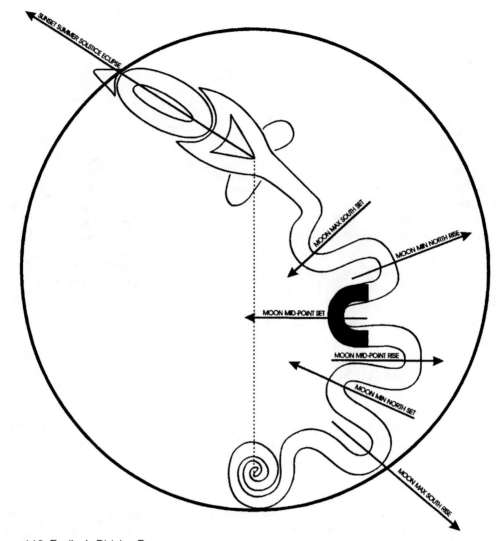

Figure 112. Epsilon's Divining Bar

Using the Delphi Circle, the lunar mid-point setting position offers an alternate explanation for minuscule epsilon's divining bar.

The two *E*'s were given special notice in the alphabet as separate entities. They for all intent and purpose represented the ethereal or fifth condition and electricity, through which the etheric state of matter is made dense or dense matter is dissolved back into the etheric stuff. The eta likely replaced the now extinct episemon bau, the thunderbolt of creation and destruction.

Figure 113. The Thunderbolt of Creation and Destruction

The Zeta Symbol

As the sixth letter of the Greek alphabet due to the removal of digamma, zeta is valued at seven. Its construction is determined using the geometry of the sacred cut.

Scholars attribute the origin of the zeta consonant to the combining of sigma with delta. Pronouncing an *s* and slowly bringing a *d* into it, the *z* sound is discovered. Of old, the sigma-delta pairing was as acceptable as any of the double consonants.

The three symbols zeta, omicron, and psi, valued at 7, 70, and 700 in the Pythagorean system, are linked in the study of the seven coils. Zeta is represented by the seventh from the head, omicron by all seven, and psi as the seventh from the tail of the creature.

As a space identical to the segmented ABGH, CDEF begins the isolation of the majuscule, finalized by JKFE, made feasible by the lateral division IK. Using the bounds set up by the majuscule, the minuscule was isolated. Its small end loops are proportionally shrunken parts of the adjoining form. This interesting practice was employed to modify the characters while preserving them from becoming indiscernible connections to the progenitor of the alphabet, the

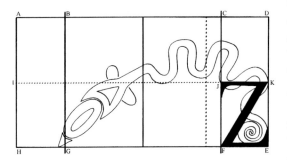

Figure 114. Majuscule Zeta

Figure 115. Minuscule Zeta

Great Serpent. These abbreviated portions are outlined delicately in black on the Serpent in Figure 115, while a modern style minuscule is placed to the left for clarity.

The North Semitic *zayin* (from which the Greeks are believed to have appropriated their original majuscule zeta form) is similar to the capital Roman I. In examining the iota two symbols ahead, note that it is based in the square of ten, containing the seven coils of the Serpent. Zayin was the Semitic seventh symbol.

Were zeta evaluated numerically using the familiar zeta-eta-tau-alpha spelling, it would add 7 + 8 + 300 + 1 producing 316. Interestingly, not only does the number 316 reduce to 10, but 3.16 is an approximation of the square root of 10. As noted, 31.6 is a key foot measure, unlocking much of the geometrical meaning of the Serpent Mound structure. However, were either eta replaced with epsilon or tau replaced with theta, the term would reduce to 7. From these facts and alternatives, it may be extrapolated that 7 and 10 were closely associated, like the beast that had seven heads and ten horns.

The Eta Symbol

Valued at eight, the term *"eta"* would apparently have given rise to the word *"eight,"* as in the Old English it was *eahta*. Eta is believed to have been created as a long *e* alternative to the short e of epsilon. The eta along with the omega was introduced from the Samian to the Athenian alphabet around 403 B.C.E., "under the archonship of Euclides."[117] Before this the *H* was used to indicate "rough breathing," just as we use the letter today. In fact, were one to attempt the spelling-out of the English H, it would be *aitch*, reminiscent of *eight* or eta.

Eta being introduced with omega was conceivably done out of necessity. The all-encompassing omega, carrier of the Great Power of the Word, was valued at 800. In this numerical appointment, omega was likely associated with Hermes or Mercury. To legitimately conceive the long e sound, the omega may easily have been joined

Figure 116. Theraen Double Square
[Ωε]τα The first appearance of the symbol's likeness is considered Phoenician, around 1200 B.C.E. Subsequently the Cretan (1100 B.C.E.) and the Theraen used the rectangle or double square box.

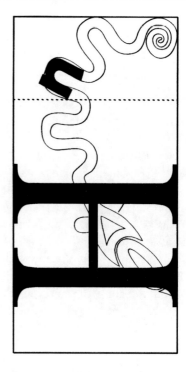

Figure 117. Majuscule Eta
The majuscule form utilizes the golden box, being therein of perfect proportion, pleasing to the eye. The symbol indicates the head and throat of the Serpent, ideal for describing "the rough breathing."

with the epsilon in a covert marriage to give birth to the eta, valued at eight. This practice is similar to the pairing of *o* and *e* to get a long *e* sound such as in the term *phoenix*. The omega would influence the epsilon as in the French *eu* or in the German practice of the umlaut. In this, the actual pronunciation of eta would be between a long and a short *e*.

It should be borne in mind that the Samian alphabet might have been strongly influenced by the Pythagoreans, as the philosopher was known as Pythagoras of Samos. He held classes and workshops there by any evidence. A further connection with omega is the location of the secret marriage of omega with epsilon would have disappeared visibly, yet have been very present in weight, i.e., numerical value. Thus omega (800) + epsilon (5) + tau (300) + alpha (1) add to 1106, subsequently reducing to 17, and finally to 8.

The Theta Symbol

In 1918, Harvard's Peabody Museum sent Charles Willoughby to measure and sketch the Serpent. He interpreted the head and oval area as representative of a head and eye, but was not the first to do this. Did this good scholar see an underlying and well-concealed fact in the Serpent's original design, a design perhaps dating back to the time of Egypt's pyramid builders?

Theta is valued at nine in the Greek system, and upon examination the cursive theta resembles the Arabic 9, used commonly around the world.

Theta claims three distinct variations, two of which are the minuscule and majuscule as commonly used. Figure 119 shows the similarity between the Egyptian Eye of Horus and the Serpent Mound head area. Horus was a formidable solar aspect, well known to govern matters of the soul. The Serpent overtaking the solar disk in its approach from the side gives rise to the elliptic, which in turn serves to sympathize with the minuscule and majuscule thetas. A thin line running through their short axes characterizes these thetas, and when the symbols are turned on their sides, they resemble the eye of a serpent or cat:

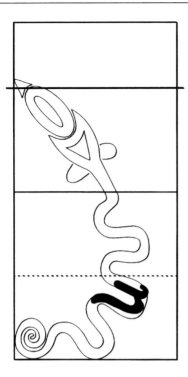

Figure 118. Minuscule Eta

The script form of the minuscule eta infers the vestigial third and fifth coils, not unlike the zeta's inference of the helix and the sixth coil. In the case of eta, these inferences join to represent 5 + 3 or 8, the value of eta. Since there is no eighth coil, the practice of vestigial delineation was logically employed. It also points out the probability of the Serpentine image being extant prior to the creation of the symbols.

minuscule eta on the Serpent form. Like the minuscule omega, the little eta uses the fourth coil from the tail, extending the right leg into the area of the third coil. This may have been for purely aesthetic reasons, but does serve to remind the user of the symbol's origin, at once distinguishing it from the other symbols needing to use the fourth coil or inferring its use, such as the omega.

After the theorized creation of the eta, the

However, one form of majuscule holds within its ellipse a defined majuscule iota:

This iota represents the inner power of the theta, and in ascribing this seed power of ten, theta is the *Ennea,* a term used to describe the nine muses of Apollo. The iota majuscule is also used in the creation of the majuscule phi, this time exceeding the ellipse, thus denoting the divining power of ten, inherent in the phi.

Considering these things, and thinking of the thetan oval to be a digestible solar orb or egg, the Serpent is on its way to devouring all conceivable cosmic power (9), only to discover that at the core of this power is the Unity, small though it seems.

As a testimony to this sacrifice, the cursive theta was developed with the intent of artistically describing the entire body of the Serpent with emphasis on the head area. ϑ is thus a symbol hinting that the full concept of theta is not confined to the solar ellipse but is transferred to the whole form of the divine creature, ultimately to transform this beast.

The Iota Symbol

Any reliable dictionary will closely compare iota, the symbol valued at ten, with the meaning "a very small quantity," "jot," or "whit," associating iota with synonyms like "bit," "atom," "particle," "grain," and "mite." The original intent of the symbol is likely relative to these comparisons, but with yet a little more substance.

The assignation of iota to the ten value is mainly attributable to the association of the symbol with the square of ten in the Pythagorean Theorem. Figure 120 shows the majuscule as indicative of the north-south orientation of the Serpent, while the minuscule is that portion of the creature admitting itself to the ten square, the first part of the first coil from the head. Spelled iota (10)-omega (800)-tau (300)-alpha (1), the term adds up to the curious figure 1111. However, merely by replacing the hard tau with

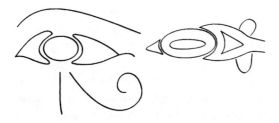

Figure 119. Comparison Between the Eye of Horus and the Serpent's Head

Were the eta removed from the second position in the spelling of the term "theta," the value would change from 9 + 8 + 300 + 1 or 318, to 9 + 5 + 300 + 1 or 315, subsequently reducing to 9.

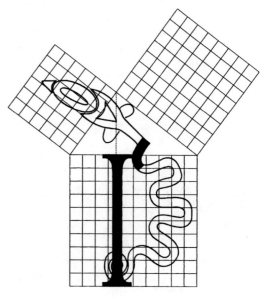

Figure 120. Iota

the softened tau of theta, the numerical value becomes 820, subsequently reducing to 10.

The Kappa Symbol

One of the more erudite in concept of all the symbols included in the serpentine offering, the kappa is assigned the premises of the sacred cut, joining gamma, zeta, and eta.

Kappa is poetically taken to translate as rim of the cup. It is related to the Hebraic *kaph,* both occupying the same position in their respective alphabets. Kaph suggests the palm of the hand.

The value of kappa is 20 by Pythagorean standard. The addition of the letters numerically gives 182, half the solar figure 364. Since 1 + 8 + 2 equals 11, finally reducing to 2, the kappa may be seen as having two meanings, perhaps adding the sacred nuance of divining.

An understanding of the rim may be discerned from the geometry of the golden section in Figures 121 and 122. Turned on its side, Figure 122 reveals the alternate form of the majuscule kappa. Like the rim of a cup, the golden section is placed at the top.

Figure 123 reveals the method for isolating the minuscule kappa. As with the beta, the Serpent is doubled over itself. A greater separation than the two Serpents comprising beta is notice-

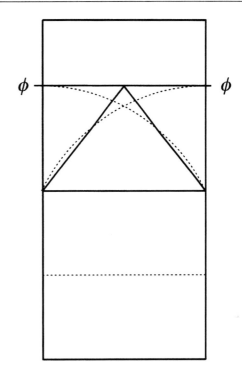

Figure 122. Majuscule Kappa

able, however, a particular detail understood by the Mystery College. Even as the term "kappa" reduces to 1 + 1, so the first coil from the head is used to create the minuscule, unlike the beta that uses the second coil to create the majuscule.

The wisdom of *the palm of the hand* is brought to life through a specialized geometry of the same sacred cut. The phrase is likely intended to describe the two palm lines brought together in a ceremonial reversal, and isolated and joined the two Serpents form what may be termed the "golden vesica," a revealing blueprint of the phi ratio exhibiting a sublime knowledge of the sacred cut. Figure 124 uses, for the virtue of its vesica, the same geometry as Figures 122 and 123.

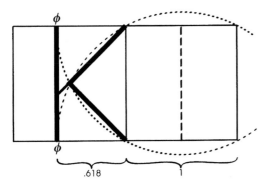

Figure 121. Majuscule Kappa and the Golden Mean

THE MYSTERY OF THE SERPENT MOUND

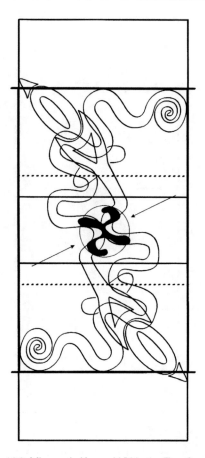

Figure 123. Minuscule Kappa Within the Two Serpents

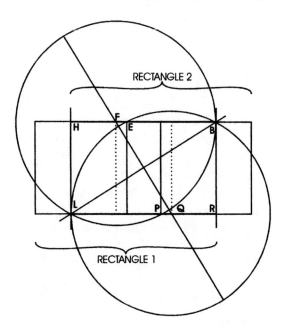

Figure 124. The Golden Vesica Details the Geometry of Kappa

The golden vesica details the geometry isolated in diagram 123 to show the minuscule. From pivot Q is formed the arc BEL, based upon the double-square rectangle 1. Similarly, rectangle 2 is the basis for arc BPL from pivot F. BHLR is the perfect golden box, HB + LR divided by HL + BR being phi or 1.618. LB divided by FQ is thereby also phi.

The Lambda Symbol

The lambda symbols are classified as dental in enunciation, and thus the head of the Serpent may be looked to for discernment of these symbols. While the minuscule may appear to be a modified version of the majuscule, in fact they are patterned after different features of the creature.

In order to comprehend these features, the Serpent should be seen in a three-dimensional form. Majuscule lambda differs from majuscule delta in this respect, though both symbols are derived or extrapolated from the triangular moundwork. A small three-sided pyramid, having the same height as base measure, would stand for the fang or tooth necessary in the restraining of the solar or thetan disk.

Interestingly, the spelling of the term "lambda" reveals the measure of this mound, 31.6 feet. Lambda equals 30, alpha (also associated with the triangular feature) equals 1, making 31. Then mu, valued at 40, combines with beta, valued at 2, with the reduction of the two

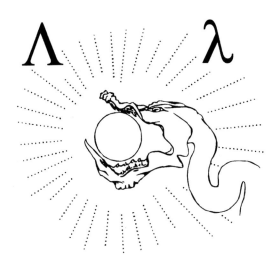

Figure 125. Lambda

figures being 6—hence the figure of 31.6 feet. Recalling that beta is used to stop or retain a vowel, to lend power to any exceeding it, it may be understood how the mu and beta would have been combined numerically. Exceeding beta then is delta, which, as a dental, releases power into alpha again, ending the term. Granted, this interpretation is speculative, but it should be understood that the Pythagorean genius was highly intuitive, extending even to the comprehension of the future natural course of mathematics—in this case the use of decimal fractions.

The Greek term "ambix" *(cup)* purportedly gave rise to the term "alembic," an important vessel used by the early chemists and alchemists. An alembic is directly connected with the source of heat with a view toward distillation. It is described as a vessel with a peaked head or cap. The term itself became used as a metaphor for anything instrumental in purifying, subliming, or transforming. In comparing the alembic to an ark-energized pyramidal altar, little imagination is needed to equate such an instrument of spiritual

chemistry with that of a divinely engineered powerhouse. Being situated at the head of the great beast (the primeval serpent, Revelation 12:9) the proposed lambda altar functionally could draw down fire from heaven (Revelation 13:13). Further, there is a direct relationship between the Lamb of God and the lambda of the gods, stemming from Greek philosophy and its mythology. Were an alpha placed before the term "lambda," the word alambda would add up to 79, the atomic number of gold. Interestingly enough, the numbers 1 through 79 added together equal 3160.

The minuscule lambda could be interpreted to represent a structure such as the Celtic quoit (pronounced keet), which is described as a huge slab of rock slanted on supporting upright slabs. To enter into such a structure meant a descent into the Underworld or Otherworld, according to Irish tradition. The quoit was and is considered a "female" contact point with the Earth. This symbol, by itself, brings the concept of the design of the Great Serpent into three dimensions.

Appearing respectively as the fang and wide-open jaws of a serpent, these two lambda symbols combine to take on a highly esoteric interpretation. With the oval feature between these two lambda symbols, the understanding of the solar disk (representing light) or the umbilicus (representing life) are illustrated. According to one source, the theta stands to mean thought, indicating the highest material plane, i.e., where Spirit utterly dominates and matter is extremely pure and rarified.

In this interpretation, the Serpent is a spiritualized creature, formidable in substance and created by God to represent the Word or Principle of Sound, the Spiritual Son (or Sun). In an alternate interpretation, the Sun charges the True Light into the creature, philosophically inducing a transformation from within, construed as evolutionary and virtually ensouling this controversial beast. The two interpretations, one of swallowing and the other regurgitating, again pronounce the dissolve-and-coagulate axiom of the Spiritual Chemistry.

Hence Michael in a celestial struggle with the Great Dragon, an account that is no different in principle from the myth of Apollo and Python, save that the Python is slain while the Beast is merely bound up for half an astronomical age.

The Mu Symbol

Successfully creating an enriched vibrational tone through the closing of the lips, mu is the labial of sound inclusion, allowing the breath to escape only through the nasal passages. This complete sealing of the mouth combined with an attempt to voice a vowel demonstrates how the long *u* and *o* cause the lips to vibrate most. Therefore we see the spellings mu-upsilon and mu-omega in the Greek. The shutting of the Serpent's mouth enclosing the theta reminds one of the Old English *muth,* the term for "mouth" stemming from the Icelandic tongue.

The spellings of omicron and omega show the emphasis placed upon the use of the mu for putting across the idea of *om,* the primary Vibratory Principle, as explained earlier in this section ("The Power of the Word," part III). It is the containment of vibration that enriches the Atom, as well as the human being in the higher sense of the Word. The containment of the Solar Principle in the mouth of the Serpent is the enrichment of the soul, the Atom, and commences the evolution or creation of Man. The Spiritual Power is no longer brilliant and free like a sun, but is restrained and contracted to do the work of evolution. The Word of God is thus illuminated even as the "Sun" or Son of God is fully empowered.

This divinely conceived symbiosis is complete

Figure 126. Mu

with the appearance of the Perfect Man and the disappearance of both the Archangel and the Serpent. They literally join, each sacrificing their separate identities in becoming Man. In alchemical metaphor, this is the integral conjoining of the sulfur and mercury principles, creating the Divine Cinnabar. This is the substance of the revelatory throne of the One, analogous to the Primal Atom comprised of the twenty-four elders, the four beasts having six wings, etc.

Valued at 40 on the Pythagorean scale of symbol-number correlation, the mu was constructed on the same premise as the delta minuscule before and the upsilon minuscule following. Mu minuscule extends a leg, paralleling the pattern line of the hexagon, distinguishing it from the upsilon minuscule, even as the gossamer distinguishes the little delta. The majuscule mu underscores the importance of sealing the spoken word as a rich utterance from deep in the throat, a point of design brought home in the noting of the position of majuscule upsilon (pictured later).

Through the inferred presence of alpha, the

value of mu-omega is increased from 840 to 841, subsequently reducing to 4. However, the explanation is simplified in the mu-upsilon spelling, showing the use of the fourth coil twice.

The Nu Symbol

From ancient Egypt we have inherited the term "Amen," a recalling or invoking of the sacred Name or Word of the Divine. The exceeding of the labial *M* with the nasaled dental *N* ensures first the sealing of the mouth by closing the lips. This is followed by the closing off of the throat through the placement of the tongue used to form the *N*. The speaker thus creates vibration through a vowel, then translates the sound into the diaphragmatic labial *M*, finally neutralizing that internalized vibration with nu: Amen.

According to the myth, Zeus took as his consort Mnemosyne, she of certain memory. She conceived and gave birth to the nine muses, divinities outwardly associated with the humanities of the era. They also served as a metaphor for the nine portals or orifices of the human Temple. There was an earlier divine, Mneme, who was one of three sisters governing the three aspects of mystical asceticism. It is believed by some that the seven-and-two muses of Apollo were inspired from the original three muses, though in view of what these three represent, there is no reason to support the notion of the ennead supplanting them. Mneme, who meant Remembrance, was connected with her sisters Aoede, *Practice,* and Melete, *Song,* for the art and science of Spiritual devotion. Practice was the attitude of correct posture and concentration of the attention, while Song was the objective of religious supplication, i.e., listening to the divine Song or internally comprehended Music of the Spheres. The nine muses, based upon correct knowledge of the nine external orifices or

"amusements" of the Temple, owed their existence to their mother, and a similar worth may be ascribed to Mneme, for she invoked both the Light and Sound Principles of human culture, without and within.

Drawing in the *True Substance* from beyond the matrix of the hexagon, i.e., the Spiritual Essence that precedes all matter, the Serpent converts this to *M,* then to *N,* with a view toward assimilation down through the seven coils and helix. The captive sun or Son brings this Essence with him, and thus begins the joining of the two, initiated perhaps by a strong appetite on the Serpent's behalf. Thus is the Word brought into illumination, commencing the memory of the sacred Temple, the institution of Man, through the invoking of the Holy Breath, i.e., the aforementioned Spiritual Essence. In the Greek this is called pneuma *bio-* valued at 618, but added to bio (life), sealing it within. It is also *Holy Spirit, Holy Ghost,* and a *Spiritual Being.* In this is intimated both the Breath that enlivened Adam and the wind alluded to by Christ in John 3:8.

The symbols mu and nu occupy the twelfth and thirteenth positions in the order of the alphabet; between them the collection is divided. It is notable that the minuscule nu is in the same place as the already-discussed minuscule gamma, as well as the crux of the majuscule mu. In enunciation, the nu converts to gamma before a gamma or the other three gutturals kappa, chi and xi. This interesting practice of the Greeks is highlighted in Figures 127 and 128. The majuscule nu, while a true dental, is valued for its lingual placement. Its sound is associated with the back of the throat. In this can be discerned the roof of the mouth and the hermetic seal allowing for proper assimilation of the Spiritual Essence and the Breath of life.

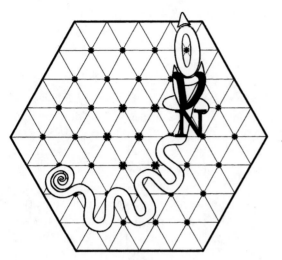

Figure 127. Nu

Figure 128. Gamma and Nu

Figure 129. The Holy Spirit filling Adam with the Breath of Life, Making Man

The Sikh religion refers to this hallowed Principle of Peace as *Nam* or *Naam,* and this is no less than the eternal Music of the Spheres mentioned by the ancient philosophers, or the Singing of the Angels known to true mystics. This enlivening Vibration is heard by the inner ear of Man, at first caught by the initiate on the right side, eventually coming from above. This Sound Current eliminates stress and revitalizes the seven "coils" or sacred centers of the human body, mentioned as the seven churches of John the Revelator's preliminary vision (Revelation 1:9), the mystical Body of Christ. This Sound stirs up and makes abundant the Light of Spiritual Comprehension, ultimately filling the body, illuminating the mind, and dispelling the shadow of Ignorance.

It is in the memory of the soul (Greek. mne) that this principle exists inactive before the creation of the Atom; and the Word, say the Master Saints, wonderfully restores all the virtues through gentle recollection.

From the tip of the Sacred Serpent flows the Universal Life Energy extracted and distilled from the Sea of Spirit. This tip, representing the majuscule lambda, brings in the Am (Word) or Lamb of God, the gentle, everlasting power of the Son, whom the Egyptians called Amen-Ra.

The Xi Symbol

Xi was also once indicated by a double consonant, variously compounded of gamma-sigma, kappa-sigma, and chi-sigma. It is pronounced zï, sï, and kse. The change to a single symbol came along with the eta from the Samian alphabet and was, in this, probably affected directly by the Pythagorean School.

The geometry underlying the two aspects of xi is focused on the six-pointed star, the hexagram (Greek: hexagrammon). The surviving records of the Pythagoreans show that special attention was given to this figure, due to the hexagon within it, the cube seen in the hexagon, along with the celebrated tetractys contained within the equilateral triangle (Figures 131, 132, 133, and 134).

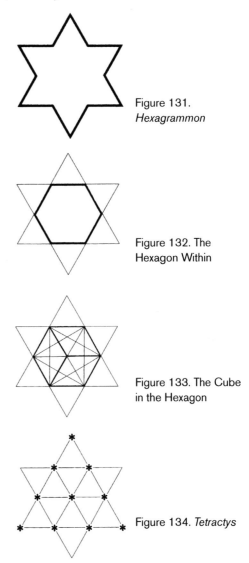

Figure 131. *Hexagrammon*

Figure 132. The Hexagon Within

Figure 133. The Cube in the Hexagon

Figure 134. *Tetractys*

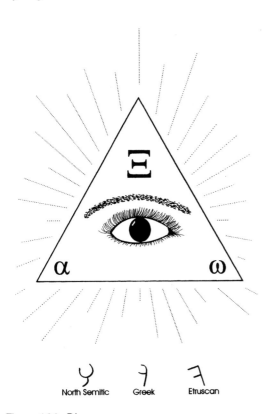

North Semitic   Greek   Etruscan

Figure 130. *Digamma*

The all seeing eye represented as one of the "twenty-four elders" was meant to convey "sight." The digamma (bottom) apparently meant double the value of gamma, i.e., six, but this version offers insight into the possibility of digamma's having originally been associated with the double square box, as gamma.

Figure 135. Fifth and Seventh Coils

Figure 136. Majuscule Xi Upon the Coils

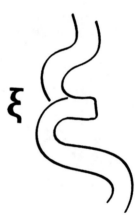

Figure 137. Apollonian Severance

Figure 138. The Grafting of Minuscule Xi

The majuscule and minuscule xi are shown in Figures 135, 136, 137, and 138. Note that the fifth and seventh coils from the tail of the subject touch into the hexagram in Figure 135. Figure 136 shows the majuscule lined-in according to the coils, the star, and the hexagon pathways. Figure 137 shows the line of Apollonian severance, removing the sacred sixth coil and joining the fifth to the seventh, analogous to the removal

of the rib of patriarchal Adam. Of possible interest to the alphabetologist is the probability of this missing sixth coil being used to effect the digamma (see Figure 130 bottom), once valued at six but excluded as a most sacred item. The practice of grafting also occurs in the creation of the minuscule omega, though the numerical reasoning is different.

The cryptic star of Figures 132 and 135 contains twelve equilateral triangles with twenty-four 81.6-foot sides—the same measure, collectively, of the solar hexagon perimeter. As the hexagon contains 96 equilateral triangles, it is compared to the brow and crown nerve centers of the human being, related to the mechanics of spiritual vision and realization, respectively. The 96 and 960 spokes or petals referred to in Indian and Tibetan records are in the theory of Spiritual Science conceived of the solar hexagon's triangular parcels, i.e., numerically conceived. In this, as already suggested, the throne of the One preceded the creation of the human form. The hexagram represents this idea in a concise and condensed form.

Thus in Revelation 5, beginning at verse 6, it can be seen how the throne is concentrated by virtue of the Lamb standing there. The seven eyes of the Lamb are seven of the thirty-seven eyes of the four beasts, who subsequently prostrate themselves before the Lamb when he shows his authority. These seven eyes, at the center of the throne, are complemented by seven horns, six of which are the wings of the hexagram and the other coming straight at the viewer, introduced by the concept of the cube in Figure 133. To further enforce the authority of the Lamb, the twenty-four elders also prostrate themselves, condensed to the twenty-four sides of the triangles composing the star. It bears repetition that the three sides projecting from the cube (Figure 133) make up the seventh "horn," while the other six are the sides of the hexagram. The Lamb merely has seemed to be sacrificed; i.e. the mystery of the Lamb's secret identity as the Son of the One seated on the throne is openly revealed, that is, the secret is sacrificed. Thirty-seven eyes take away 7 leaves 30, the value of the symbol lambda.

Figure 139 shows the Star of David (the Lion of Judah, the Root ... Revelation 5:5), as well as

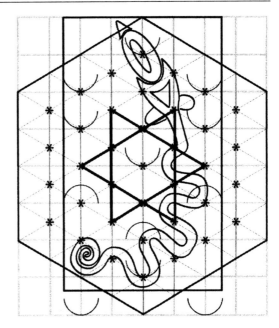

Figure 139. How Xi Represents Sight

the Seal of Solomon, the son of David, as projected into the ark (see Figures 61, 62, and 63). As explained in "The Serpent and the Ark," all is concentrated within the precinct of the ark. Xi is at the focus of the throne and is thus equated with the focus of the all-seeing eye. So it is extrapolated that xi represents sight Ξ, through which Masters and Adepts of the Spiritual Science witness the internal light of the Divine.

The Omicron Symbol

The omicron was given the value of 70 in the Pythagorean School. Omicron is translated to mean the *little o,* the greater being the omega. The original Semitic, Greek, and Latin form was more circular in appearance, the elliptic effect in some modern majuscule forms being a matter of shading.

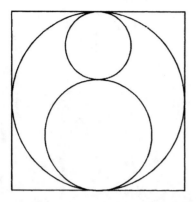

Figure 140. The Delphi Circle, the Arbelos and the Phi Ratio

Describing the number of degrees in a circle, this 360 may apply to either of the two circles contained within the Delphinian Circle. Recalling that the encompassing circle of Delphi is 360 feet multiplied by φ (1.618) or 582.49 feet, the internal circles detail a relationship between measure and geometry that is pleasing to the eye.

A description of the inner circles' measure is of interest to the serious student. Figure 140 shows the Delphi Circle with the Arbelos contained within it. Figure 141 shows how the phi ratio reveals itself. The Serpent's true north alignment creates twin 45-degree slices with the bisection of the two circles. As AD equals 582.49 feet, so ED is exactly half that multiplied by phi: 471.246 feet. AE is therefore 111.246 feet, and AB twice that at 222.49. Subtracting AB from AD determines the diameter of BD at 360 feet, majuscule omicron. For the discerning eye, this diagram offers a clue to the determination of the decimalized foot as the preferred unit of mea-

While the value of 7 is given to zeta—the symbol using the seventh coil from the head— the formation of *psi* (valued at 700) uses the seventh coil from the tail. Omicron, being 70, approaches the problem of its representation by literally encompassing all seven coils.

In order to achieve the correct circling of all seven, the *Arbelos* is used, first shown in the previous section on the Golden Mean. For the omicrons, the Delphi Circle is a matrix for this geometry attributed to the inventive Archimedes. But since Archimedes (287–212 B.C.E.) lived some time after Pythagoras, this particular form of the Arbelos is probably more accurately the discovery (or rediscovery) of the Pythagorean College.

The spelling of omicron reduces like this:

Omicron	70
Mu	40
Iota	10
Kappa	20
Rho	100
Omicron	70
+ Nu	50
Omicron	360

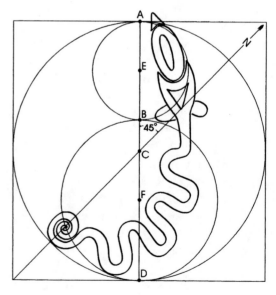

Figure 141. The Serpent Revealing the Phi Ratio

sure. As an added note of interest, DF multiplied by φ is DC, the center of the Delphi Circle.

The Sages of the Mystery College possessed the God-given ability to not only *rise above* the illusion of the Atom, because they understood its internal construction as well, having thoroughly penetrated it with their attention.

Just as the hexagon reveals in flat dimension the internal construction of the Primal Atom (soul), so the ancient Science of Spirit was familiar with the precise nature of that contained within the outer shell of the ordinary atom—without smashing it. The beginning of this knowledge was concerned with the inner circles being in proportion by means of the phi ratio. Sub-protonic particles were possibly thus discerned long ago as governing every aspect of physical and metaphysical law through a profound and acute discernment of the divine proportions ascribed to φ. What science today terms leptons, bosons, quarks, etc., became the seed form of the human being-shaped creature. Once properly embued with a living spiritual entity and in certain fashion directing the Universal Logos (the Greater Word, Omega), this miniature seed of compacted qualities (omicron) became Man.

So it is perhaps that the numerical value of omicron reduces to 9, for it contains the full wherewithal and potential power for the highest conceivable creation. Representing the Atom, omicron is correctly circular in design, not unlike a sphere. The wisdom of pi and its symbol, π, is also intimately a part of this knowledge, and this symbol immediately follows omicron.

The number 7 is the only one of the first 10 whole numbers that does not divide evenly into 360, instead creating a rational yet endless decimal.

Figure 142. Construction of the Two Omicrons

The above diagram shows the construction of the two omicrons, revealing how shading creates the elliptical effect.

The Pi Symbol

Like omicron before it, pi is based upon the phi-oriented Arbelos. It is the sixteenth symbol in the Greek alphabet. Pi was supposed to have developed from the North Semitic *pe,* meaning *"mouth."* However, the symbol has never resembled any sort of mouth that comes to mind, supporting the probability that the Pythagorean version of the symbols developed differently from what we have come to believe. *Pe* somewhat resembles an angled shepherd's staff, and pi in its familiar majuscule form is quite different. Nevertheless, there are sufficient similarities, as can be seen in any good dictionary or encyclopedia. The Etruscan and North Semitic versions were virtually the same. Like beta, pi is a consummate labial, strongly affecting vowels.

Because it is derived from the same area of the Arbelos as the minuscule omicron, pi may have been confused with that mouth-like symbol.

Since there is no eighth coil, the values of eta

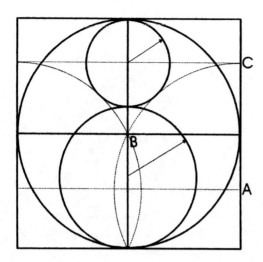

Figure 143. Plotting the Arbelos

This illustration shows the plotting of a proper Arbelos. Taking the horizontal dotted line at A as the middle of the lower quadrants, the same arc that creates the golden mean at point B defines the placement of the horizontal dotted line at C. Using the line taken from the line at C, the smaller circle is constructed.

---

(8), pi (80), and omega (800) were considered either a product of the third and fifth coils or simply a doubling of the fourth coil. In the case of our pi, it is both. In Figure 146, note the segmentation of the fourth coil, making two parts: $4 + 4 = 8$.

As stated in the previous symbol analysis (see "The Omicron Symbol"), the diameter of the Delphi Circle is 582.49 feet, 360 x π. The use of the golden mean to conceive the pi symbol creates a mystical and sacred bond of practical implications. It is thought that the introduction of this symbol in its minuscule form by Englishman William Oughtred (some say William Jones, English mathematician, 1706) in his description of the relationship between the diameter and circumference of a circle is an interesting *coincidence*. Such inspiration was also known to the

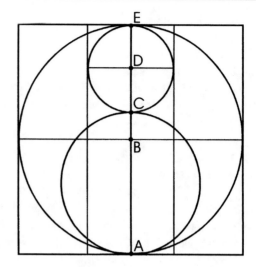

Figure 144. Interesting Features of the Arbelos

$$AB = BE$$
$$AB \div BD = \phi$$
$$AC \div CE = \phi$$
$$DC \div CB = \phi$$
$$BD \div DE = \phi$$

The Arbelos relates to phi, 1.618034, in some interesting ways. If φ is multiplied by π and then taken to the fourth power it is equivalent to the numbers 1–36 added together, 666. Thus phi, pi, and the square of 6 in its graphic form are all related in a sacred and mystical methodology.

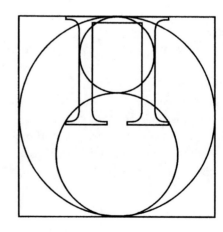

Figure 145. Majuscule Pi

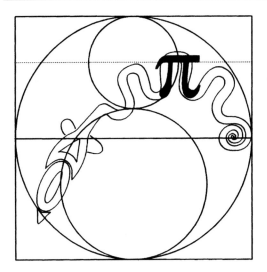

Figure 146. Minuscule Pi

Pythagoreans and may be attributed to the subtle resurfacing in the subconscious mind of lost and forgotten verities. The Indian Masters say that it is a relationship of karmas returning, not unlike seeds planted, awaiting even years before the right conditions present themselves for germination. In this, we are inescapably linked to our past. The attributing of "mouth" to the symbol could be similarly explained.

The numerical value of pi being 80 may be the result of its intimate link-up with the phi geometry. When enunciating the powerful labial *P* into *I*, breath is necessarily released. Otherwise the sound would more resemble *B*. This "rough breathing" is characterized as eta. However, since the announcing of phi (a fricative labial) uses potentially greater breath, the eta of pi is not present as a vowel. The numerical value is there, however, for it reflects a record of the science involved: pi = 80, eta = 8, and this 88 added to iota's 10 and reduced goes 98 to 17 to 8. It should be understood how eta being valued at 8 only makes this arrangement more logical—

as in using upsilon after mu to construct the spelling of mu.

The Rho Symbol

As the ancient dragon-slayer proceeded to dismember the Great Serpent, it was more like fine surgery than butchery. Each part was to be preserved as recognizable. Thus it is restated that if these alphabetical symbols were put together *in a certain way,* i.e., with knowledge of how they were originated, the picture of the Great Serpent Python would be revealed.

The rho occupies the seventeenth position in the gallery of the Greeks and is among the more elegant symbols due to its simple premise. It is valued at 100. Recalling that neither alpha nor iota uses the first coil from the tail, we see that rho was partially composed on this feature of the Serpent map. In addition, it should be of interest to note that the only other reference to the helix is in the idea of the majuscule omega being the *Last* of the scriptural *First and Last.* The small triangular feature, as mentioned, represents the *First* or alpha majuscule.

Either *O* or *U* may be considered best in forming the uvular *R*. Enunciating these vowels, little effort is required to bring the uvula close to the flow of air. While rho is spelled ρω in the Greek, the English incorporates the *h,* indicating the breath. In this, the rho is technically spirant. In the Latin *spira* means *"to breathe,"* being relative to the Greek *speira,* meaning *"coil"* or *"spiral."* To make this connection is of some importance, for in the view of the ancient phonetic science, the serpent was the *power of the breath,* which uncoiling gave rise to the word of speech. Hence here is one connection between the breath and *spirit.* The Indian Yoga Adepts, masters of breath control, make a similar connection.

The helix of the Great Serpent represents the

last portion of the creature remaining coiled after its possibly striking-out at the solar disk. In another interpretation, the coil is the reserve of power as the creature (Logos) is engaged in the act of bearing the soul of Man. In the first interpretation, the disk represents its contact with Sound Principle or Logos, supplying the active breath necessary to animate language. In the alternate explanation, Man himself is the off-spring of Logos or Word, his parental figure owning a stored and inexhaustible resource of power—the legacy of Man.

This last portion of the coiled entity is fit for describing the rho sound, for it is a deep and low utterance. *Ouraios,* a Greek term meaning *"of the tail,"* influenced the term for the Egyptian headdress *asp,* called *Uraeus* (see explanation in "The Serpent and the Cross: The Mystery of Distillation").

The classical minuscule uses the helix, extending a tail, indicating the first coil. The modern minuscule loses its little hook, perhaps indicating a loss of knowledge concerning the symbol's original intent. The majuscule simply appears patterned after the minuscule, using the larger

Figure 148. Majuscule and Minuscule Rho

omicron circle of the Arbelos, the figure turned upside down from its position depicting the pi symbols, maintaining the north alignment as its central axis. The larger circle touches the back of the throat, the column of the majuscule *standing through* the fourth coil, used to make the upsilon (three symbols ahead).

Thus to properly develop the *r* sound, O (70) + U (400) would be used to commence the action. These vowels situate the practice deep in the throat. The rho is created but then must go into the omega (800) to properly qualify it as an expression of the Great Word. An alternate expression would be *Ra,* but it would not capture the mechanics involved, simply being a hallowed syllable utterance. Thus these three symbols conspire to create an envelope giving rise to the deep *r* sound, the spirant *h* losing itself in the support of their triune—recalling the Greek spelling. Thus 70 + 400 + 800 equals 1270, reducing to 10 and 1.

The Egyptian Uraeus

Figure 147. The Egyptian Uraeus

The Sigma Symbol

Following the rho, sigma is the eighteenth symbol in the Greek system, valued at 200. Numerically, the term reduces thus:

Sigma = 200
Iota   = 10
Gamma = 3
Mu   = 40
Alpha = 1
Sigma = 254 = 2+5+4=11 = 1+1 = 2

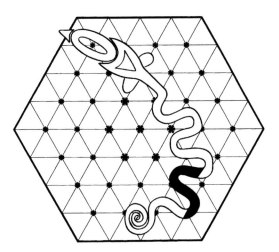

Figure 149. Stau

As captioned in "The Serpent and the Cross: The Mystery of Distillation," when sigma precedes tau in a term, the two may be consolidated to be valued at 6. Greek scholarship avers caution against mistaking the symbol *stau*, valued at 6, for a sigma. Stau, which sounds like an abbreviated sigma-tau, was likely the result of the multiplication and reduction of the two, viz. 200 x 300 or 60,000, reducing to 6.

The Greek rendering of the Revelation to John 13:18's beast reads χξϛ', adding 600 + 60 + 6. Chi sounds like *kh,* and xi like *ks*.[118] According to the rule, the *beast* could have appeared χξστ, the sigma-tau duo at the end combined to arrive at the 6 value.

In consideration of the stau and sigma, Figure 150 reveals the minuscule form of the sigma, the one to the left being the basis for the English *s.* Note that the one on the right suggests a parallel with the line of the solar hexagon. Both these minuscule forms appear to use the second coil from the tail, expressing the sigma value, 200. Again, the symbols involving a doubling— viz. 2, 20, and 200—all utilize a double Serpent. Further, were the figure on the left inverted and the third coil emphasized, the stau is made apparent (Figure 149).

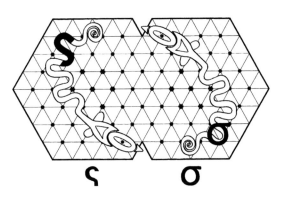

Figure 150. The Dual Serpents of Minuscule Sigma

In the majuscule illustrations, the hexagon itself demonstrates the two more familiar versions. Perhaps by coincidence, they also imply the approximate length of the Serpent *sans* the oval feature. The draping or overhang of the majuscules brings their measure to about 666 x 2 feet.

Etymologists concur that the English *six* is derived from the Greek *hex* as well as the Sanskrit *sas*. The number 666 is well represented in

— 179 —

Figure 151. Majuscule Sigma

Figure 152. Majuscule Sigma Using Rotated Hexagon

the 96 triangles of the hexagon, each having 5 units of 666 square feet.

Sigma: The Final Doubling and Separation

As with the figures representing the beta and kappa, the symbology of the sigma purposely uses the serpentine form twice in order to express its imagery. As the majuscule sigma is recognizable in both forms pictured in Figures 151 and 152, so the two minuscule forms are familiar, the one on the left used almost exclusively to end words.

For the serious student or philosopher, it may be of interest to note the evolution of the symbols expressing the value of 2. Beta, the first, is seen as a close knitting of the Serpent form with itself. Kappa, the second, begins a separation of this matching. The third, as seen in the sigma diagram of the twin serpents, completely separates the two, leaving only the philosophic salt of the geometry.

The philosopher may divine much from this simple diagram, understanding the nature of the three constituents. There is some salt in sulfur, as the mercurial element, just as there is some mercury in sulfur and vice versa. In the end, the twin serpents and the salt combine to give rise to the sacred phoenix, which in essence is immortal due to this most wise separation, purification, and amalgamation. It is in the fiery nest, say the Adepts, that the phoenix is reborn (see "The Chi Symbol").

Pythagoras and the Sigma

As explained in "The Number of the Beast," the name of the first philosopher may add up to either 864 or 666, in accord with the discrimination of the wordsmith. Pythagoras' name had a most sacred meaning to his elect. It is said that they (his disciples) only addressed him as *Master,* or as a mark of great respect, *That Man.* The name ascribed to him by history thus contains a possible two-fold interpretation, one revealing the numerology of the solar hexagon, and the other the magic square of 6.

Πυθαγορας to Ιησους (Pythagoras to Jesus)

The number 864 is interpreted by some as 96 x 9, the Foundation. This could account for the name *That Man,* as Pythagoras' works served as a great foundation for the future reference of philosophers, musicians, and mathematicians, etc. However, the number 864 is also 24 x 36, clearly reminiscent of the multiplication used to form the name of Jesus in the original Greek. To achieve the figure 888, the 37 interior eyes of the four beasts are multiplied by the 24 points about the solar hexagon (Ιησους).

Perhaps it was that the Pythagoreans did not consider the central point of the solar hexagon as numerable (asterisk point number 19), the sacred center of the throne. The later Essenes or Gnostics, penetrating this mystery, may have seen the central point as numerable, and thus Pythagoras may have been seen as *he who precedes the Christ or Anointed: the Ante-Christ.* This theory is backed up when recalling that PYTHAGORAS may be summed up to 666. Since 24 x 37 is 888, a sacred link between the Pythagorean and Neo-Pythagorean Schools is apparent. Thus the era of Apollonius and the ante-Nicene Christians had a distinct role in forming the scripture used by the later Church. The Mysteries were preserved even through the lengthy period of the uneducated and uninitiated editorship of the so-called "Church Fathers."

> *There is need for shrewdness here: anyone clever may interpret the number of the beast: it is the number of human being, the number 666.*
>
> Revelation 13:18

The Tau Symbol

The tau symbol, nineteenth in the Greek order, is one of the more simplistic. While the other dentals—delta, theta, lambda, and nu—seem to converge upon the head area of the Great Serpent for their symbolism, the tau (like the rho and sigmas preceding it) seems to prefer an identification with the *tail* of the subject. Tau is valued at 300.

North Semitic *tav* or *taw* was originally a simple cross +, but the Greeks and Etruscans endowed their majuscules with the more familiar T shape. As explained in "The Serpent and the Cross: The Mystery of Distillation," it would have been difficult *not to include* the esoteric wisdom of the cross symbol in the teaching of alphabetical science, for it was key to understanding the most holy of mysteries, that of passage beyond the physical world. The semblance of the ank or crux ansata became an important part of this collective knowledge. The cross has come to symbolize that which must be overcome and *risen above.* Hence the interpretation of the *tail* (in conjunction with the cross) as representing the base of the Cosmos.

As illustrated in "The Serpent and the Cross: The Mystery of Distillation," the cross of the Mysteries represented the lower regions of the seven-leveled Omniverse. These regions, previously described in the geometric analysis of Kircher's diagram, are of the material atom. As the proverbial *cross* that is carried in life (the human form), it precedes the heavenly regions proper—symbolized by the great orb atop the ank. This orb bears a possible resemblance to the Great Oval at the head of our Serpent, the Creature (as Logos) sustaining all spheres, including the highest.

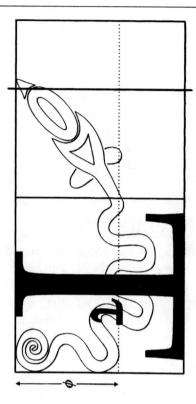

Figure 153. Tau

As illustrated previously, the "tail" of the "dragon" may include most of the Serpent's form starting from below the head—hence the majuscule tau umbrella-like over the seven coils. The taking of the phi segment emphasizing the area of the third coil is prerequisite to understanding the concept of the furnace, wherein the phoenix is immolated and the worm begins the process of regeneration (see "The Chi Symbol").

Valued as it is, the third coil *from the tail* was used—likely because the majuscule came first—and it, originating possibly as the Semitic *tav,* was identified with the tail. In order to correctly reduce the term of the symbol to 3, its enunciation must be closely considered. The dictionary guide pronounces *tau* as *tou.* As the lesser or short *o,* omicron most easily comes after forming the *t* sound. The mercurial aspirant is present,

creating the gentle plosive effect. With upsilon at the end, the term would be constructed numerically 300 + 8 (the aspirant) + 70 (omicron) + 400 (upsilon), summing to 778. As noted, the number 777 is indicative of the cross or transitional element in the transformational process. In accord with the rules of the ancient canon, words or phrases could sum to within one or two digits as a whole term, though not as a reduced term. Three sevens reduce to 21 and finally to 3.

The familiar spelling of tau-alpha-upsilon is also of interest, for its value is 701, reminding one of the terms *ophion* and *phoinix,* both valued at 700. As Oroboros, Ophion would have *eaten his tail,* just as the phoenix's *worm* survived on the remnant of its parental bier. In consideration of *one linear process* as enjoined by initiate philosophers, the serpent (or dragon) is often depicted as eating its tail. Sometimes the dragon is called *tail-biter.* In this wisdom, tau is considered *dental,* for the head and tail become joined in the circle representative of continuing life.

In careful consideration of this understanding, recalling from an earlier illustration that alpha and omega are identified with the triangular feature and the helix, respectively, the wisdom of tail-biting would bring together the *first* and the *last,* regenerating the *Word* as a linear expression.

In essence, this process of self-regeneration reconstructs the Serpent as a whole entity, like a resurrection or revival of the original Word of God (the Logos) prior to the slaying and separation of its parts used to construct the spoken word. This resurrection is part of a *most sacred* divine process, ultimately serving to enlighten the philosopher as mystic to the connection between matter and Spirit, nature and Divine Nature. The addition of tau-alpha-omega comes to 1101, reducing to 3.

Figure 154. Oroboros

Interpreted to represent one cyclical and one linear process, the worm or serpent is identified as dragon, for it owns feet, indicating earthly mobility, the nature of the philosophic mercury principle. As Uroboros from Uranos "Sky," "Heaven" plus Boreos, the primal wind that descends from above (the North Wind)], the worm of the dragon or phoenix is a thing from heaven fated to be integrated on Earth. As Ouranos has the double meaning of "tail" (from extrapolation of the root "oura"), it can be understood how Oroboros or ouroboreos is an intriguing and enduring symbol.

This is the dragon that both creates and ends its own existence, described in the Revelation to John 17:8, where it is written: "… the beast was once alive and is alive no longer, and is still to come."

The Upsilon Symbol

The upsilon is one of the more mysterious in the Greek offering, occupying the twentieth position in their alphabet. The majuscule character is believed to have stood at one time for the digamma, although this appears to be relative to digamma's minuscule. Digamma however, was a consonant, and thus the figure's transition

to a vowel form gave rise to the spelling Y–ψιλον, logically referring to the minuscule placement upon the fourth coil. In this, it became similarly distinguished as *E*-psilon, also a vowel.

As discussed under the rho symbol, the utterance of the *u* sound expresses the depth of the throat. A majority of the words beginning with upsilon have as their second letter *pi, phi* or *psi*. These letters seem to wholly capture the up thrust created through upsilon's enunciation.

The numerical value of upsilon can be determined using the same method as described under the epsilon symbol. Taking the *ps* as pi-iota-sigma, the term is evaluated 400 + 80 + 10 + 200 + 10 + 30 + 70 + 50, adding up to 850 and subsequently reducing to 4.

Having the meaning *"slender"* in the Greek, upsilon's majuscule is created upon the uppermost portion of the serpentine body where it begins to become the head, i.e., the depth of the throat. It branches into the finlike excursions extending on either side, as mapped.

It is taught that Pythagoras considered upsilon to be the symbol denoting the *forking of the ways*. The branching to the right was held as that

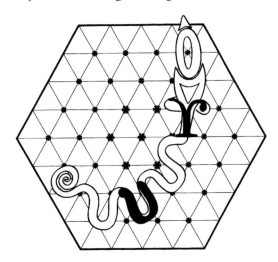

Figure 155. Majuscule and Minuscule Upsilon

of *Divine Wisdom,* while the one to the left was that of *Earthly Wisdom*. The majuscule form at times includes a small roundish ball collected upon its right horn, apparently symbolizing the cumulative presence of the *Spiritual Essence.* The *Music of the Spheres* or *Holy Sound Principle* is said by the Great Masters to be *caught* on the right side, a fact known to the initiates from the first day of their training. With a slender strain of the Divine Music heard at the outset, the concentration and regular efforts of the aspirant ultimately open the inner ear entirely, allowing the various sounds characterizing the inner planes or levels to become fully audible. This enrichment of the inner life usually precedes the restoration of the inner vision, and thus is called *the Door.*

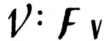

Figure 156. About the English V

The English *v* is related to the old digamma. The majuscule upsilon has the characteristic *V* at its crux. This logically is also the area characterizing the minuscule gamma and nu.

The Phi Symbol

In the English alphabet, it is the letter *f* that stands as the closest equivalent to the Greek phi. Technically, however, phi is a bi-labial fricative, while *f* is a labial-dental fricative. This means that phi uses both lips and *f* uses the bottom lip with the top teeth. Beta is also considered a bi-labial fricative by phonemicists. Because phi is an unvoiced labial aspirate, it is considered unique, with positions similar to beta when the breath is considered important in putting across the idea of a strong vowel. The Latin transliter-

ation always showed it as *ph,* passed on from the older pi-eta. In other languages, the *b* and *p* are considered bi-labial plosives, indicating the subtle differences of the Greeks.

Since the phi in the form of a geometrical and mathematical term is intimated to be a part of the Great Serpent's construction, care has been taken to discern its origin in both the minuscule and majuscule forms. The majuscule appears as the majuscule theta (representing the sundisk/umbilicus/representation of heaven) turned on its side with the majuscule iota growing out of it. This is to say that the iota is expanded to become a more important characteristic, i.e., the presence of the masterful number 10.[119] Understanding that such a proposed sundisk is actually a circular concept positioned so it may appear as an ellipse, a certain elliptical form may well have been isolated for the majuscule phi.[120] Since the Serpent Mound oval was apparently dictated to a certain extent by several stars, any argument stating that the oval is purely geometric would not stand up to scrutiny. Thus is the door opened for the oval's meaning to be interpretable.

Figure 157 describes how the oval form for the majuscule phi may have been conceived. This is only a technical point, however, assuming that the Great Oval was considered a disk/umbilicus being approached from its side. Figure 158 appropriately uses the Serpent form first introduced in the section "The Serpent and the Golden Ratio," but including Romain's lunar alignments. On the fifth coil from the tail is the *minuscule phi.* An alternative would be using the fifth coil from the head.

By esoteric tradition carried into the present day, phi is valued at 500. There is no recognized etymological link between *phi* and *five.* It is feasible that with the loss of symbol-number correspondence in the adaptation of the Greek sym-

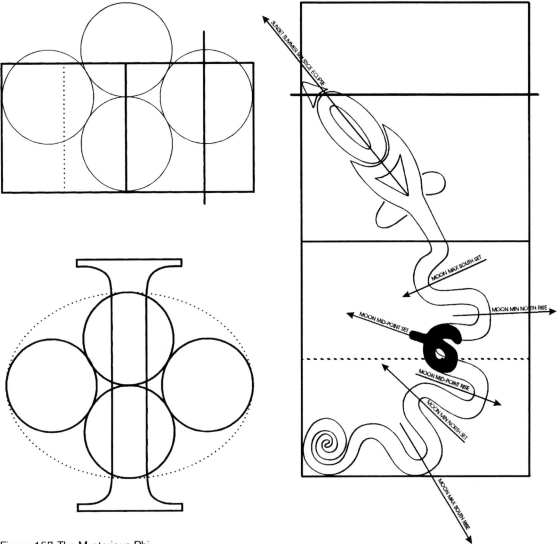

Figure 157. The Mysterious Phi

Since the phi and chi are mysterious in origin to that school of thought insisting that the Greek collection is derived strictly from the Semitic, there are two theories explaining the elliptic of the majuscule. The first is the four circles method. Enclosed in the double square box, the sacred cut reveals an almost exact bisection of the circle to the right. The second is in the extraction of the great oval from the Tree of Life as made from the magic square of eight. This same oval is shown resting atop the Horus depiction.

Figure 158. The Alignment of Minuscule Phi

The fifth coil from the tail, divined by the moon's midpoint setting position, explains the slightly slanted line, familiar in many forms of minuscule phi. The perpendicular line version is more indicative of the majuscule.

bols into Latin and later English, the disconnection could be accounted for. Etymologists have traced the word *"five"* back to the Old English, associating it with the Dutch, German, and Icelandic tongues, making it difficult to trace further. As previously noted though, when one considers the Old English *eahta* (eight) being so similar to *eta* (valued at eight), the connection seems more logical.

When adding the ascribed values of the cursive or "lesser" phi (.618034) and minuscule phi (1.618034), the result is the square root of 5.[121] The multiplication of these twin-like figures produces unity or 1. Hence the logic of phi (Φ) representing the 5(00) value at once featuring the majuscule iota growing out of it, being as unity, and, subsequently, the sovereignty of the majuscule form.

The spelling of phi in the Greek is Φι, which reduces to 510. However, were the aspirate added as shown in the English spelling, it would appear φηι, becoming 518, reducing to 5. It should be recalled that this is a bi-labial fricative—lots of breath. Eta in this instance is strictly relative to the aspirate or breath. So while not visibly present in the Greek spelling (this perhaps being assumed due to its uniqueness), it is very much a part of the expression.

The Chi Symbol

As the twenty-second letter of the Greek system, chi is one of the symbols not traceable or logically attributable to any Semitic form. It occupies the same counted position as the antique *taw,* and therefore scholars have perceived a probable connection between that Semitic creation and the later Greek chi. It is believed by some that chi may have developed from an earlier form of the xi, but in essentials they are looking for a cross or something turned from a cross as it is generally perceived: + > x (χ).

The origin of the symbols phi and psi (Φ, φ, Ψ, ψ) are a mystery to scholars however, and with chi between them, there is reason to consider its origin as recondite as its neighbors.

Numerically, chi is spelled (χι in the Greek, giving it the value of 610. Like phi preceding it, chi was considered a double consonant. Thus the aspirate is once again not visible—even as the breath is not visible except during cold weather—yet it is well integrated into the enunciation. Including the numerical value of the eta therefore, the value of chi comes to 618, reducing to 15 and finally to 6. The English spelling is *ch,* not *kh,* reminding one of the xi (ζ), valued at 60.

Chi is represented in the minuscule as contained within the graph of the sacred cut, using a portion of the sixth coil from the tail as well as a portion of the fifth, indicating the influence of phi. This is demonstrated in the proportions used in the diagram, the effigy partitioned by the ratio of 1.618 to find .618, χ. It would appear that every representation for the value of 6 is mysteriously missing or interrupted. This number was most sacred to the philosophic school of thought, and could hardly be compromised to the status of ordinary. Because chi is valued at 600, it of necessity had some extraordinary circumstance in its creation. The majuscule aptly demonstrates this, it being taken from the space resonant as .618, while angled with its crux by 1.618. Similarly, the sixth coil is not wholly taken as the mold for the minuscule, but rather the fifth and sixth.

It is through such an intimate interaction of 1.618034 and .618034 that philosophic unity is established, for the two terms multiplied produce 1. In this, the chi geometric structure has been likened to the *furnace* of initiate philosophers from which the phoenix arises. The twin

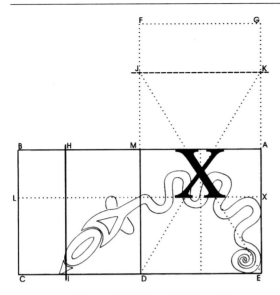

Figure 159. Majuscule Chi Extends Beyond the Visible

The box DFGE is identical to ECBA. MFGA is therefore a hypothetical extension, thus marked by a dotted line. Just as HI marks the sacred cut of the first box, so JK is the mark of the sacred cut on the second. EK x JK = 1.618. KA divided by JK therefore equals .618. KD crossing JE creates the framework for the majuscule, defining AX as stated. As seen in the creation of the chi majuscule, the element of the unknown or unperceived is present, i.e., the X factor extends beyond that which is visible.

abling it to express the instructions of the God-man, Christ, or Messiah. To the initiate, the mortal foibles associated with the first school of thought are untenable. The majuscule characters were given out first, the minuscule believed to be too revealing of the sacred Serpent's bodily constitution.

Both the majuscule and minuscule share a common line of intersection, going from the upper right to the lower left, KD. An identical line from upper left to lower right, JE, creates the framework for the majuscule. The bounds for the shaded-in majuscule are determined by multiplying the length of AE by .618, creating AX and subsequently XL. In selecting this manner of surgery our Python subjugator has made chi worthy of its enigmatic predecessors, digamma and xi.

principles of sulfur and mercury amalgamated into a perfect fixation therein.

Whoever believes that the majuscule characters of this alphabet were created long before the minuscule is not familiar with the Mystery College's intent. Thus there are two schools of thought in this regard. One is the mundane school that draws conclusions from evidence found in libraries, ruins, and graves. The other is the philosophic school, which believes in the intentional creation of the alphabet in complete wholeness, lending it Godly sanction and en-

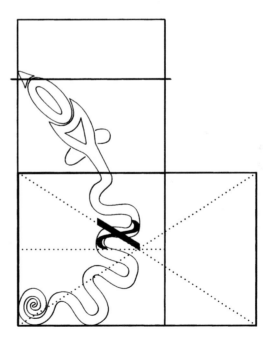

Figure 160. Minuscule Chi in a Graph of the Sacred Cut

The Psi Symbol

The psi symbols are in the twenty-third position of the alphabet, next-to-last in the collection. Psi came into the Athenian from the Samian, along with eta, xi and omega. It is enunciated as a double consonant, compounded from sigma and a labial. Thus we find βσ, πσ, and φσ in earlier examples before uniformity. The psi was and is valued at 700, and in this it might be discerned that the Samian architects created it from the phi-sigma, 500 + 200 being 700.

The minuscule form is not unlike the phi minuscule in that they both have the line of what is termed *divining*. Xi and chi, also double consonants, utilize distinctive *divisions* in their geometries, while phi and psi incorporate lines apparently originating from the lunar paths across the fifth and seventh coils.

The majuscule form is evidently intended to carry a great message. The alphabet was perceived as an entity, and through a certain inspiration and insight, was meant to relate a won-derful revelation of life, death, and resurrection in the highest meaning of the Word. It is thus not a great stretch of the scholar's imagination to see that the purpose of this alphabet directly relates to the message of the New Testament.

Immediately following the complete separation of the elements with the sigmas, the tau commences the wisdom of the process of regeneration. The upsilon captures the Spiritual Essence on the right side—fuel for the fire. Then appears phi, the integrating and amalgamating factor of the philosophic Stone (the soul). Following in correct order then comes the chi, joining the fifth coil to the sixth, even as the *volatile* and the *fixed* referred to by philosophers of science. Out of the sophic furnace of mysterious chi comes the light-laden *phoinix*, transformed from the lair (world or realm) of the worm and dragon. In the Greek, this term adds to 700, the same as the term *ophion,* serpent.

In Figure 162, the Tree of Life, divined by science and art of the magic square of eight, has its

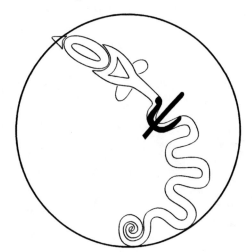

Figure 161. Minuscule Psi

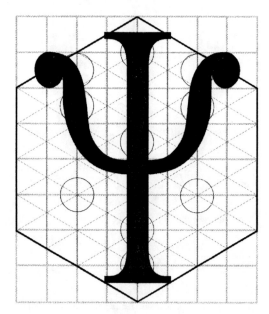

Figure 162. The Tree of Life Becomes the Phoenix Rising

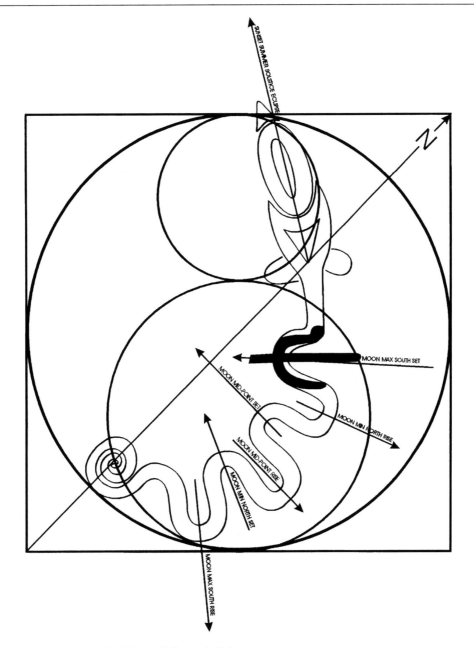

Figure 163. Completing the Definition of Minuscule Psi

As illustrated under "The Omicron Symbol," a 45° angle is established to the west of Romain's north-south alignment. Making this line parallel to the top and bottom of the page, a correct angle to discern the minuscule psi is made. The lunar maximum south setting position alignment divines the seventh coil from the tail, again emphasizing the method of the ancient cosmologists.

seven levels and ten focal points connected in a different fashion than previously described in "The Traditional Tree and the Great Serpent." Thus the ank, the tree, and the psi majuscule all have a common source or inspiration. This is likely the original idea behind the majuscule, and may perhaps have arisen *after* the creation of the minuscule shown in Figure 163. Here the seventh coil from the tail is used, recalling that the zeta minuscule incorporates the seventh from the head while the omicron encompasses all seven coils for its majuscule.

When enunciating the *ps,* the long *i* is popularly used to carry it out. This divining iota represents the power of 10 and is similarly present in the majuscule phi. In this case, however, the tree with its *ten horns* or *coronets* complements its *seven levels,* the value of psi. In the highest conceivable symbolism, the celebrated tree interpreted as the psi majuscule graphically represents the phoenix. Risen out of the ashes, wings outstretched, our Phoenix brilliantly leads into the omega, a return to its true home in the Great Word.

The Omega Symbol

The alchemical sage Zosimos of Panopolis interprets the omega majuscule as having been inspired by the notion of its circle representing the circle of Okeanos. This great life-giving river or *current* of the Sea of Life is nothing less than the Greater Word, Ω.

The *o*-mega, meaning the *great O,* is the last symbol in the Greek system. As discussed in "The Power of the Word," the fifth angel of Revelation's chapter seven represents the Controlling Power, that which creates order out of chaos. It is the primal Vibration said by the Masters to be constantly uttered directly from the mouth of God. It is enunciated as *am* with a slight change

to a circular formation of the open mouth, lending it its characteristic sound.

The majuscule omega encompasses the Serpent, utilizing the Delphi Circle. It is a symbol of enduring *love,* that which encompasses all, working ceaselessly toward unification in harmony of all. Omega is the greatness of the *first and last,* and like the alpha majuscule using the vesica piscis the one and only time, the use of the Delphi Circle without the Arbelos is a one-time use only. In this, the alpha and omega majuscules are unique.

Just as the omicrons are seen as closed circles, so the omega, encompassing their space, is a greater circle, opened to symbolize the ever-giving heart of all that is creative. This is the First Cause and Great Giver of life. It is the Grand Vibratory Principle, sympathetically empowering the omicron or lesser Om and enlivening the countless atoms of Creation. Hence we see omega surrounding the omicrons.

Figure 164 reveals the majuscule, while Figure 165 shows the method for creating the minuscule. Similar to the way the ξ was created, the grafting technique is practical. Since there is no eighth coil, the fourth was removed and the third joined with the fifth. The pi minuscule performs a similar operation, but does not entirely cut away the fourth coil, curling into the third and fifth coils from the tail or head, whichever is preferred. Similarly, the eta *infers* the third and fifth coils through the vestigial technique first shown in the zeta minuscule. In this, each symbol denoting the value of the 8 has a different method of description, yet utilizes the combination of 3 and 5 to make 8.

Figure 164. The Feet of Majuscule Omega

The great square surrounding the Delphi Circle gives rise to the Arbelos as described under "The Pi Symbol." In order to create the podium feet of the majuscule omega, the square is here maintained, referencing the omicrons.

Figure 165. Grafting Minuscule Omega

The practice of grafting, evident in the xi majuscule, explains the unique minuscule omega. When pronouncing a long *O*, the lips purse lightly, creating the English *W*. In fact, the omega is valued the same as two upsilons (double-*u*), 4 + 4, after reduction. Whether this was done unconsciously by English alphabetology is a matter of opinion.

However, scholarship avers the *w* sound to have been represented by the Semitic waw, which in the Greek alphabet became the digamma and upsilon. Thus the enunciation of omega simply prepares the way for the *w* positioning.

Epilogue

THE MYSTERIES SURROUNDING SERPENT MOUND will withstand time and reveal themselves to future generations with an inspiration overdue to those who would celebrate a superior heritage. If you, patient reader, have taken the time to read this entire book with some thoughtful intent, then you must know something of the preparation involved in the design and proper placement of this majestic dragon in the Ohio wilderness. Uncounted generations of Native Americans kept the site intact. Putnam's arrival was similarly crucial in the analysis and preservation of the effigy. But our Harvard professor was a rare exemplar among the Whites, for most men of the race simply preferred to plunder and rape the antiquities of North America, concerning themselves very little with their preservation and interpretation.

There is a fundamental divergence between the Old European and Native American approach to ancient and sacred sites. In its endeav-

oring to explain away the ancient mysteries in terms of its science, nineteenth- and twentieth-century archaeology has only enslaved itself to the material retrieved from the inadvertent desecration of uncounted gravesites. These mysteries by their nature are barely attached to the tomb-robber's evidence, and thus the newly emerging proponents of archaeology seek to enlighten its shadowy domain through the skillful application of previously unacceptable modes of investigation. Among these are astronomy, comparative mythology, folk traditions from around the world, and even first-hand mystical experience. Such noble efforts to see through the eyes of the ancients have yielded promising results, but not without the customary reins of biting criticism imposed as a device for equalizing and tempering. Unfortunately, both jealousy and plagiarism infect many branches of research science — the cause and cure for which may be grasped through observation of these sciences' histories.

The European invasion of the Americas sought first gold, jewels, and sculptures fit to display in public and private collections. While efforts were made by some to record and understand the multi-faceted native tradition, the Europeans considered the indigenous people both ignorant and savage to a great degree. Because the Native Americans were a militarily conquered race, they were ruthlessly subjugated and oppressed during the post-Revolutionary period, and this bigotry has continued to this day. In hindsight, materially oriented archaeology has ruined exponentially more than it has preserved, and has correctly deciphered a little more than nothing. Is it any surprise that the native community is indifferent, their love stymied?

In the Ohio Valley, the ancestral land authority has taken measures, installing critical safeguards against the selfish curiosity that has threatened the theft of sacred relics from their resting-places. As a boy, I remember skeletons on exhibit at the Cincinnati Natural History Museum. Such artifacts were on display as well at the Serpent Mound Museum until just a few years ago. Finding an arrow point or sinew stone in the field is one thing, but methodically looting an ancient resting-place is obscene in light of Native American beliefs concerning the status of the dead. Yet it goes on even today.[122] Any number of these gravesites were constructed directly over or by converging streams of earth energies, and the placement of burials at such locations and the placement of the burials at such locations facilitated the creation of a sanctuary for the Earth-spirit.[123] Little needs be said on the vital nature of such localities. But the White Man was and is to an extent blind to such natural rhythm and flow, a condition unfortunately afflicting modern man in general.

The Rosetta Stone Metaphor

After the fall of Egypt and the rise of Rome with its modified form of Christianity, the early Church violently carried out the systematic removal from the face of the Earth all that might betray the pagan roots of its new imperialism. The middle of this first millennium marked the death of the keepers of the last bastion of the exquisitely subtle Egyptian Tradition, and the last interpretable hieroglyphs were chiseled from the remaining sanctuaries' pillars. As though seeking the cov-

Figure 166. The Cincinnati Tablet

The famous Cincinnati Tablet bears the careful engravings of a style more than once related to the high art of the much later Mayan stoneworkers. It was found in a tall, massive mound in what is now downtown Cincinnati in an astronomically oriented position. It may be held in the palm of the hand and on its reverse is a figure similar to the French fleur-de-lis. This tablet and others like it are theorized to have been part of a single collection at one time. Their individual members have been found spread out over the broad Ohio Valley in tombs, indicating that they may have been distributed among various tribes at one time, and used as powerful or politically significant amulets.

eted limelight created by the institutionalized rape of the Valley of the Kings, North American archaeology has similarly looted, logged, and leveled what are only now being realized as astro-nomically oriented and naturally spirited cere-monial locations. Perhaps because Christians tra-ditionally bury the dead in a box and vainly wave a marble flag overhead, a blind eye has been cast on the three or more dimensions of thought embodied in Native American sacred sites.

In 1799 at the mouth of the Nile, the town of Rosetta yielded a slab of stone that, through par-allel Greek inscription, would at last tell the meaning of the lost Egyptian hieroglyphics. The Great Serpent Mound, in a class of art and archi-tectural planning that transcends any known earth or stone effigy, is analogously a most excel-lent Rosetta Stone. Respectfully regarded and thoughtfully studied, our Stone—which is made of earth—may one day be seen as a timeless treasure upon which no price may be established. In this mature approach, the Serpent Mound will be rediscovered as an important repository of the ancient wisdom, the retrieval of which re-quires less of the objective reasoning and more of the subjective.

When perhaps the greatest traditional philo-sophic writer of the twentieth century, Manly Palmer Hall, states openly that the Serpent Mound is an indicator of the presence of the Mysteries on the North American continent,[124] a knowledgeable person should take notice. On the other hand, it doesn't take a good philoso-pher to intuit the Great Serpent as connected to a culture possessing Godly awareness and a penchant for describing what may not be eluci-dated in words.

It would seem that approximately every 2,160 years, one-twelfth of a precessionary age, an extraordinary amount of energy finds expres-sion among one or more factions of the world populace. The explosive innovation of the Adena People, finding their height of promising expres-sion in the Hopewell era, offers yet another pos-sible illustration of such a theory. Like the pyra-mid builders of Egypt who had no peers in their art before or after them, the Adena-Hopewell seemed to come from out of the darkness of pre-history with exceptional techno-artistic and orga-nizational ability. All considered, these unknown people left a wonderful and mysterious legacy that our best investigators are just now seriously unraveling.

There are unmistakable signs that either a real genius was effectively nurtured in Ohio's prehistory, or the people here were privy to a tradition of what could only be interpreted as truly insightful and of superior intellect. It is not out of the question to suggest that the Archaic Allegheny culture's influence underscored the dynamic cultural expressions ascribed to the Adena-Hopewell.

The Ohio Historical Society, headquartered in Columbus, has done some exemplary work in the field and the library, rediscovering, after the groundbreaking work of Colonel Reeves dur-ing the 1930s, what may likely prove to be an ancient road of sixty miles in length. It is straight to the fault of being inexplicable and extends between the two Hopewell bastions of Newark and Chillicothe. Such a road, having parallel earthen walls going the distance, would have required a politically strong and centralized gov-ernment, or an inspiration extending from a for-mer time, or both. It has gently shocked the archaeological community in that it is pre-Mayan and pre-Anasazi in design and construction. One should be reminded that far more harsh seasonal changes take place in the Ohio Valley than in places further south, making such an effort more difficult. This ceremonial highway, mystically (though not physically) connecting the two sites of Newark and High Bank, bears a strong and compelling resemblance to the later overland projects of the Central American cultures.

Are Newark and High Bank themselves effigies to the ancient Grandmother Spider and Great Turtle mythologies, still kept alive among the stories of the western nations? Perhaps more intriguing would be the possibility of the two sites having been in existence prior to these myths, and that the stories of the Spider and Turtle were the inheriting cultures' ways of explaining the meaning of these gigantic monuments. We may know the answer to this question some day, even as we understand the antiquity of the Great Serpent effigy. Now believed to be of a design older than the earliest Hopewell due to several pieces of new evidence, the Great Serpent may be an embodiment of a very ancient premise of world myth, perhaps unific to the prehistoric world. If the Hopewell had extraordinary energy and genius, who designed the Great Serpent more than two millennia before predecessors, the Adena? Could these grand works of serpent, spider, and turtle have been the design of the Allegheny People?

Since the first edition of this work, the star pattern was discovered, and the dominant influence of the Great Dragon over the ancient world has made itself apparent. I have learned as well through sources of traditional philosophy that the ideal of the Great Serpent is one of a repository. It is not composed of clay, stone, and topsoil, but of compressed, compounded, and interactive information, the deciphering of which has required this amateur years and years of continuous research and meditation. As related in "The Great Magnetic Line," there are believed to be other types of repositories as well, all over the world, numbering in the multiple hundreds. Theories about their purpose are well beyond the scope of this little book. These unseen, intentionally concealed structures considerably predate the icon of the Great Serpent. A part of the purpose of this work is therefore to introduce the exceedingly wise and meaningful design of our Great Serpent as relating to the hidden purpose of the subterranean order.

The Vision

In the vision I describe in "The Great Magnetic Line," the Seal when activated was sustained by the cities and towns encompassed by it. Yet it had a *single point of ignition*. The light energy of the Seal revealed in reverse order the stages that had culminated in the cooperation of the cities.

Revered as a powerful symbol of democracy and freedom, the Great Seal may not have been the invention of elitist Masonry or the political icon of Colonial statesmen, but an intimate part of Native American tradition. Yet even as the human soul is forgotten, buried in the flesh and made to witness its slow decay, so the Seal is all but lost to the memory, being anchored and fully resonant in the subtler tissues of Gaia's body. Yet now it sleeps, lost to the memory of even the wise, blanketed by the silts and soils of untold millennia, waiting for its revival, at long last.

Four thousand eight hundred years or more may have passed since the inception of the sacred and ceremonial Great Serpent in what is now Adams County. By the evidence presented, it was a project designed to mark the *place of the initiation* for the rebirth of the Great Eagle, the world Phoenix. By implication, a wonderful occurrence was foreshadowed in the ancient forestlands of the Ohio, for the Serpent is a grand sign of the wisdom of the ages, and the manitou of power, grace, and majesty.

It is not out of the question that much of our traditional religious temperament and ethos has a foundation in what is this possible future event. Fragments of its proposed ceremony survive in our various scriptures, mythologies, legends, and folk traditions as though it were a singular Flower, the petals of which were distributed to every corner of the world. Yet its deeply buried bulb remains hidden where it was planted long ago, that it might release its bloom and spring to life once in a grand age, after the passage of uncounted stars. Now, the Western Continent may be destined to host the restoration of the Great Seal, a custom returned by the hand of Fate that ultimately may offer the *cup of light* to the entire world.

In this tradition, the Serpent Mound stands as an allegorical symbology of the Wisdom, the Gnosis, the full import of which may not be simply handed over to a general populace still struggling for domestic and international peace. Nevertheless, it is the world's fate to inherit its legacy. The fine matters of creation, reflected in our culture, must be realized before the reconnection to a paradisiacal Earth may be effected.

The Seal is a great medallion of light, and its detailing would require much education and sacrifice. Racial, religious, and economic barriers would have to be put aside. So much depends upon non-violence alone that even though we advance technologically, we are caught in the gyres of relearning the spiritual ropes. Hatred by its quality prevents love from taking over the rule of the human heart, for love is the evolutionary force—the real Power. This is the beginning of wisdom. This beginning took the form of a humble earthwork based upon an astral pattern thousands of years ago. Who designed and constructed it we do not know. Perhaps we are not intended to know.

As soon as the dragon found himself hurled down to the earth, he sprung in pursuit of the woman, the mother of the male child,

But she was given a pair of the great eagle's wings to fly away from the serpent ...

Revelation 12: 13, 14

The successful accomplishment of the reactivation will initially martial a specific region, unveiling, however temporarily or permanently, the subtle region of the Earth, Gaia. Her son, the ensouling pattern of the throne, is at first insufficient for the Dragon's enormous celestial majesty. Thus his power moves out across and through the landscape, like a rarified magnetic field. It is the power of the ark that lends the Dragon life, and the "light" extends from his lair, its lucid projections affecting the minds of men and women—especially in the long night of "tribulation" that is to come.

But even the inference of a millennia-lost Edenic environ does not come without atonement, and the awesome "beast," the Serpent of Yaweh, survives, roaming unchallenged and uncontested through this time. For it is the period of dissolution when good is rewarded and past evil atoned until the playing field is leveled.

The beast was allowed to mouth its boasts and blasphemies, and to be active for forty-two months.

Revelation 13:5

While the many ministers and priests from their pulpits and sanctuaries pronounce the beast to be some sort of God-forsaken confederacy of European, Mediterranean, North African, or Asian countries, in reality it may very well take the form of an actual creature of a divinely engineered nature. All the signs and ingredients are there, including the seven heads and ten horns, the tail sweeping one-third of the stars from the sky, and even the "little beast." Why should we look confusedly to political signs for an accurate fulfillment of scriptural imagery? Utilizing the same sort of power and magnetic aura as a radio and television station, this "beast," the true Old Serpent and tempter of Eve, may well rise to the occasion of prophecy from his lonely sanctuary in Adams County.

> *So the angel set his sickle to work on the earth, and harvested the whole vintage of the earth and put it into a huge winepress,*
>
> *The winepress of God's anger, where it was trodden until the blood that came out of the winepress was up to the horses' bridles as far away as sixteen hundred furlongs.*
>
> Revelation 14:19, 20

But if not supported and sustained what some would term *predestination,* the Dragon is a mere fantasy and myth for the imagination, as also will be the expediency of the hoped-for *Rapture,* or the enactment of the celestial Light War, long awaited as the *Armageddon.* For the latter occurrences depend wholly on the former, even as the phoenix will not rise save through the mitigating circumstance of a certain sacrifice, that of an international discipline based on love.

But beware the worship of the wondrous beast, for it is an ephemeral thing, its purpose calculated to cleanse the earth of bloodstains from past civil wars through calling down the backlog of reward and punishment. The Great Serpent has carried with it in its descent to the earth the hallowed *seed of light,* and the end of its brief reign will commence the restoration of the Tree of Life, the leaves of which will heal the nations, the fruits of which will restore the Spirit.

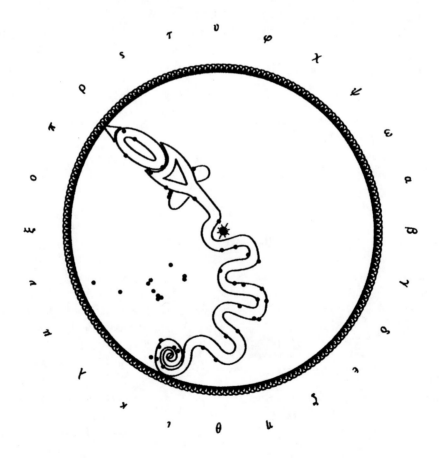

Notes

1. Adena *(Ah-dee-na),* from the Greek root αδεν—meaning "enough of" or "lacking nothing," was a name bestowed by Thomas Worthington, an early governor of Ohio, on an unnamed race of people who lived in the Ohio Valley region beginning about 1000 B.C.E. (before the common era of the Christian calendar) to about 100 C.E. (Common Era). Archaeological opinion differs by as much as two centuries on the cultural extinction. It is believed that they were related to the prehistoric aboriginal Lenni Lenape, "the Ancient Ones."

2. The Hopewell were named after Mordecai Cloud Hopewell, a Revolutionary War Captain who settled in the area. This native group followed the Adena, and probably lived in the Ohio Valley until no later than about 500 C.E. Thus it is thought that the Adena and Hopewell cultures overlapped beginning around 200 B. C.E. It has not been ruled out that they were the result of the commingling of the races of the prehistoric Alleghan-Lenape and the ancient people called by Heckewelder, Mengwe, creating a vigorous hybrid culture.

3. The Fort Ancient People were so named because they inhabited the site of Fort Ancient a number of centuries after its being abandoned by the Hopewell. The Fort Ancient People were a very early branch of the Mississippian Culture whose descendents are theorized to have met with the first Spanish, French, and English explorers. Many of the great earthen structures throughout the Mississippi Valley are attributed to these people. Yet their structures are not to be confused with the much earlier earthworks of the Ohio Valley. This time period beginning after 1000 C.E. is filled with much speculation due to ancient accounts that were transcribed from native oral history by early missionaries and settlers.

4. This map is the first known to have attempted a topographic view of the effigy, roughly revealing its varying heights.

5. See "The Draconis Mystery" next section.

6. As reported by Hancock in his *Heaven's Mirror,* a series of first millennium C.E. temples in Cambodia possibly referenced Draconis for their situation.

7. Discovered by Reca (ree-sa) Jones, this group of mounds constitutes an oval-shaped enclosure more than 800 feet across at one point. One mound is over 20 feet high and the others vary between 3 and 14 feet, according to one source. The group is believed by archaeologists to be as old as 5,400 years—older than the pyramids at Giza.

8. The fact that there were many trees and much topsoil present when Squier and Davis first appeared on the scene coupled with the fact that there is no soil beneath the effigy creates a simple choice. Either nothing ever grew there before (which is highly unlikely) or the outcropping was indeed cleared.

9. Between Putnam's first visit and his second, it is written that vandals and treasure hunters had left the effigy scarred, giving the professor concern for its future. The oval embankment appears in subsequent renderings to Squier and Davis as possibly made of soil parted along its ellipse, creating a wishbone feature. Logically speaking, Putnam followed the clay core for his pattern, restored the oval, and eliminated the strange earthen bank. The star chart coupled with Romain's map nicely confirms Putnam's correct restoration to a high degree.

10. The excavation team's methodology reflects greater sensitivity to the Native American philosophy, a very important step forward.

11. The clays found commonly in the area were used to make those first crude ceramics, and although the Adena People's particular kiln techniques aren't known, many examples of their pottery exist today, mostly in shard form.

12. There are massive "borrow pits" on the park property, and possibly on an adjacent private property. The meaning of the term "borrow" is precisely

what it sounds like.

13. There is also an "official" position on the matter of depth of soil. It is stated that the materials from a brief primitive farming concern could have been incorporated into the soil depth. Even if this were true, such material would add only a fraction of an inch, if that, given the very short span of the gardening. Besides, the mound proper was possibly not farmed at all. In addition, the whole park was blanketed in deep, rich "vegetable mold," i.e., topsoil-like earth, not just the effigy. Why would these people have covered the whole park with topsoil? To top it off, Squier and Davis reported the effigy to have considerably higher embankments than observed by Putnam! Thus, even if the builders added some topsoil (for ceremonial purposes), why the entire area and not just the Serpent? Why would they have added topsoil to the floor of their meticulously smooth and level oval earthwork as well as between the already narrow spacing of the tail coil? There was no dark soil found beneath the effigy, only inorganic material, like stone and stone-clay. Did they find the area bald or did they clear it? If they cleared the whole area as is evident, why would they then bring topsoil back in when they could have simply left it there, saving much labor?

14. The Fletcher and Cameron map as well as the Hardman map would also work adequately in this particular demonstration.

15. This is believed derived from an early Arabic root, meaning "of the serpent or dragon's head."

16. There were actually three steps taken—one at a time—as my thinking evolved. First, I was curious to see if the size of Stonehenge and the size of Serpent Mound were relative in terms of horizon sightings. They were. Then the hexagonal geometry was added (see "The Great Serpent as Universal Template"), and it was amazing to see that the replica of the Stonehenge circles fit precisely inside a smaller hexagonal configuration. But when the asterism of Draco was added, it was hard to believe at first. Here was some obvious proof that not only was Serpent Mound related to Stonehenge by astronomical proportion, but Stonehenge probably was based, like Serpent Mound and the Pyramids at Giza, upon a star pattern.

17. Pythagoras or the Pythagorean College under the Master's guidance successfully engaged in a number of areas of study. They were believed to have been into medicine, astronomy, botany, zoology, mathematics, and geometry, to name but a few areas of endeavor. Unfortunately for us today, little remains of the direct teachings of this proto-philosopher.

18. With regard to these supporters, it was after his return to the site in 1885, and after being informed of the owner's plans to level the Serpent for farming space, that Putnam took upon himself to raise the funds. After his return to Boston, he writes that were it not for a small group of Boston ladies, he might not have raised the $6,000 necessary to wrest the landmark from the intended grasp of the short-sighted agricultural project.

19. Iconograhic science deals with the study of symbols and images (from the Greek icon, meaning "image").

20. How the Shaman Stole the Moon by William Calvin.

21. Due to the policy of rewriting history to match its ambition, the first Christian millennium witnessed the systematic chiseling of the last interpretable hieroglyphs from the remaining bastions of the Egyptian Tradition. It was not until 1799 when the town of Rosetta yielded the famous stone tablet revealing three corresponding forms of the same passage that the mystery was solved.

22. The celestial motion of precession has been a godsend in the quest for accurate archaeological dating. It is approximately 25,920 solar years in duration and is characterized by a nearly imperceptible wobbling in the Earth's axis of rotation. It has been compared to a top rapidly spinning yet listing at the same time. An example of the attention given to it comes from ancient Egypt. Draconis-gamma was known as Isis in 3500 B.C.E. and was visible through the central light-passages in the temples of Mut at Thebes and Hathor at Denderath. Well over a thousand years later, the temple of Ramses at Karnak incorporated these stars' light in an internal passage 1,500 feet in length. There are other examples of similarly oriented temples, each in its own time abandoned for another, due to precession. In fact, the Greek astronomer Hipparchos (190–125 B.C.E.) is now believed not to have

been the discoverer of precession, but rather reported well on the close proximity of certain religiously oriented temples, rebuilt as the greater motion of precession rendered them disoriented—out of alignment.

23. The term "asterism" means "a grouping of stars," which is to say, a subset of a larger or constellatory province.

24. In 2750 B.C.E., Draconis-alpha (Thuban in the Egyptian) was less than 10 feet from true north, while now it is about 26 degrees. Its light, thought to have been more brilliant then, could have been seen even during the day from the "bottom of the central passage" of the Cheops pyramid, as well as the two pyramids at Abousseir.

25. The Great Oval at the mouth of the Great Serpent Mound may well be a rendering of such an understanding.

26. In Indian tradition, this is termed *Sat,* the True Substance.

27. Further, 12 will fit around the six, 24 about the 12, etc.

28. This is apparently because of the Creator's six days, mentioned in Moses' writings.

29. There are other ways to divide the seven circles to prepare the hexagonal form, but this method uses the pinion points of the compass, all radiating through the central pinion point.

30. The seed mind, intellect, lower mind, and ego (the condition of experiencing a seemingly separate existence from the Creator) all comprise the higher, Causal Body of humanity. This body is considered archangelic, not yet actually humanoid in shape, but, for practical analysis, more spherical. While the seed mind, intellect, and lower mind all comprise fine sheaths of the body, the ego automatically establishes itself as a sort of partner to the seed mind when that primary organ of thought arrives by the action of Universal Love *(Chit).* This could be described as the spiritualizing of an Atom. Like the electrical current used to change common iron into a magnet, the force of conscious love creating a conscious entity quickens the primary form. Thus the throne of the Divine (all-conscious knowledge), represented as the hexagon, gives rise to the concept of the Son, the offspring of the Invisible which ultimately becomes Man.

31. The five organs of sense include the eye, ear, nose, skin, and tongue. The five objects are therefore seeing, hearing, etc. The five organs of action include the foot, hand, genitalia, rectum-anus, and again the tongue, this time in the capacity to form intelligible words and sounds for communication. The five conditions of matter are noted above. The quality of fire is contained in the metabolism. There is a general misconception concerning the "ether." The ethereal condition sustains the other four, like a subtle substrate or background. It is also considered the pre-creation state of matter and is often associated with electrical forces. It is sometimes considered to be a viscous fluid or gaseous substance existing between the stars and created worlds, super-penetrating all. The Masters relate that the active and pure ethereal condition is abundant and ascendant in the human being, allowing a greater comprehension of the other conditions as they all work together. It provides a clear intellectual atmosphere or dimension for proper contemplation of higher realities. It is a positive aid in helping the individual to determine correct behavior from incorrect and right from wrong. In short, it is that which enables human beings to "hold dominion" over other life forms.

These conditions of matter and one other (electricity) are brought into their distinguished states through the interaction of the *four qualities.* These are hotness, coldness, moistness, and dryness. These four are important in that they affect the ether, subsequently aiding in the creation of matter in its many forms.

In their combinations, they produce six states. Hotness and dryness produce the fiery condition; hotness and coldness the liquid condition; moistness and coldness cause solidity; and moistness with hotness produces the gaseous condition. Finally, the sixth state of electricity comes from coldness meeting with dryness. Electricity is the liaison or projected Will of the Universal Ether and serves in the creation of matters from the etheric condition to the numeric condition of protons. It is like the gene and chromosome touching upon the simplistic and pristine matter within the unfertilized egg. The Will brings about an intelligent structuring of the Ether, subsequently creating Matter. It is also through such Will that Matter is returned back to the Ethereal State. Hence whole universes go in and out of creation or comprehension with the passage of Great Time.

32. A similar reverence for the pi ratio was found by Thom is his analysis of many of the stoneworks in Britain. The ancient designers there are believed to have deliberately created elliptical circles in order to reduce the numerical value of pi to 3, thereby making their unit of 2.72 feet (the Megalithic Yard) nicely proportionate. But like the mysteries of the Serpent Mound's measures, there was more to Thom's discoveries.

33. The reader can repeat this using a simple hand calculator. The side of each equilateral triangle equals approximately 81.6 feet. Dividing one of the triangles perpendicularly in half and by using the Pythagorean Theorem to determine the hypotenuse of each triangle, the hypotenuse equals the square root of 4995 feet or 70.67 feet. Multiply 70.67 by 8 to determine the long axis of the hexagon which equals 565.36 feet. Dividing 565.36 by 3 will determine the diameter of any the seven circles underscoring the hexagon, 188.4 feet. Dividing 188.4 by *pi* (3.1415926) yields 59.99, virtually 60.

34. The effigy is constructed on a massive deposit of dolomite (magnesium-limestone) that characterizes the area. This fact raises the question of whether the builders cleared the entire area of earth or if the area was barren when they arrived there. A fairly uniform amount of topsoil has accumulated over the effigy and its peninsula-like setting since its construction, lending support for the case of the area having been cleared.

35. "Pyramid" is a term of enigmatic origin, but it may mean "divine fire." Within the Great Pyramid is the Tet, a phallus-like instrument thought to be the transforming device for energies created and admitted into the Tuat, the encompassing matrix of heaven or all-nature. This Tet, resembling a sort of gabled roof with tons of granite piled below, causes a condition (due to the quartz content of the rock) termed "piezoelectric." Piezoelectricity indicates conductivity within the rock; actual electricity is released through pressure, transforming the granite which is normally a poor conductor. Percolating slowly through the conducting column of the Tet and spreading out into the

upper body of the massive structure from its gabled roof, tremendous energy emitted from the sealed King's Chamber ultimately converging at the tip of the Great Pyramid. When the geometry of the Great Pyramid was still intact, a well-tempered and digested form of the ark's product was released. The warm energy would deliberately rise ever upward toward heaven, refining and culturing itself through the chemical filter of the limestone.

The secret of the ark's mystical power may be uncovered by examining its construction and materials. The box, as well as the table and incense burner described in Chapter 37 of Exodus, were built to the proportions of the phi series, ratios known to the Pythagoreans in their musical theory: 1:2, 2:3, and 3:5. The resonance produced by the ark would therefore enter into a mode of harmony. The use of pure gold to line the ark within and cover it without is the most important key to the instrument's function. The extremely heavy mercy seat with its angelic ornaments could have provided the necessary hermetic seal, crucial to producing an electrical reaction within the ark. In this, the twin ornaments may have served as anode and cathode contacts, directing the polarized energy as it rose.

Calcium is a metallic element, atomic number 20. In its common calcium carbonate form, limestone is a poor conductor but a great accumulator of electrical energy. Forming the bones of humans and many animals, calcium is key in the ability to sustain the bioelectrical energies needed for gradual growth and continuing health. Being a living, semi-conducting framework material, the bones (Latin: *ossi*—similar to Osiris) retain a considerable resonance of life force energy suitable for promoting healthy and vital bone marrow, key to blood cell production. Polished limestone can approach a nacreous sheen, for it is the same thing pearls are made of. A fine polish like this is comparable to a dentist's polish on a crown, effectively sealing off the internal body of the subject from natural corruption. Most investigators assumed that the casing stones of the Great Pyramid were once capable of reflecting sunlight.

36. The pyramid's base, measuring around its existing casing stones, averages to 755.7 feet per side (Petrie and Cole).

37. The Indian *Sants* are Mastersouls who grant initiation into Spiritual Science. A Sant is a Mastersaint or Master of saints. In order to be a Mastersaint, one must be a Mastersoul, i.e., one who can help others rise above body consciousness. A saint may be a member of any religion and a member of any race. The Great Master's work is to initiate the souls who are ready for the spiritual life.

38 . Called variously the gentry, the jinn, the sidhes, the good people, etc., their lives are generally very private, most preferring a separate existence from the general populace humankind.

39. Also called the third eye, the yogic eye, the all-seeing eye, etc., this specialized organ corresponds to the pineal gland in the physical body.

40. The age of the Serpent effigy precludes any historical documentation of its method of design or inspiration. What archaeologists, amateur and professional, have pieced together over the last 150 years has been largely based upon physical evidence.

41. The kabbalistic (from q'abbalah, meaning "something passed down" i.e., from tradition) tree is a particularly unusual arrangement of 10 orbs, difficult to construe by any geometric formula. Thus it has been attributed purely to the "spheres of existence" by most. Its advocates suggest it was created to embody the fruits of the tree of life and that these fruits are the essence of the tree. In reality, the geometry came first. But so excellent was this geometric form's design, serving as a visible body for this universal knowledge, that the origin of the form has been lost.

42. It is stated that the first magic squares did not "surface" until the ninth century of the common era. The public knew little of these "occult" figures of numerology until then, although they were used by initiates from prehistoric times. Some believe that God used magic squares to do certain creative works, including the layering of the Great Universe itself.

43. A couple of books including one on number puzzles and one on magic squares and cubes helped. A friend and I set to work constructing all the magic squares from 1 to 100. We stopped before we got to 30. Odd-numbered squares have a different starting method from even-numbered ones. Prime numbers presented us with little difficulty, but those that were twice a prime number (6, 10 etc.) were really tough. The magic square of eight is definitely the simplest, yet has the most possible combinations, until you reach the square of 16.

44. Esoteric tradition holds that the ank is key to understanding both the microcosmic and macrocosmic forms, i.e., the humanoid and the Universal. The Sages logically patterned their Cosmos after the macrocosm. This they subsequently related to the human form. As there are seven distinct levels to what is termed the Omniverse (the Grand Universe) the top four levels comprise the regions of non-material Spirit and the bottom three levels comprise the regions of the material atom. These bottom worlds form the image of the cross by the wise and holy of some faiths. It is a fact that the cross is held as sacred to nearly all ancient world cultures, and takes on many different forms. The symbolic cross of Christendom, however, is long-held as a disconnected fragment of the holy ank, purposely separated from its mother form as an act of forbearance with respect to the Mysteries.

In fact, an important correlation is made between the knowledge possessed by the Revelation author and the complete geometric and astronomical knowledge of Serpent Mound. Pre-Christian civilization has apparently borrowed heavily from the specific image, and therefore lore, of the Great Serpent. The rise of Christianity's flower seems to have its roots firmly embedded in this tradition, drawing to its bloom its essential elements of form and life. The creature's fantastic presence both begins and ends the Bible, having grown into a majestic and terrible dragon by Revelation. The New Testament itself was originally penned in the style of the numbers, geometries and coils of the Father's most mysterious creature.

45. This is the beast having seven heads and ten horns. In actuality, it is the association of the Serpent design with the ank-tree of life symbol which has confused the imagery of the tree of life with the image of the "beast" or Great Dragon.

46. After constructing the square, the point between the numbers to be connected was marked, and the compass pin was placed there. Subsequently, a half arc was drawn, revealing the figure, number by number.

47. This is the balancing of the hexagon and its

attributes with the square of eight and its expressions. The Great Serpent serves as intermediary joining two forces of nature together.

48. So in one sense, the Serpent is regurgitating, in another it is swallowing, and in yet another, simply attaching itself to something. It all depends upon one's point of view.

49. As one member of the American Society of Dowsers noted, a coiled rattlesnake will appear similarly when striking out at its prey. When considering that the design simultaneously embodies specific geometry and astronomy, it is not difficult to surmise the true meaning behind the mound.

50. See the next section and the section entitled "The Revelation."

51. The ancient Egyptians had a cubit equal to 20.736 inches. Divided by the link (7.92 inches) this figure becomes the square of the golden mean, 2.618. After a little thought, I realized that it was the ratio of 3:5 that was important, not the determination of cubit used by Moses. The box, along with the table and incense burner described in Chapter 37 of Exodus, were made to the strict proportions dictated by the phi series. These were the same ratios as those used by the Pythagoreans in their musical scales, 1:2, 2:3, and 3:5.

52. In 1961 a group of Minnesota College students attempted successfully to reproduce Moses' ark on a smaller scale. When they placed the mercy seat on top, nothing happened. Then someone had the idea to fill the gold-lined box partially with silicon. After the lid was placed back on it, an electrical reaction began to take place. The students had to dismantle the thing, and not without some difficulty. Their ark generated a very alarming static charge.

53. Earthlights are believed to be static discharges within various gases, usually seen at night. They may appear to take on actual forms as clouds do at times.

54. The "shaking tent" was one of the more interesting rituals in the cyclical planting and reaping of the Innu nation of ancient northeast Canada. It consisted in a believed direct communication with selected animal masters, as well as with "cannibal spirits." The shaman created the tent of caribou skins, and his power was said to have derived from the number of animals he had slain in his lifetime. This practice

basically reflects the form of worldwide degeneration known as ritualized animal and human sacrifice. This practice forces the spirit of the creature or man to exit from the form at the will of the murderer, thereby creating a temporary breach in the etheric bond separating the spirit world from the material. It was due to a loss of knowledge blending the terrestrial and atmospheric energies that the practice of ritual sacrifice came on the ascendant, for in the peaceful blending of the opposing force of nature, the opening to the spiritual resource was attained, thereby eliminating the practice of sacrifice.

55. See the phi section in "The Great Serpent as Universal Template" for the illustration of this ley line.

56. A good example is from the life of Francis Xavier. After an early death at age 42, his body remained incorruptible—even when covering it with lime for quick decay. His body remains mummified in spite of the fact that the limbs have been removed as "holy" relics. Another excellent example from America in modern times was the incorruptibility of Paramahansa Yogananda after his natural death. Yogananda taught a certain type of mental and physical discipline which had the side effect of producing this phenomenal non-decaying of the physical body after death. Xavier is also believed to have had some knowledge of the *HolyBreath* through which attunement with the immortalizing Essence is secured.

57. *Prana* has no transliterated version in English, so is defined as meaning "vitality." Prana may indeed be compared to the *vital airs*, experienced through a certain method of breath regulation. Prana is the literal breath of the soul exhaled into the body, enlivening it. It has been compared to the Oriental *c'hi;* the little known Polynesian *mana* which was said to enliven inanimate objects such as stone; the even more obscure *odyle force* of ancient Europe and Scandinavia by which the *Yggdrasil Tree* was preserved; and finally the perfected *collyrium* of the Saints. This collyrium literally is a *bath for the eyes*, and is conveyed directly from Master to disciple, aiding in the withdrawal of the attention to the sensorium region. When received, a single glance may relieve an individual of his senses for some time. Moslem poets like Hafiz and Kayyam compare it to wine, the Master representing the Cupbearer.

58. The control of *prana* or "life-force" is preceded by careful preparation of mind and body, often requiring years. The spiritual experiences related by the Mystic Adepts are the result of gaining mastery over death through consciously and methodically withdrawing from the sense faculties. Once the soul collects its currents adequately behind the eyes, then the words of Paul, and others who declare a routine or daily passing through the mystery of death, become clear.

59. Primary integers consist in the figures used to make up all others, i.e., 1,2,3,4,5,6,7,8,9 and 10.

60. Prime numbers are odd numbers, with the exception of 2, that are only divisible by themselves and 1. Three is a prime number, but not four. Five is prime, but not six. Seven is prime, but not eight, nine, or ten.

61. An excellent example of these sub-figures of 666 is found in the work of Bligh Bond, a scholarly British investigator who wrote early in the twentieth century. Bond's careful analysis of the ruined Glastonbury Abbey measurement remains an important discovery. The Church of England had purchased the land holding the ruins of this ancient site, and appointed Bond to find its forgotten foundations. Bond figured the original length of the structure was been 592 English feet. From this he was able to deduce a grid composed of 8 parts, each part being a 74-foot square.

62 . The table of Kircher offers several interesting examples of the kabbalistic science's 666. The following were names attributed to the antichrist: Τειταν, Λαμπετις, Αντεμος, and Λατεινος. Later, it was applied to Nero (Neron Caesar by the Hebrew method), Hadrian, and Mohammed. Later still, the Catholics made it apply to Martin Luther, and, as Asimov notes, the Protestants returned the favor by summing up the names of several popes as beast incarnations.

63. A logarithm is an exponent of a selected base figure intended to describe a greater or master figure. For example, 2 is the logarithm of 100, based upon 10. In the case of Thom's Megalithic Yard, 2 is the logarithm of a figure fairly relative to the golden mean, about 1.65 (the golden mean is approximately equal to 1.62).

64. The ratios, to be considered "Pythagorean," are always in whole numbers. Since a right triangle can be made without using whole units dictating the length of each side, versions of the right triangle using whole units had a sacred meaning to the ancients. Some of the examples discovered by Thom were 3–4–5, 5–12–13, 8–15–17, 12–35–37, and 9–40–41. Through using these special right triangles, coordinate points within the triangle could, among other things, be plotted. Many of these formations, while not "true" ellipses, nevertheless have been theorized to utilize the same methods of production.

65. Is it a coincidence that the modern protractor has 720 half-degree marks?

66. The figure 816 relates itself to the foot in an interesting way that may account for the foot being divided into inches. The one-fortieth part of 1 MY is .068 feet. Multiplied by the inch (1.2 tenths of a foot)equals the figure .0816.

67. The reason that this version of the Serpent seemed so well fixed is obvious through observing that some of the lines of the geometry when extended touch into key points on the effigy.

68. Surely a true North Star line would have to be created on the spot. Lunar and solar alignments taken from the sun and moon's appearance on the eastern horizon are affected by landmarks. The appearance of the arc of the rising sun or moon would change in accordance with mountain or sea level viewed from the observer's position.

69. This figure of 1.8 feet is the base for the logarithm of 2 for the golden mean as 1.62. It is also the *germ* of the square of Mercury, which, combined with the germ of the square of the Sun, 1.36, equals the proposed height of the missing capstone area of the Great Pyramid, the square root of 1,000 (in feet). The germ of a square is basically related to the square root of one of the square's cells. 1.36 is the germ of the Square of the Sun, arrived at by taking the square root of 1.85, the 1/36 value of the square with the decimal moved over 1 place to the left. Similarly, the germ of the Mercury Square (the magic square of 8) is 1.802. The two figures, 1.36 and 1.802, added produce the square root of 10. This figure of the square root of 10 (or 1,000) is also identical to the height and base measurement of the small triangular feature at the head of the Serpent Mound.

70. This measure of 340 feet is already shown to house the Serpent figure in one of the two hexagonal geometries, a well as the hypotenuse of the 6–8–10 Pythagorean Theorem.

71. Ohio Archaeologist, winter 1988.

72. Romain also conducted an analysis of many Hopewell geometric structures, and found a possible unit running through them all of very approximately 1.053 feet. This figure, or one similar to it within a few thousandths of a foot, may be an important key to the division. This figure is also very consistent with his _ Serpent Mound Unit, 126.4 feet, found at the head of the effigy.

73. One of Marshall's right triangles is a true 3–4–5. Others own whole numbers on two of their sides, the right angle most commonly displaying them. These right angle sides include 1–1, 2–1, 8–5, 5–2, 7–1, 13–3, and 17–4.

74. The "Hopewell" earthworks, although not suspected to be in association with star patterns by the archaeologists, may prove in time to be intimately linked with the stars' influence along with the influence of the sun and moon.

75. Marshall demonstrates the 264-foot unit. He states that this unit is the diagonal of a square with sides of 187 feet. Hence the relativity of the 187- and 264-foot units. In reality, however, the 264-foot unit does not own a diagonal of precisely 187 feet. Nevertheless, the figure of 264 feet is 3,168 inches, which is 400 surveyor's links of 7.92 inches each, and 4 surveyor's chains of 66 feet each. All these measures are used in English-speaking countries. Thus there is a striking coincidence between the prehistoric measurements suggested by Marshall and the system widely in use today.

76. The figure 55 is found repeated within several enveloping figures, it being the result of adding the primary integers 1 through 10 together to create the master figure of the double 5. An example of its possible use is found in the long Egyptian cubit, 1.728 feet. Through the multiplication of true pi by .55, a very close form of the cubit is discovered. Further, the measure of 176 feet, 6 of which make up the diameter measure of the circles at the Newark and High Bank earthworks, and being _ the 264-foot unit, is a simple multiple of half the square of 8, i.e., 32, by 5.5.

77. The figure of 79, apart from its being the atomic number of the precious metal gold, becomes 3,160 when its numbers are added. Romain found this figure to be 31.6 feet, as the base and perpendicular bisector of the small triangular mound at the head. As the _ SMU, this figure also bears a resemblance to the square root of 1000. (See note 1 above and also "The Delta Symbol".)

78. There is a like misunderstanding as to the nature of "Satan" or "the Devil." Spiritual Science Adepts have always stressed the fact of it being the Mind itself that is the great Enemy.

79. It is believed that a very large number of repositories exist from a very ancient time, and that they were originally "marked" on the surface through the creation of beauty spots. At a much later time, some of these places were also defined through the creation of stone and earth structures (such as Serpent Mound). Whether this was done unwittingly or with knowledge of the system of repositories is not well understood at this time.

80. The office of the Pythia was that of the Oracle spokeswoman. It is not known how many women held the seat. The title is of course taken after the name of the Python.

81. The Principle of Sound or Vibration is discussed under the heading of "The Vesica Piscis." Its relationship to the soul, i.e., the entity represented as Gaia, is like that of the flame to the wick of the candle — virtually inseparable. Thus Python was not only the first Oracle of Gaia, but also the natural oracle.

82. The small triangular feature at the west end of the effigy is not wholly contained in some of the geometric studies of the Serpent survey. Like Apollo's addition of the tripod after the work of "slaying" the serpent, this mound seems to have been added to complete the geometric form of the Thuban centric circle.

83. Interestingly, the Ark of the Testimony or covenant has been associated with the tripod structure. Knowing the early Church's design to eradicate all influence of the great pagan Oracle, it is assumed that the inference of any resonance between the Oracle Seat and the Voice of the Ark was insufferable to the Church Fathers.

84. The reality of the imagery of Serpent Mound coupled with its "messengers" or accompanying

geometries fits so well the descriptions of the Book of Revelation that certain thoughts arise regarding the depth of influence the Pythagorean School had on the pre-Church era.

85. The Mysteries of Eleusis celebrated the myth of the goddess Demeter (Ceres) and her daughter Persephone. It is today believed by scholars to have been one of the more important Mystery rites of ancient Greece. It very likely used a specially prepared essence of ergot from wheat combined with wine to produce the vision of Persephone's return once a year from the realm of Haides (Hades). The ergot "brew" was astonishingly effective.

86. The Mysteries of Isis required much learning and listening. Isis, considered by philosophers a world-class divinity, is identified with a number of goddesses and often was considered a daughter of Saturn, the most aboriginal father figure. She is held to have given birth to the Sun, but also to have been a pupil of Hermes. She has been identified with Wicca craft on one hand and Spiritual Science, through the myths, on the other hand. Her all-encompassing persona is also believed by some to have been the model of the archetypal woman appearing in the heavens in the Revelation to John.

87. The Mysteries of Adonis (Adoni) were an annual ritual in Egypt as well as Phoenicia. Like the birth of Jesus, Adonis was believed to have been born on December 24th at midnight. His mysteries may well have been astronomical to a certain extent, although the symbolism of his myth joins him to the rites of fertility. The Jews later borrowed the term Adonai to mean the Lord.

88. The Spiritual stronghold of ancient Hindustan or India has remained a virtual oasis for the God-seekers of the world. Every major religion may trace its roots there, signifying a rich source of Spiritual knowledge, which underscores the tenets of the established faith systems. In today's demanding materialistic world, those seeking enlightenment still feel the calling to return there in the fervent hope that a true Master will be contacted. This, is essence, is the attraction of the subcontinent for the spiritually hungry, for there living Saints still make Themselves available to the public weary of the failings inherent in the social religions.

89. Because of the probable influence the Neo-Pythagorean College had on the writings of the New Testament, not only the Pythagorean Theorem but the hexagon and its vesica piscis are likely attributable to the Sage's influence as well.

90. King James authorized version.

91. "Apostle" is a term from the Greek literally meaning "one who is sent out." Christ is believed to have had as many as 70 apostles.

92. It is around this time that the Oracle of Delphi mysteriously loses its influence and vanishes from the public view. The early Church, especially after the Council of Nicea, very quickly became a source of politically oriented power, exercising its domination in threatening and wrongful ways, leading directly to the Dark Ages.

93. The name of Jesus in the original Greek was valued at 888. The spelling of the name changed to a *J* from an iota as imperial Rome gained more and more influence. This holy name was created with the intent of invoking the Son through proper numerical-verbal structuring. In short, the Revelation was intended to be read by the initiates of the period. Ultimately the text was corrupted by later ecclesiastical editorship, thoroughly discrediting the true founding fathers' original intent.

94. Apollos was born in 4 B.C.E. according to my Encyclopedia Britannica. The dates may vary according to the bias of scholars, but this is probably the correct telling. It was in the spring of that year that the phenomenon of the Star appeared in the eastern heavens, being chiefly the light of Jupiter. Like Pythagoras before him, the birth of Apollonius was heralded by an angelic presence. Many signs accompanied his birth, and like Pythagoras, it was predicted that the child would grow to become a great teacher and leader of men. The life and works of Jesus of Nazareth are to a broad extent based upon the life and miracles of Apollos. Apollos was named *the Antichrist* by the later "Church Fathers" in an effort to downplay the historical figure Apollonius and bolster the existence of the non-historical figure Jesus. There were too many similarities in the lives of the two men to continue the support of a Jesus as the Messiah, and thus an all-out attack on the life of the great Sage was instituted. In 325 C.E. Jesus Christ was truly "born"—at Nicea.

95. Apollonius was a strict follower of the Pythagorean School. He did not cut his hair. He practiced chastity and abstained from both strong drink and the eating of animal tissue. He wore clean white linen and presented himself as a paragon of a man: tall, stately, and vigorous. He was thoroughly dedicated to the art of healing and was known to have performed a number of miraculous cures.

96. Constantine I took over Rome in 324 C.E. In 325, the Council of Nicea convened. A deal was struck at that time that would allow the cult of Christianity to be liberated from the underground, while at the same time consolidating Constantine's power base. The doctrine of the Neo-Pythagorean School, like the Pythagorean before it by 500 years, insisted on vegetarian diet coupled with a lack of alcohol and the observance of continent behavior in public and private. Such a lifestyle miraculously evolves the light of the inner man, and the ensuing peace can be infectious. Thus the Messiah appears from time to time to remind humanity of the connection between true living and spirituality—the highest goal and purpose of human life. Constantine was not spiritually inclined, and thus the life and works of the messianic messenger were struck out of the records. It is written that 17 temples commemorating Apollos' life and work existed at one time in and around Rome. But the sacrifice of giving up wine and meat was not suitable to the Roman emperor, much less the early pagan Fathers of the Nicene travesty. Thus the beautiful life of the true messiah began to be forgotten, replaced with the politics of murder and wholesale destruction. Perhaps the final stroke and best example was the intentional burning of libraries. Most notable was Egypt's great library at Alexandria that housed an unknown number of works concerning the life of the philosopher Apollos, proving his impact on the culture. The Church decided, in its now ruthless method of destroying evidence, to burn that repository to the ground. The chief arson was Pope Theodosius, whose edict of 389 C.E. fueled a crazed Christian mob to destroy everything about Apollonius and other related "problems." By this method, their new Messiah, based on the life of a late ante-millennium Jewish martyr, Jehoshua, renamed Jesus Christ, could take the foreground.

97. "Know Thyself" is an ancient and timeless axiom of philosophy. Knowing what we are apart from body and mind requires a certain amount of self-analysis and deep meditation coupled with prayer. Once one achieves this Self-realization, then his life takes on a completely different order of priorities.

98. Common cinnabar may be created or simply bought from the mines. Philosophers' cinnabar appears somewhat the same and weighs virtually the same, yet is compounded differently, ultimately having a completely different effect.

99. Guru Nanak, the first of the Sikh Masters, makes mention of the souls being created in the highest region which is characterized by a lack of material (Mind) substance, Sat Lok. In his autobiography, Paramahansa Yogananda relates of an experience he had with his Master, Sri Yukteswar, wherein the Master appeared to him and disappeared even as a scroll rolling up with the aspects of light and subtle thunder. In this it is apparent that the Sages understand the nature of the body and mind as wholly subservient to that of the soul.

100. The human form, being patterned after the subtle attributes of the spiritual entity, therefore entertains the presence of the soul, seated at the sensorium. The two get along like great roommates, and the exchange of the energies from the spiritual realm whence the soul comes with the material which the body is composed of is fluid and virtually unimpeded in good health.

101. See the explanation under the chapter titled "The Hexagon."

102. The terms *qi* or *chi* are equivalent to the Indian *prana*.

103. The evidence for the presence of "straight tracks" has been found as well in Europe, Britain, the Mediterranean, Northern Africa, Australia, and the Americas. Alignments of ancient sites over distances on very straight lines were believed to have been astronomically inspired, but this has not proven to be the case in a number of instances. A very subtle yet powerful flow of magnetic current beneath the landscape on straight lines has begun to create a new interest in the as yet unexplained phenomenon worldwide.

104. Alfred Watkins coined the term "ley line" in his research of the ancient straight tracks in Great

Britain. The names of many of the places having these lines pass through or by end in –ley, hence the term.

105. As noted previously, a number of Native American nations had strong memories of the mythical thunderbird, which sported after the serpent. From the Dakotas, Minnesota, Ohio, east to the Onondaga of present-day New York, the Micmac of the extreme east, and northwest to the Great Lakes' Cree, the legends of the great Firebird are as widespread as any expected to be of great antiquity. The bird is held to be divine, and the thunderbolt is a flaming arrow flashing from its eyes.

106. The tradition of the ancient Greek language names the serpent *ophion*.

107. A syllabary is a catalog or listing of syllables, or a set of written symbols, each symbol representing a spoken syllable.

108. Width (land), depth (sea), and height (tree).

109. This is the Spirit of the Divine prior to entering into the Primary Atom or Chitta, the Heart of Creation. It is the soul entity as it exists prior to being attracted into the Creation Sphere (Omniverse or Grand Universe).

110. Revelation 7:2.

111. The 144,000 mentioned in Revelation 7:4

112. Jiva has as its only comparison in English something akin to *uninitiated, unenlightened* or, in religious terms, *sinner.* It refers to not having gained the experience of rising above body consciousness, i.e., incarnate until the time of initiation at the hands of a competent Christ-Master.

113. This refers to Maharloka, the region of the Primal Atom, i.e., the Great Causal Sphere.

114. Messiah refers to the Commissioned Master, i.e., the one through whom the God-into-expression Power works the miracle of whole, complete, and legitimate salvation.

115. Both the beast of Revelation and Apollo's Python are relegated to abysmal shafts in the Earth, places beyond comprehension. Rev. 9:11 hints at the possible influence of the Greek myth when the "Angel of the Abyss" is named *Apollyon,* conceivably a mockery of Apollo or a reference to a part (-on) of Apollo's mythologem. Similarly, smoke rises up from both shafts in the Earth (Revelation 9:2).

116. The Hebraic culture had, like others, a system of writing. We now refer to any system of writing as an alphabet, but originally, it was the Greeks who "fixed" their assortment of letters into a closed system. Their alphabet was the first numerically-corresponding system of letters.

117. Liddell and Scott, Greek English Lexicon, Oxford, 1974.

118. The serpent-man myths of Mexico and Central America name Quetzalcoatl and Kukulcan as emissaries of the traditional wisdom. Perhaps by coincidence their names use similar gutturals, leading to the thought of the Serpent Mound, as Putnam averred, being created by a pre-Mayan culture.

119. See "The Serpent and the Golden Ratio."

120 . It is noteworthy that in Marshall's extensive researches of the geometric forms in Eastern North American prehistoric architecture, no true ellipses were discovered.

121. $\phi + \varphi = \sqrt{5}$

122. I have friends in the Anderson area near Newtown, who on New Year's Day just a few years ago witnessed the lifting of a whole skeleton on a slab of stone from the Turpin Mound. The skull was so fragile that it just fell apart on the spot due to the amateur handling. This mound and many like it are totally unprotected and easily accessed by vandals at any time.

123. Just as we today create parks in and around our cities to preserve forest growth or to allow for areas of recreation, so it is believed the ancient indigenous people created sanctuaries for the continued protection of both the natural beauty and inherent spiritual energy of a place.

124. *Secret Teachings of All Ages,* page CXCIII.

Bibliography

Allen, Richard Hinckley. *Star Names-Their Lore and Meaning.* New York: Dover, 1963.

Alter, Robert and Frank Kermode, eds. *The Literary Guide to the Bible.* Cambridge: Belknap Press of Harvard, 1987.

Andrews, W.S. *Magic Squares and Cubes.* New York: Dover, 1960.

Arundale, G.S. *Kundalini, An Occult Experience.* Madras: Theosophical Publishing House, 1974.

Asimov, Issac. *Asimov on Numbers.* New York: Bell Publishing, 1977.

Atwood, Mary Anne. *A Suggestive Inquiry into Hermetic Mystery.* New York: Arno Press, 1976.

Besant, Annie. *Seven Great Religions.* Madras: Theosophical Publishing House, 1966.

Bishoff, Dr. Erich. *The Kabbala.* York Beach, ME: Samual Wiser, 1985.

Blavatsky, H.P. *Isis Unveiled.* Madras: Theosophical Publishing House, 1972.

_____. *The Secret Doctrine.* Madras: Theosophical Publishing House, 1972.

_____. *Collected Writings.* Madras: Theosophical Publishing House, 1888.

Brose, David S. and N'omi Greber, eds. *Hopewell Archaeology: the Chillicothe Conference.* Kent, Ohio: Kent State University, 1979.

Burkhardt, Titus. *Alchemy.* Longmead, U.K.: Element Books Ltd., 1987.

Campbell, J.F. *The Mysteries—Papers from the Eranos Yearbooks.* Princeton, New Jersey: Princeton University Press, 1955.

_____. *The Celtic Dragon Myth.* North Hollywood, California: New Castle Publishing, 1980.

Cowan, Wesley. *First Farmers of the Middle Ohio Valley.* Cincinnati, Ohio: Cincinnati Museum of Natural History. 1987.

Devereux, Paul. *Places of Power : Secret Energies at Ancient Sites: A Guide to Observed or Measured Phenomena.* London: Blandford, 1990.

_____. *Earth memory: Sacred Sites—Doorways Into Earth's Mysteries.* St. Paul, Minnesota: Llewellyn Publications, 1992.

Dragoo, Don W. *Mounds For The Dead.* Pittsburgh, Pennsylvania: Carnegie Museum, 1963.

Frazer, Sir James S. *Appolodorus I and II.* New York: G. P. Putnam's Sons, 1921.

Fletcher, Robert, Terry Cameron, and Bradley Lepper. "Serpent Mound: A Fort Ancient Icon?" *Midcontinental Journal of Archaeology,* spring, 1996.

Fulcanelli. *Le Mystere des Cathedrales.* 2nd ed. Translated from the French by Mary Sworder. London: Neville Spearman, 1971.

Goldwater, Leonard J. *Mercury: A History of Quicksilver.* Baltimore: York Press, 1972.

Glotzhopper Robert C. *Serpent Mound: Ohio's Enigmatic Effigy Mound.* Columbus, Ohio: Ohio Historical Society, 1994.

Hall, Manly P. *Man: Grand Symbol of the Mysteries. Essays in Occult Anatomy.* Los Angeles, California: The Philosophical Research Society, 1972.

_____. *The Phoenix: An Illustrated Review of*

Occultism and Philosophy. Los Angeles, California: Philosophical Research Society, 1983.

_____. *Secret Teachings of All Ages: An Encyclopedic Outline of Masonic, Hermetic, Qabbalistic, and Rosicrucian Symbolical Philosophy: Being an Interpretation of the Secret Teachings Concealed within the Rituals, Allegories, and Mysteries of All Ages.* Los Angeles, California: Philosophical Research Society, 1988.

Hamilton, Ross. *The Mystery of the Serpent Mound.* Cincinnati, Ohio: Gaiasophical Society, 1993.

_____. "Mystery of Ohio's Serpent Mound." *Ancient American,* May-June, 1997.

_____. "Ancient Genius of Ohio's Serpent Mound." *Ancient American,* January-February, 1998.

Hancock, Graham. *Fingerprints of the Gods.* New York: Crown Publishers, 1995.

Hathorn, Richard. *Greek Mythology.* Lebanon: American University of Beirut, 1977.

Hawkins, Gerald. *Stonehenge Decoded.* London: Souvenir Press, 1966.

Head, Joseph, and S. L. Cranston, eds. *Reincarnation: The Phoenix Fire Mystery: An East-West Dialogue on Death and Rebirth from the Worlds of Religion, Science, Psychology, Philosophy, Art, and Literature, and from Great Thinkers of the Past and Present.* New York: Julian Press, 1979.

Heckewelder, John. *History, Manners, and Customs of the Indian Nations.* The Historical Society of Pennsylvania, 1876 (originally published in 1819).

Jackson, Howard. *Zozimos of Panopolis on the Letter Omega.* Missoula, Montana: Scholars Press, 1978.

Johnson, Obed. *A Study of Chinese Alchemy.* New York: Arno Press, 1974.

Jones, James Athearn. *Traditions of the North American Indians.* London: Colburn and Bently, 1830.

Jung, Carl. *Psychology and Alchemy.* Princeton, New Jersey: Princeton University Press, 1968.

Ko Hung. Translated and edited by James R. Ware. *Alchemy, Medicine, and Religion in the China of A.D. 320.* New York: Dover, 1981.

Lawler, Robert. *Sacred Geometry: Philosophy and Practice.* London: Thames and Hudson, 1982.

Leadbeater, C.W. *The Chakras.* Madras: Wheaton, Illinois: Theosophical Publishing House, 1994.

Lepper, Bradley. "Great Serpent." *Timeline,* September-October, 1998.

Liddell, Henry George. *Greek-English Lexicon.* Compiled by Henry George Liddell and Robert Scott. Oxford: Clarendon Press, 1974.

Longfellow, Henry Wadsworth. *The Song of Hiawatha.* Rutland, Vermont: C.E. Tuttle Company, 1992.

Michell, John. *The New View Over Atlantis.* New York: Thames and Hudson, 1995.

Morgan, William. *Prehistoric Architecture in the Eastern United States.* Cambridge, Massachusetts: MIT Press, 1980.

Otto, Martha Potter. *Ohio's Prehistoric Peoples.* Columbus, Ohio: Ohio Historical Society, 1980.

Putnam, F.W. "The Serpent Mound of Ohio." *Century Magazine,* 1890.

Romain, W.F. "The Serpent Mound Map." *Ohio Archaeologist,* winter, 1988.

_____. "Terrestrial Observations at the Serpent Mound." *Ohio Archaeologist,* spring, 1988.

_____. "The Serpent Mound Solar Eclipse Hypothesis." *Ohio Archaeologist,* summer, 1988.

_____. "Ancient Eclipse Paths at the Serpent Mound." *Ohio Archaeologist,* fall, 1988.

Silverberg, Robert. *The Mound Builders.* Athens:

Ohio. Ohio University Press, 1986.

Singh, Kirpal. *Naam or Word.* Delhi: Ruhani Satsang, 1960.

_____. *The Wheel of Life: The Law of Action and Reaction.* Delhi: Ruhani Satsang, Sawan Ashram, 1965.

_____. *Godman.* Bowling Green, Virginia: Sawan Kirpal Publications, 1979.

Sivan, Nathan. *Chinese Alchemy: Preliminary Studies.* Cambridge: Harvard University Press, 1968.

Smith, Piazzi. *The Great Pyramid: Its Secrets and Mysteries Revealed.* New York: Bell Publishing Company, 1978.

Steiner, Rudolph. *Knowledge of the Higher Worlds.* New York: Anthrosposophic Press, 1961.

Starr, S.F. *Archaeology of Hamilton County, Ohio.* Cincinnati, Ohio: Museum of Natural History, 1960.

Swami Sri Yukteswar. *The Holy Science. Kaivalya Darsanam.* Los Angeles: Self-Realization Fellowship, 1972.

Walker, Barbara. *The Woman's Encyclopedia of Myths and Secrets.* San Francisco: Harper and Row, 1983.

Wasson, R. Gordon, Albert Hofmann, and Carl A. P. Ruck. *The Road to Elusis: Unveiling the Secret of the Mysteries.* New York: Harcourt, Brace, Jovanovich, 1978.

Webb, William S. and Charles E. Snow. *The Adena People.* Lexington, Kentucky: University of Kentucky, 1945.

Woodward. Susan L. and Jerry N. McDonald. *Indian Mounds of the Middle Ohio Valley.* Newark, Ohio: McDonald and Woodward Publishing Company, 1986.

Wurmbrand, Michael and Jane Huang. *The Primordial Breath.* Torrance, California: Original Books, 1987.

Yogananda, Paramahansa. *The Science of Religion.* Los Angeles, California: Self-Realization Fellowship, 1982.

Index

1

1111, 164

4

47th Proposition of Euclid, xx

6

666, 58, 89, 90, 91, 92, 93, 94, 97, 119, 124, 144, 159, 179, 180, 181

8

888, 41, 119, 122, 123, 124, 181

A

acacia wood, 71, 134

Adam, 17, 24, 25, 33, 123, 169, 172

Adamic Earth, 126

Adams County, xiii, xviii, xxii, 5, 18, 38, 107, 115, 196, 198

Adena People, xvii, xxiii, 6, 8, 115, 137, 151, 195, 196

Adonis, 112

aether, 72

Ahamkara, 33

alchemy, xvii, 45, 125, 126, 127, 128, 130, 159

alembic, 167

aleph, 150

Algonkin, 81

alkahest, 53

Allegewi, xxiv, 12

Allegheny Mountains, xxiv

Allegheny River, 12

alpha, 24, 141, 144, 150, 151, 152, 153, 177, 182, 190

amber, 72, 75

ambix, 167

ambrosia, 130

Amen, 37, 41, 169

American Congress, 133

American Society of Dowsers, xiv, 29, 67

Amrit, 130

Anasazi, 195

Ancient Monuments of the Mississippi Valley, xix

Andersen, Hans Christian, 133

angel, 87, 148, 190, 198

Angkor Wat, xx

ank, ankh, xxvii, 56, 62, 64, 67, 68, 69, 85, 86, 89, 105, 114, 128, 181, 190

Ante-Christ, 181

anthropocosmic, 33, 34

anthroposophic, 33

antiquities, 4, 9, 193

Aoede, 169

Apollo, xv, xxvii, 108, 109, 110, 111, 112, 113, 150, 164, 168, 169

Apollonius of Tyana, 110, 112, 114, 115, 181

apostles, 113

arbelos, 145, 174, 175, 178, 190

archaeoastronomy, xviii, xix, 14, 108

archaeology, xv, xvii, xxiii, xxv, 5, 9, 14, 29, 150, 151, 193, 194

archaeometrology, 102

archangel, 168

Archimedes, 174

arithmetic, xiii, xv, xvii, xx, 32, 89, 93, 111, 143

ark, 38, 55, 56, 58, 71, 73, 84, 85, 86, 87, 128, 130, 134, 167, 173, 197

Armageddon, 142, 198

artifacts, xvii, xviii, xxiii, xxv, 3, 6, 53, 54, 194

asp, 178

astrology, xvii, 11, 29, 69

astronomical alignments, xxiii, 5, 96

astronomy, xvii, xviii, xix, xx, xxvii, 4, 5, 11, 12, 14, 17, 29, 44, 46, 64, 69, 94, 95, 98, 99, 103, 108, 111, 112, 141, 145, 193

Athenian alphabet, 162, 188

Atlanta, 135

Atum, 24

Aum, 41, 142

aura, 68, 76, 122, 197

Australia, 38, 79, 81
Australian Aborigines, 79
Avidya, 38, 133, 148
awareness, 69, 148, 195
Azhdeha, 17
Aztec, 16, 37, 134

B
Babylon, xv, 17, 18, 111
Bani, 143
Barton, William, 133
Bel, 17
beta, 141, 144, 150, 154–56, 165, 167, 175, 180, 184
beth, 150
Bible, 66, 71, 91, 104, 113
Big Bang, 25
blind spring, xiv, 78
Blosser, Jack, xxiii
Blue Jacket, 3
bosons, 175
breath of life, 147, 169
Britain, xxii, xxvi, 3, 7, 20, 94, 95, 97, 131, 135
Brittany, 94
Brush Creek, xiii, 3, 84
Buddha, 149
Buddhi, 33
Buddhist, 78, 143

C
Caesius, 17
carbon dating, xx, xxiii, xxiv, xxv, 6
catacombs of Rome, 40
Cathars, 16
Celts, xxvii, 78, 131, 167
Central America, 5, 7, 195
chaos, 42, 89, 148, 190
chemistry, 132
chi, 141, 159, 186–87, 188
Chinese, 18, 75, 128, 130, 131, 132
Chippeway, 81
Chit, 34, 35, 36
Chitta, 33, 34, 35, 146, 148
Christ, 122, 127, 128, 147, 149, 150, 169, 181, 187
Christianity, 194
Christians, xvii, xviii, xxi, xxii, xxvii, 23, 24, 26, 30, 37,
    41, 62, 78, 105, 113, 114, 119, 121, 128, 145, 146,

149, 181, 195
Christmas, 132
Christos, 121, 149
Cincinnati, xxiii, 3, 4, 53, 54, 55, 78, 80, 135, 194
Cincinnati Historical Society, 4
cinnabar, 126, 168
circle, xxvi, xxvii, 25, 26, 27, 30, 31, 32, 33, 35, 39, 41,
    42, 43, 53, 57, 58, 68, 80, 90, 92, 94, 95, 99, 127, 145,
    174, 176, 178, 182, 190
Circle of Okeanos, 190
Circle of Thuban, 92, 99, 102
Circleville, xiv
Clement of Alexandria, 23, 134
Columbus, 195
comma, 157
Connolly, Robert, xxiii, xxiv, xxv, 6
consciousness, 36, 130
copper, 6, 8, 9, 69, 72, 75, 81
Copper Age, 8, 75
Cosmic Egg, 25
cosmos, 24, 33, 73, 142, 181
Council of Nicea, 41, 91
Cowan, Clinton, xxiii
Cree, 81
crocodile, 18
cross, 62, 114, 128, 181, 182, 186
crucifix, 128
crux ansata, xxvii, 62, 105, 181
crux gammata, 105
cryptoexplosion, 82
cubit, 71

D
daleth, 150, 157, 158
Daphnis, 108, 109
Darwin, Erasmus, 16
Davis, Edwin H., xix
Delaware, the tribe, 12
Delphi Circle, 145, 174, 176, 190
delphos, 145
delta, 144, 150, 153, 157–58, 161, 166, 168
dharma, 73
digamma, 161, 172, 183, 187
divine music, 184
divine nature, 64, 84, 87, 111, 125, 133, 142, 182
divine ratio. *See* phi

divine reciprocal, 53
divine wisdom, 184
Draco, xv, xix, xxv, xxvi, 16, 17, 18, 19, 21, 146
Draconis, xvii, xxv, 17, 18, 39, 45, 97, 98, 99, 101, 102
dragon, xvi, xxii, xxvii, 16, 19, 23, 56, 61, 66, 67, 68, 69, 73, 77, 79, 86, 105, 108, 116, 117, 118, 119, 130, 131, 132, 134, 151, 152, 177, 182, 188, 193, 197
dragon path. *See lung mei*
Dragoo, Don, 6
drakon, 18
druid, 78
Druidic College, 132

E
eagle, 35, 122, 133, 136, 138, 197
eahta, 162, 186
earthlights, 72, 79
earthly wisdom, 184
earthworks, xiii, xvi, xviii, 7, 12, 54, 78, 80, 98, 101, 102
Edison, Thomas, 72, 73, 112
Egg of Brahma, 126
Egypt, xiii, xv, xviii, xx, xxvii, 7, 9, 17, 24, 37, 44, 56, 57, 58, 62, 64, 85, 111, 114, 115, 126, 132, 133, 143, 144, 149, 163, 169, 178, 194, 195
Egyptian pyramids, xv, xx, xxvi, 44, 195
electra, 72
electricity, 71, 72, 73, 75, 76, 79, 131, 146, 160
electron, 72, 147
eleph, 150
Eleusinian Mysteries, 112
Elizabeth I, 72
Ennea, 164
episemon bau, 160
epsilon, 159–60, 162, 163
Erato, 70
Eratosthenes, 18
Erebos, 133
Eros, 42
Essene, xviii, 111, 115, 116, 181
eta, 113, 159, 160, 162–63, 165, 171, 176, 177, 186, 188, 190
Eternal Substance, 64
ether, 72, 77
Etruscan alphabet, 156, 157, 175, 181
Euclides, 162

Europe, 7, 78, 81
Euterpe, 69
Eve, 25, 197
Eye of Horus, xxvii, 163

F
Faraday, Michael, 72, 73
Father of American Archaeology, xxii, 94
Fibonacci, Leonardo, 49
firebird, 133
fish, 40, 41
five conditions of matter, 33
five currents, 148
five electricties, 145
five organs of action, 33, 34
five organs of sense, 33, 34
Flammel, Nicholas, 128
Fletcher and Cameron, xix, xxi, xxiv, 15, 20, 44
flint, xxv, 6
flower of life geometry, xiv, 22
Fort Ancient, xvii, xxiii, xxiv, 151
Fort Ancient People, xvii
four angels, 148
four beasts, 34, 87, 168, 173, 181
four ideas, 34, 35, 36, 37, 119, 147, 148
four winds, 148
France, 128, 131
Franklin, Benjamin, 72

G
Gaia, 17, 42, 81, 108, 109, 145, 196, 197
gaiametria, 144
Galileo, 16
gamma, 144, 150, 156–57, 165, 169
Garden of the Hesperides, 17
gematria, 91, 144
geo-astronomical alignments, xix, xxvi
geomancy, xx, 67
geometria, 91, 144
geometry, xiii, xiv, xvii, xviii, xx, xxv, xxvii, 12, 14, 15, 16, 22, 26, 27, 29, 30, 31, 33, 41, 43, 44, 45, 46, 52, 53, 55, 57, 62, 64, 68, 85, 91, 92, 93, 94, 95, 103, 104, 111, 112, 114, 117, 118, 126, 127, 141, 143, 144, 145, 153, 156, 157, 161, 165, 171, 174, 177, 180
giants, xviii, 54, 61, 79
Gilbert, William, 72

gimel, 150
Giza, xvii, 22, 56, 57
Glenford Fort, 9
Gnosis, 197
Gnostic School, xviii, 111, 181
gold, xiii, 69, 71, 80, 130, 142, 167, 193
golden mean, 49, 52, 53, 80, 93, 94, 157, 174, 176
Grandmother Spider, 196
gravity, 27, 82, 134, 143
gravity anomalies, 82
Great Dragon, 17, 168, 196
Great Hopewell Road, 80
Great Lakes, 135, 136, 137
Great Magnetic Line, 135–36, 137
Great Norwood Mound, 55
Great Oval, xiii, xiv, xv, xix, xxi, 14, 22, 181, 184
Great Pyramid, xiii, xxv, xxvii, 22, 50, 55, 56, 57, 58, 61, 81, 99
Great Seal, xvi, 133, 196, 197
Great Turtle, 196
Greek alphabet, 142, 157, 159, 161, 175
Gulf of Mexico, 135
gunas, 34
guru, 133

H
Hall, Manly, 133, 195
Hardman, Clark and Marjorie, xiv, xix, 6, 14, 29, 101
Harmonic Convergence, xxi
Harrison, William Henry, 3, 53, 55
Harvard, xiii, xxi, xxii, 3, 94, 193
Hashteher, 17
Hawaii, 71
Hawkins, Gerald, xxvi
heaven, 11, 17, 24, 31, 37, 43, 56, 87, 104, 116, 118, 119, 133, 145, 147, 167, 184
Hebraic culture, 38, 57, 91, 111, 114, 115, 143, 144, 150
Helena, Montana, 135
Helios, 109
helix, xiii, xxi, 22, 82, 169, 177, 178, 182
Hermes, 122, 132, 162
Hermod, 64
Hesiod, 42, 149
Hes-mut, 17
hex, 179

hexagon, xxvii, 26, 27, 29, 30, 31, 33, 35, 36, 38, 39, 42, 43, 58, 62, 67, 68, 69, 85, 86, 87, 90, 92, 95, 97, 118, 123, 124, 126, 127, 128, 141, 154, 168, 169, 171, 172, 173, 175, 179, 180
hexagram, 171, 172, 173
hexagrammon, 171
Hiawatha, 77, 132
hieroglyphics, 144, 195
High Bank, 12, 103, 195, 196
Hindu, 17, 143
Hipparchos, 18
Hively, Ray, 103
Holy Breath, 147, 169
Holy Ghost, 169
Holy See, 16
Hopewell Culture, xvii, xxiii, 6, 8, 9, 101, 137, 138, 151, 195, 196
Horn, Robert, 103
Horus, 163
human form, 33, 34, 36, 38, 62, 69, 84, 87, 90, 104, 116, 118, 120, 121, 126, 134, 146, 147, 173, 181

I
Ikhnaton, 149
imam, 38
India, 7, 112, 146
iota, 150, 161, 164–65, 177, 184, 186, 190
Iroquois, 14, 138
Islam, 87, 143

J
Jain, 143
Jefferson, Thomas, xviii, 12, 54
Jelaludin Rumi, 27
Jesus, 41, 111, 113, 114, 122, 123, 127, 149, 181
jiva, 33, 36, 148
Jnanavatar Yukteswar, 73
Jnanendriyas, 33
John of Patmos, 113
John the Revelator, 23, 116, 130
Joseph and the Pharaoh, 62
Jupiter, 79

K
kabbala, 114, 115
kabbalists, 69

Kalliope, 69
Kalma, 143
kaph, 165
kappa, 157, 165, 180
karmas, 130, 177
Karmendriyas, 33
Kenabeek, 132
Kepler, Johannes, 27, 112
Khufu, 56
Kircher, Athanasius, 181
Kleio, 70, 143
komma, 157
Krishna, 73, 149
Krita Yuga, 73

L
Ladon, 17
Lamb of God, 167
lambda, 93, 153, 158, 166–68, 173
Lamp of Hermes, 128
Lansing, 135
Leonardo of Pisa, 49
leptons, 175
Levi, Eliphas, 76, 79
Lexington, 135
ley lines, 135
Library at Alexandria, 149
limestone, 81
lion, 35
Lion of Judah, 173
Little Dipper, xxvi, 19, 21
Little Eagle, xiv
lodestone, 24, 72, 75
Logos, xxvii, 23, 42, 67, 87, 105, 107, 110, 120, 127,
    128, 141, 142, 143, 145, 146, 147, 151, 159, 175,
    178, 181, 182
Lord of Hosts, 41
Louisiana, xiii, xxi
Lovett, xxii
lunar and solar alignments, xxvi, 7, 19, 20, 105
lung mei, 75

M
MacLean, J.P., xxii, 7
magic square of eight, 65, 69, 188
magic squares, 65, 67, 69, 89, 90, 91, 103, 181, 188

magnesia of the wise, 41
magnetism, 27, 67, 72, 73, 75, 76, 77, 79, 84
Maha Mantra, 143
Manas, 33
Mandan People, xxiii
manitou, xiv, 196
mantra, 146
Marshall, James A., 101, 102, 103
Masters of Spiritual Science, 84, 121, 135, 146, 150,
    184
Mastersoul, 27, 130
mathematics, 29, 33, 46, 53, 64, 91, 102, 111, 167
maya, 148
Maya, 16, 195
measurement, xviii, 15, 22, 29, 44, 45, 90, 91, 98, 99,
    101, 127
megalithic rod, 94, 99, 103
megalithic yard, 94, 97, 99, 102, 103
Megissogwan, 77, 132
Melete, 169
Melpomene, 70
mercury, 68, 69, 77, 85, 122, 123, 125, 126, 128, 130,
    156, 168, 180, 187
    as dragon-master, 66
Mercury, 56, 64, 67, 162
mercy seat, 71
Merkaba, xviii, 121
Messiah, 24, 26, 41, 111, 114, 121, 130, 149, 187
metrology, xvii, 46
Mexico, 5, 7, 14, 44, 101, 102
Michelangelo, 112
Michell, John, 40, 55
Michigan, xviii, 8, 9, 136, 137
microcosm, 33
microsoul, 27
mikro, 147
Millon, René, 101, 102
Minnesota, 136
Mississagua, 81
Mississippi Culture, xvii, xxiv
Mississippi River, xiii
Mississippi Valley, 40
Mneme, 169
Mnemosyne, 69, 70, 169
Mnesarchus, 91, 111
Mohammed, 149

Mongolia, 130
Moses, 23, 55, 71, 84, 136
Mound Builders, xvii, 94
mounds, xiii, xviii, 6, 12, 53, 54, 55, 78, 80
mu, 158, 167, 168–69, 168, 169, 177
music, 36, 37, 112, 143
Music of the Spheres, 37, 111, 143, 169, 184
muth, 168
Mysteries of Isis at Thebes, 112
Mystery Schools, xv, xviii, 25, 26, 30, 34, 56, 62, 64,
    87, 104, 105, 110, 111, 116, 119, 121, 122, 165, 175,
    187
mythos, 108, 110

N
Naam, 143
Nad, 143
Native Americans, xiv, xx, 3, 7, 14, 22, 30, 67, 68, 77,
    101, 102, 115, 128, 132, 133, 137, 138, 151, 193,
    194, 195, 196
Nehebkau, 24
New England, 3, 136
New Testament, 41, 94, 104, 114, 116, 188
Newark earthworks, xiii, 12, 14, 195, 196
Nicodemus, 149
Nile, 143, 195
nix, 133
Nix, 133
North and South Dakota, 136
Northern Lights, 72
nu, 169–71
Number of the Beast, 89, 91, 181
numerology, xvii, 41, 89, 94, 115, 181
Nun, 24

O
Ogdoad, 119, 122
Ohio Archaeologist, xix, 103
Ohio Historical Society, xxiii, 3, 195
Ohio Valley, xxi, 3, 5, 6, 8, 9, 12, 40, 54, 78, 80, 94, 98,
    102, 194, 195
Ojibway, 81
Old English, 162, 168, 186
Old Testament, 62, 71
om, 147, 168, 190
omega, 24, 113, 147, 148, 152, 153, 162, 163, 168, 172,

173, 177, 178, 182, 188, 190
Omega Word, 147, 148
omicron, 41, 147, 161, 168, 173–75, 178, 190
Omniverse, 181
Ontario, 82
ophion, 182, 188
ophis, 18
Oracle of Apollo, 149
Oracle of Delphi, xv, xxvii, 91, 110
Oread, 108
Orion, xx
Oroboros, 182
Orphic College, 24
Orphic Egg, 126
Osiris, 57
Otherworld, 167
Oughtred, William, 176
ouraios, 178
Ouranos, 81
Oversoul, 25, 33, 34, 147

P
Panch Sabda, 145
Pancha Tattwa, 145
Parthenis, 91, 111
Parthenon, xiii, xv, 50, 81, 111
pe, 175, 190
Peabody Museum, 3, 163
pedogenesis, xxiii
perfect number, 26
Perry County, 9
Peru, 5
Pharisees, 149
phi
    as numeric constant, 49, 52, 53, 58, 92, 165, 174,
        175, 177, 186.
    as symbol, 141, 159, 164, 184–86, 188, 190
phi ratio, 49, 53, 165, 174, 175
Phoebe, 108, 109
Phoebos-Apollo, 145, 150
Phoenician Mysteries, 112
phoenix, xvi, 57, 122, 130, 132, 133, 134, 137, 162,
    180, 182, 186, 190
Phoenix, Arizona, 135
phoinix, 133, 182, 188
physics, 33, 69, 76, 143, 147

pi
   as numeric constant, 92, 94, 95, 175
   as symbol, 159, 175, 178, 183, 190
piezoelectric effect, 82
Plato, xviii, 112
pneuma, 25, 169
Polaris, xxvi, 15
pole star, xxv, xxvi, 15, 18
Polyhymnia, 70
Posidonius, 5
prakritas, 26, 33
prana, 84
precession, xxv, 12, 16, 73, 75, 195
Primal Atom, 33, 36, 38, 122, 133, 168, 175
Primal Consciousness, 25
Prometheus, 150
Proto-Atom, 25, 34, 36, 38
psi, 141, 159, 161, 174, 183, 186, 188–90
psilon, 159, 183
psyche, 148
Putnam, Frederic Ward, xiii, xix, xxi, xxii–xxiii, xxiv, xxv, 3–4, 5, 6, 7, 9, 14, 15, 22, 44, 81, 94, 193
pyramid, 57, 166, 195
pyros, 57
Pythagoras, xviii, xxvii, 26, 43, 45, 46, 72, 90, 91, 94, 103, 111–12, 111, 112, 113, 115, 116, 134, 145, 150, 151, 159, 174, 180, 181, 183
Pythagorean School, 90, 91, 114, 115, 116, 141, 171, 173, 174, 181
Pythagorean Skein, xviii
Pythagorean Theorem, xx, 29, 43, 44, 45, 67, 94, 101, 126, 145, 159, 164
Pythia, 108, 110, 150
Python, xv, xix, xxvii, 43, 45, 46, 91, 108–13, 142, 150, 159, 168

Q
qabbalah, xvii
qi, 130
quarks, 175
quartz, 35
Quetzalcoatl, 134
quoit, 167

R
rajas, 34

Rapture, 146, 198
rattlesnake, 14
Rebus of the Masters, 112
Revelation, 17, 22, 26, 30, 31, 36, 56, 67, 69, 79, 87, 89, 91, 113–19, 130, 144, 145, 148, 152, 167, 173, 179, 190
   quote, 24, 30, 32, 35, 37, 40, 68, 69, 87, 89, 104, 105, 116, 117, 118, 148, 152, 181, 197, 198
rho, 91, 153, 177–78, 181, 183
Roc, 133
Romain, William F., xiv, xix, xxvi, 14, 15, 20, 86, 99, 101, 102, 184
Rome, 16, 40, 113, 149, 194
rosary, 145
Rosetta Stone, 16, 195

S
sacred cut, 29, 53, 145, 157, 161, 165, 186
sacred geometry, xv, xxvii, 29, 30, 31, 32
sacred sites, xxii, 81, 84, 103, 138, 193, 195
Saint John the Divine, 113
salt, 156, 180
Salt Lake City, 135
Samian alphabet, 162, 171, 188
Sanskrit, 33, 133, 179
Sant Kirpal Singh, 130
sas, 179
Satan, 36, 105, 119, 147, 148
sattwa, 34
Sault Ste. Marie, 135
Scotland, 94
Seal of Solomon, 173
seat of the soul, 146, 148
Secondary Serpent Unit, 101, 102
seed mind, 33, 34, 35, 120, 148
Semitic alphabet, 38, 113, 141, 144, 150, 157, 158, 161, 173, 175, 181, 182, 186
Seneca Tribe, 14
sephiroth, 114, 128
Serpent Mound map, xiv, xvii, xix, xxv, 14, 15, 17, 19, 20, 21, 22, 44, 98, 101, 102, 177
Serpent Mound Unit, 93, 99
seven seals, 87
shaman, xiv, 12, 14, 38, 77, 79, 80, 81, 98
Shi-shu-mara, 17
sigma, 91, 161, 179–81

Sikh, 143
Simran, 146
Snow, Charles E., 6
solar disk, 163, 167, 178
solar eclipse, 14
Solar Eclipse Hypothesis, xix
solar hexagon, xiv, 22, 57, 58, 69, 116, 118, 119, 145, 173, 179, 181
Solar Mysteries, 109, 119
solar rule, 90, 122
Son of God, 34, 87, 148, 168
soul, 4, 24, 25, 27, 33, 34, 35, 36, 62, 67, 68, 69, 75, 78, 81, 84, 87, 109, 114, 121, 122, 126, 127, 128, 130, 133, 134, 138, 142, 146, 147, 148, 159, 163, 168, 175, 178, 188, 196
Sound Current, 41, 110, 148
Sound Principle, 31, 35, 41, 110, 111, 125, 143, 145, 146, 150, 169, 178, 184
speira, 177
sphere, 25, 27, 34, 175
spira, 177
spiral, xxi, 29, 177
square, 45, 57, 58, 65, 80, 157
square of Mercury, 65, 126
Square of the Sun, 90, 122, 126
Squier and Davis, xxii, 6
Squier, Ephriam G., xxii, 6
Sraosha, 143
St. Augustine, 26
St. Bernard of Clairvaux, 27
St. Patrick, 132
Star of David, 173
stau, 179
Stonehenge, xxvi, xxvii, 3, 14, 20, 21, 22, 44, 108
Sufis, 27
sulfur, 77, 82, 122, 126, 156, 168, 180, 187
sulfur springs, 82
sundisk, 184
Syria, 5, 111

T
Tallahassee, 135
tamas, 34
Tanmantras, 33
Tartaros, 42, 137
tau, 128, 181–83, 188

tav, 181, 182
taw, 181, 186
Tecumseh, 3
Temple of Solomon, 55
ten coronets. *See* ten horns
ten horns, 117, 162, 190, 197
Tenskwatwa, 14
Teotihuacan, 102
Terpsichore, 69
Tesla, Nikola, 72, 73
tetractys, 171
Thales, 18
Thalia, 70
The Creator, 24, 25, 31, 33, 34, 36, 38, 64, 87, 109, 120, 126
The Muses, 69, 87, 128, 164, 169
The Two Bears, 18
Themis, 108, 109
Theogeny, 42, 149
Theosophists, 37
theta, 158, 163–64, 165, 167, 168, 184
Thom, Alexander, xviii, 54, 72, 94, 95, 101, 102, 103
Thoth, 64, 67
Throne of God, 30, 36, 42, 57, 87, 92, 118, 120, 122, 123, 133
Thuban, xxv, xxvi, 18, 19, 92, 97, 99, 101
thunderbird, 81, 133, 138
Tiamut, 18
Tower of Babel, 55
Transcendental Sound, 143
triangle, xiv, xx, xxvi, xxvii, 31, 42, 43, 44, 45, 46, 57, 58, 92, 94, 97, 101, 123, 124, 157, 171, 173, 180
True Substance, 24, 169
Tsi Kung, 18
twelve Olympians, 42
twelve Titans, 42
twenty-four elders, 26, 32, 33, 35, 36, 87, 159, 168, 173

U
Uktena, 115
umbilicus, 116, 145, 151, 167, 184
Underworld, 68, 109, 136, 167
Unifying Principle, 64, 143
Universal Ether, 72
Universal Love, 34, 36
upsilon, 41, 158, 168, 177, 178, 183–84, 188

Uraeus, 178
Urania, 69
uroboros. *See* oroboros
Ursa Major, 18
Ursa Minor, xxvi, 19, 21

V
Valley of the Kings, 194
versorium, 72
vesica piscis, xxvii, 29, 30, 36, 40–43, 69, 99, 127, 153, 190
Vibratory Principle, 34, 36, 37, 41, 147, 190. *See also* Word
Vibratory Structure, 34, 35, 42
Vishnu, 73
Vishnunabi, 73, 75
Voice of the Divine, 121, 143
Voice of the Silence, 37
volt, 72
Volta, Alessandro, 72

W
Wales, 94
Water of Life, 24, 26, 42, 122, 130
Watkins, Alfred, 78, 135
Watson Brake, xiii, xxi

Western Meridian, 135
Will of God, 147
Willoughby, Charles, 163
womb, 41, 43, 109, 116, 118, 145
Word, xxvii, 24, 34, 35, 36, 37, 41, 42, 87, 105, 107, 110, 111, 121, 126, 127, 134, 142, 143, 145, 146, 147, 148, 150, 151, 152, 167, 169, 178
Word of God, 38, 134, 145, 146, 147, 150, 168, 182
worm, xvi, 57, 131, 132, 133, 182, 188

X
xi, 171–73, 179, 186, 187, 188

Y
Yahweh, 152
Yaweh, 80, 197
yoga, 84, 146
Yugas, 73

Z
zayin, 161
zeta, 161–62, 161, 165, 174, 190
Zeus, 147, 169
zinc, 72
Zosimos of Panopolis, 190